CULPRITS IN THE MIND

(Perspectives on Pakistan)

Imran Khalid Usman

Dedicated to

The religious minorities of Pakistan including those non-Muslims who chose not to live in the country at the time of its formation and their descendants, who are in all meanings of the term, the most indigenous people of this land and if the country does not belong to them to live, thrive and prosper here safe and freely, then it belongs to no one else too,

And to the remembrance of Fehmida Riaz's poem *'Tum Bilkul Hum Jaise Nikle'* ('You turned out to be just like us')

Contents

Preface 1

Muslim Nationalism 5

    Arab Muslims 9

    'Majority' Muslims 11

    'Homogenous' Muslims 13

    'Voluntary' Muslims 14

    'Minority' Muslims 17

    'Conquistador Minority' Muslims 26

    Verdict on Muslim Nationalism 51

    The Problem with Islamic 'Dogmatic' Fundamentalism 57

    About Anti-Islam and Anti-Pakistan Narratives 86

Pakistani Zeitgeist 109

    The Democratic and Institutional Legacy of the British 112

    'Muhajir' or 'Settler': The Core Factor of the Migrant in the Rural-Urban Divide 115

    Skepticism of the Majority and Diversity, Puritan Cleansing and Infinite Regression 147

    Middle Class Clichés 156

    Solipsistic Personal Prejudices 170

    Statecraft, Upper Classes 195

    Rule of Law and Corruption 226

    Pakistani Effervescence and Vagaries of the Outside World ... 249

Epilogue 258

Index 262

About the Author 273

Preface

Each country on this planet, inhabited and dominated by the human species, has a story of its own within the territorial boundaries in which it existed or exists. This story can be read like a novel.

The story can read out like a novel, with a certain cast of characters spread over generations. As time never goes back in known human perception, those characters become sealed in history as the protagonists or antagonists of the novel, never to be denied or overlooked by historians when reviewing the novel. And like for all literary works, when a critic reviews this novel, it is essential to prepare the critique by analyzing the psychological and social motivations of the characters as well as the *'zeitgeist'* in which the characters of the novel existed.

On a contemporary level, there are current events, news flashes, politicians and ministers, prime ministers and presidents making the headlines. At any given time, for any common observer as well as for leading commentators, journalists, and intellectuals, there is nothing of more significance than these contemporaneous features. These become and appear larger than life at that time, and to an untrained observer of history, it would seem that it is those leading individuals making the news who are the real drivers of history and those who will make or break the country.

However, the fact is, and scholars of history have shown the world exhaustively already, that there are undercurrent forces of economic and socio-psychological nature which determine the direction a society or country will take. On the ground, it is translated, and to the trained eye it is observable on a day-to-day basis, in the behaviour pattern of even the common people of the country. If an observer is trained enough, or has trained oneself enough, to possess deep insight into the originating points of not only the economic but also the socio-psychological trends dominating the behaviour pattern of the common people on ground, then it becomes easier to understand the *'why'* and *'how'* of the current events and of the leading politicians making the headline news in the country, and to even predict to a sufficient degree of accuracy as to what is most likely to happen next in the most important affairs of the country.

As stated in the opening remark, each country has a story of its own. Although it is true that generally the established theories of political science and social behavior predict the same kind of course in all countries if the basic triggers are the same, however, each country has its own uniqueness, of mass as well as individual behavior, depending on the unique cultural experience of the people living within the territory of the country. And for a scholastic study, it would be important to know how, through each unique experience and characteristic, societies and countries can arrive at the same results established by studies of political science for certain identical economic and social triggers. The triggers may be of similar nature, giving similar results predicted by established political science theories, but the originating points of those triggers lie in the cultural uniqueness and individual cultural experience of each country.

This could bring such a study to face the circular argument that, in fact, as a *'cause'*, it is the economic conditions which determine even the *'zeitgeist'* or *'the cultural uniqueness and individual cultural experience of each country'*, bringing each country to the same results which would be obtained by any country with similar economic conditions. So eventually, it is the economic conditions which need to be studied and addressed to understand the existing situation of a country or to find the way forward for that country.

However, such an approach would be oversimplistic, inexhaustive, and not sophisticatedly advanced enough to qualify as the correct holistic approach when attempting to understand the predicament of a country. Because the *'nature of ideas'* generated in a particular stage of economic development or retrogression does in turn have an effect on the people, at the helm as well as on ground socially, determining the next step which the country takes, as a state as well as a society. The *'cause and effect'* process between the objective economic conditions and the subjective behavior of a country's people is very much interactive and exchangeable.

This element of unpredictability and uniqueness of human response owes itself to the nature of conscious life wherein, unlike unconscious life or nonliving matter, the freedom of choice and decision is available and therefore, the response to external conditions is not identical as it would be in the case of nonliving matter or unconscious life. That is, in short, good does not always win and it is not a foregone conclusion that life and the world will go on. But self-destruction too is always a very likely possibility (some cases in point being: the two world wars, the holocausts under Nazism and under communism in the former USSR and China, the holocaust of the 1947 Indian partition, the 1971 "Operation Searchlight" and dismemberment of Pakistan, the 1970s Cambodian holocaust, the 1990s ethnic cleansing and balkanization in former Yugoslavia, theocratic rule in Iran, the Talibanization of Afghanistan, etc.).

It is in the context and with the help of the above-stated preferred approach that this book will attempt to state, record, analyze, and describe the story of a people and society within a territorial boundary, where, despite the presence of one of the most ancient civilizational heritages, the tendencies of *'religious fundamentalism'*, *'sense of supremacism'* (religious or ethnic or linguistic), *'separatism'*, *'militarism'*, *'jingoism'*, *'anti constitutionalism'*, *'anti democracy'*, *'anti pluralism'*, *'anti federalism'*, *'anti history'*, and *'authoritarianism'*, in short, fascistic tendencies, overcame their opposing positive tendencies and came to dominate the thought process of the supposedly conscious and educated class of that society. The very class from whom a country would expect the generation of forward-looking ideas built on the agreed and long-accepted modern civilizational heritage of humanism, democracy, and tolerance.

This book will also touch upon the fact that these ideas of humanism, democracy, and tolerance have been eroded and have suffered a setback in other countries too in recent times, due to the dumbing down of Western societies and increased immigration of primitive cultures into those societies. The reasons for the inability of Western societies to rise above themselves and deal correctly with these cultures will also be interrogated.

But this book's prime focus is on the uniqueness of the particular country of Pakistan, of which I, the author, with a lifetime of firsthand observation and a certain amount of political activism during my younger years, am a citizen, and where the zeroing in of the fascistic tendencies described above has been quite acute. It presents an interesting case study for those endeavoring to understand the ramifications which a region and the world can and did face at large, and the people living within that country's boundaries do and did face in particular, due to this acuteness.

The objective of this book is not an indictment of this country as a state, and neither does it deny or intend to play down the country's successes and the positive influence its people have asserted and exerted on the larger human society. Instead, the objective is to understand, as the first quarter of the 21st century AD ends and the country has already been around for more than three quarters of a century, longer than another ideological multiethnic federated country, the USSR survived, why, as a state, it has always been a state in constant internal turmoil, at war with itself, thus emanating a perception of instability and failure as a state.

The objective is to understand the *'sob story'* behind this crisis. A crisis which has always been existential and will continue to remain and be so if the real underlying story of the culprits of this crisis, internal and external, is not told. If it is not told, understood, and discussed openly and extensively, even *ad nauseam*.

Muslim Nationalism

It is very well known, and accepted universally, that the state of Pakistan was created based on the idea of 'Muslim separatism', or Muslim exclusivity, which gained ground among the Muslim population of British India. But to understand the mechanics of how the thought process of those at the helm and the policymakers of the new state functioned subsequently, the fact that needs to be explored is that the basis was 'Muslim separatism' and not a serious, well-thought-out, and as such intended ideological movement for the establishment of a structured Islamic state.

The emphasis of the scurry for the new state was more in the backdrop of an overwhelming, predominantly Hindu, non-Muslim majority and the fact that the elite of the Muslim population, again mostly from the Muslim minority provinces of British India, detested the oncoming eventuality that in a free democracy they would have to live largely under the leadership of non-Muslims, mostly Hindus.

Indeed, it is a historical fact that ideologically Islamic dogmatic fundamentalist parties like the Jamaat-e-Islami and the Jamiat Ulema-e-Hind, practicing Muslim leaders like Maulana Abul Kalam Azad, Majlis-e-Ahrar, and Muslims in overwhelmingly Muslim-majority provinces or states in the very northwest of India were up to the end not very participative in or enthusiastic for the Muslim League movement for Pakistan.

The case of Bengal, where the Muslim League won in both the 1937 as well as the 1946 elections, and Punjab need to be seen in the context of the Muslim population in these provinces not being in an overwhelming majority. The ground in Bengal was more ripe for Muslim separatism and communalism from the economic 'liberation' angle of Muslim peasants in eastern Bengal working on lands owned by Hindus. In Punjab, it was the other way around, with the Punjabi Muslim in general keeping aloof and distant from the Muslim League's politics up until the very eve of Indian partition. This was because in Punjab (mostly in the western part), the elite of agricultural landlords were largely Muslims, with Hindus mostly

5

dominating the urban centers, and as such, the Punjabi Muslim had a lesser sense of insecurity.

However, among the Punjabi middle class, there did exist scholastic yearnings and aspirations of Muslim supremacism and pan-Islamic dogmatic fundamentalism (cases in point being the pan-Islamic poet Iqbal and the Muslim League Shafi group, the Ahmadiyya sect, and the remnant followers and believers of the Khilafat movement). It was only by the time when it became common knowledge that the departure of the British from India had become inevitable and imminent that various factors like the British concern for establishing a friendly state against the USSR, the Punjabi landlords' concern regarding the anti-feudal stance of the Indian National Congress and the pan-Islamic aspirations of the Punjabi Muslim middle class coincided and complemented one another to join the Muslim League movement for Pakistan.

The case of Sind was similar to that of Punjab, with Sindhi agricultural landlords dominating the rural part and Hindus dominating the urban centers. However, Sind was different from Punjab in the sense that the proportion of the Muslim population was much larger than the Hindu population and therefore it did not face its own partitioning in 1947 as did Punjab.

In short, it would be safe to conclude that the Muslim League movement for Pakistan was based on a 'Muslim separatism' emanating more from pragmatic concerns of the Muslim elite and Muslim supremacists of being subdued or overwhelmed by a predominantly Hindu majority rather than from a structured ideological struggle for the establishment of an Islamic state. That is why, in the Muslim League's Pakistan movement, we see leaders from the Shia, Ahmadiyya, and Ismaili Muslim minority sects, minorities within the minority, at the fore. In fact, we even see the leader of Dalits, Jogendra Nath Mandal, also at the fore, who had jumped onto the Muslim League bandwagon from Bengal as a reaction against the treatment of Dalits among the mainstream Hindus. This reinforces the view that those spearheading the Pakistan movement had neither predicted nor intended that the new state they were striving for would convert into a theocratic state at any time.

Much has been written about the distinction between a "Muslim state," which is a "state for the Muslims" and an "Islamic state," which is a "theocratic state run under the laws of Islamic sharia." This book does not intend to repeat or dwell on what has already been extensively written, regarding this distinction.

But what does need to be explored is how the 'Muslim separatism' in British India, which gave birth to the state of Pakistan, was and is different from instances of 'Muslim separatism,' or 'Muslim exclusivity,' or difficulties of coexistence between Muslim and non-Muslim populations in a single state observed elsewhere in the world.

In this context, the conversion to Islam of different peoples in different lands is first assessed. Based on this assessment, it becomes possible to categorize this conversion into various groups, with each category possessing characteristics distinctly different from another category. Once this categorization is established, it becomes easier to see that the Muslims of the Indian subcontinent are uniquely alone in the category in which they fall. That is why their perceptions, their response mechanism to their non-Muslim compatriots, and their yearnings for establishing a national state solely based on the Muslim religion, regardless of shared race, language, and historical experience, are uniquely different from the Muslims of other lands.

Of course, the initial assessment of these categorizations excludes the 'Islamic dogmatic fundamentalist' movement which now pervades across the Muslim world and its adherents, who with conscious effort strive to think and act alike, with the least attachment and loyalty to the various cultures and historical heritage from which they spring forth. In fact, as will be seen later in the book, it is this very lack of attachment and loyalty to their own heritage which eases the task of ideologically indoctrinating a Muslim of any land toward 'Islamic Dogmatic Fundamentalism' or 'Political Islam.'

The assessment of the Islamic Dogmatic Fundamentalist phenomenon will be made after completing the assessment of the converted people, to the exclusion of this phenomenon.

This book proposes the categorization, and generates titles for each category, as follows:

Category A: Arab Muslims

Category B: 'Majority' Muslims: Converted Muslims in lands conquered by the Arabs where conversion was complete, or Muslims came to form the majority of the population.

Category C: 'Homogenous' Muslims: Converted Muslims in lands conquered by Muslims and where conversion was complete (or converted the majority), and the population was ethnically and linguistically homogenous.

Category D: 'Voluntary' Muslims: Converted Muslims in lands where Islam arrived not through conquest but through voluntary conversion.

Category E: 'Minority' Muslims: Converted Muslims in lands where Islam came through conversion by conquest attempts or voluntary conversion or by migration, but the Muslims remained or remain a minority and did not achieve dominance in political power.

Category F: 'Conquistador Minority' Muslims: Converted Muslims in a land where Islam came through conquest, the conversion was not complete, Muslims remained a minority, and the population was ethnically and linguistically not homogenous.

Although it is not spelled out in the titles, categories B to F are meant to signify generally non-Arab Muslims although there is overlap of characteristics in each with the Arab Muslims. Notice that Category F is defined in the context of 'a land' and not 'lands' which is because while the first five of the six categories, that is Category A to Category E, may find more than one country or land which fit their criteria, with their certain characteristics overlapping with each other, there is only one country or land which fits the entire criteria of Category F, and this is the category in which the Muslims of India fall. It would however be pertinent to mention that Category F could also have had another land overlapping with its criteria from Category E, had Muslims not been wiped out completely from Spain in the 15th and 16th century A.D.

Arab Muslims

Islam appeared on the planet in the 7th century A.D. as an Arab religion or a religion of the Arabs. This book does not intend to fixate on the historicity of the advent of Islam or debate on, or with, the newer and newer emerging research and theories regarding the origin of Islam, however it is an undeniable fact that the language, diction, symbolism, connotations and aspirations invoked in this religion are distinctly Arabic and primarily addressed to an Arabic mind of the period in which its origin is historically placed. In fact, it reads like the education of the Arabic mind with the Abrahamic message about the Oneness of God.

As such, the religion of Islam in many ways, is not a negation of the value system, traditions and heritage of the land and people among which it first appeared but a logically natural and necessary improved continuity of all those things for advancement in a changing world of its time.

Indeed, with the adoption of Islam, a fragmented tribal society was able to evolve into a viable state and its people obtained a code of life which at the time could be considered as the most progressive, forward looking and disciplined way of life. With the shedding away of pagan superstitions and polytheistic idol worship, this code of life provided initiation of serious and logical reflection about the world around them for the nomadic and tribal people who until then were limited to strife among themselves and with the harsh land in which they lived.

The strict code of conduct, the codified and harnessed self-control, and militaristic discipline which Islam provided them enabled the Arabs to spring out of their land and conquer neighboring decaying empires and harness the diverse civilizational knowledge base of the conquered people.

The Arab ascent as the pinnacle of human civilization and the center of commerce and learning continued for a good six centuries after the conquest of Mecca by the Prophet. This high point of Arab history passed through three caliphates: the Rashidun, the Umayyads, and the Abbasids, and included the period well known as the 'Golden Age' of Islam. The hadith and the life account of the Prophet were also formally written down during this period. From the mid-9th century A.D. onwards, it took a downhill path and started declining after the defeat of the Mutazilites, the rise of Imam Hanbal, the domination of the orthodox interpretation of Islam as the official ideology of the empire, and culminated with the Mongol invasion and destruction of Baghdad in 1258.

Thereafter, the zenith of the Arab Muslim dispersed into smaller empires scattered in Egypt, North Africa, and Spain and was subdued on the larger scale by the rise of the Turkish Ottoman Caliphate. In Spain, it was completely eliminated in the 15th century A.D.

The glory and pride of Arab Muslims saw a return to the global stage with the entry of Muhammad ibn Abdul Wahab and Abdul Aziz bin Muhammad bin Saud on the Arabian Peninsula in the 18th century A.D., the uprising against the Ottoman Empire in the early twentieth century A.D., the return of Arab sovereignty over Arab lands, and, finally, the discovery of oil in the late 1930s.

All along this journey, the story of the Arab Muslims from the religious point of view has been an inward looking story, a story of the self, a story in which the religion of Islam was less of an ideology brought from elsewhere, something that had to be adopted with conscious effort and more of an essential and inherent cultural aspect of their lives which was naturally and historically evolved and intertwined with their customs and daily lives. It was less externalized and more internalized. Islam was them, and they were Islam.

Indeed, it can be safely stated anecdotally and be verified through several Arab writings that for the Arabic mind, the acceptance and practice of Islam by non-Arabs, though welcomed and for some Arabs considered as affirmation of the righteousness and superiority of their own civilizational value system, is not necessarily a definite expectation from the non-Arab. In other words, to put it simplistically—in fact, crassly— the Arab Muslim does not really expect a non-Arab to be automatically a Muslim, and if a Muslim, a practicing Muslim at that, and if a practicing Muslim, then well and good, but not intrinsically expected.

That is why the Arab Muslim is more at ease with non-Muslim states and societies than is the non-Arab converted practicing Muslim. That is because for the Arab Muslim, Islam is their own civilizational value, and when interacting with other civilizations, they are genuinely interested in knowing those indigenous cultures and civilizational systems rather than seeing a reflection or cyclostyle copies of themselves in people who they know are ethnically, linguistically, and civilizationally different from them but are endeavoring to be like them.

Islam has been purported to be a religion which is above races, ethnicities, castes, and nationalities, and a brotherhood of men equal if they are just Muslims. The Prophet's famous last sermon was also a call to the same essential spirit of Islam, saying that no Arab is superior to a non-Arab and no non-Arab superior to an Arab but only by his or her piousness.

However, in reality and historically, the Arab perception of Islam has been generally to consider it as an Arab civilizational value system. References may be found in works of the likes of Hanbali scholars like Ibn e Taymiyyah whereby Arabs are tended to be seen as superior to non-Arabs, and it is rare among the more orthodox Arab Muslims to look favorably at giving away their women in marriage to non-Arab Muslim men.

In the context of the above exposition, returning to the subject of Muslim nationalism, it would seem that for the Arab Muslims, the concept of nationalism would not be religious nationalism. Instead, it is ironically a return to nationalism based on family, tribes, and historically territorial sovereignties within the Arab world. And therefore, outside the Arab world, they would expect the nationalisms to not be religious, specially Muslim ones, but based on the set rational premises of language, culture, ethnicity, and historical experience of territorial sovereignty within a land. In that sense, their perception of nationalism would be in line with the set definition of nationalism in political science, as also similarly perceived by the rest of the world, and no different.

'Majority' Muslims

With the emergence and the consolidation of Islam in the Arabian Peninsula, Arab military expeditions extended out of Arabia and defeated armies of the Roman and the Persian empires. Even under the Rashidun caliphate, the first caliphate of the four righteous Companions of the Prophet, the lands and areas of the Levant, Mesopotamia, Persia, Khorasan, Azerbaijan, and Egypt had been conquered, with expansion continuing in the direction of Northern Africa and the Sudanese Nubian lands, and into Anatolia in the Northwest.

During the Umayyad and Abbasid caliphates, the conquest of the Islamic empire was consolidated from Morocco in the West to Khorasan or Afghanistan in the East, with Transoxiana in the North and a third of Anatolia in the Northwest under complete Muslim control.

The time between the commencement of the Rashidun caliphate (632 A.D.) and the end of the Abbasid caliphate (1258 A.D.) comprises a period of six centuries and a quarter. During this time, the majority population of the aforementioned lands had converted to Islam.

Whether through forced conversions under the threat of death, or voluntary conversion to gain the privileges which would come automatically by being a Muslim in a Muslim empire, or voluntary conversion purely by being convinced of the trueness of the message of Islam, the fact is that, as time passed over several generations, the majority of people of these lands genuinely accepted and adopted Islam, its tenets, and rituals in their daily personal and social lives, and the belief systems of their pre-Islamic faiths dwindled and faded away.

However, due to the synthesis of their non-Arab cultures with the strict and more rigid Islamic code of conduct brought in by the Arab conquerors, the practice of Islam and adherence to it mellowed down to a more urbane and cosmopolitan version. Spiritual and philosophical, and less literal, ways of understanding the faith came into vogue, and extensive works of Fiqh (jurisprudence) and philosophy were produced due to this synthesis with the non-Arab lands.

The four schools of Islamic Fiqh emerged during this period, as did Sufism and Islamic mysticism, the Mutazilite movement, and the advancement of scientific thought under the likes of Ibn e Sina (Avicenna) and Al Beruni.

Due to this synthesis, the non-Arab Muslims in these majority Muslim lands became comfortable with Islam. And with the pre-Islamic faiths having all but disappeared, this new and present faith of Islam intertwined with their culture, and they moved on as Muslims but who were not Arabs.

The important point to note here is that, since there was no non-Islamic faith of any significance left in their lands, therefore these majority non-

Arab Muslims felt no sense of insecurity in continuing their indigenous culture intertwined with their Islamic faith, of course shredded of any pre-Islamic polytheistic practices.

This was supported now by the advancement and presence of a body of work of more sophisticated and virtual (less literal) interpretations of Islam, and was further strengthened and systematized with the loosening of the Arab grip on political power and the rise of non-Arab kingdoms and empires in these lands.

It is due to this reason of long historical experience of maintaining their cultural uniqueness within the ambit of the Islamic faith that the people of these lands were never unclear about their nationhood. They always saw it within the territorial boundaries in which they had existed for centuries. And at the end of the Western colonial era, starting in the second quarter of the 20th century A.D., they easily asserted their nationalism based on the territory in which they lived and did not endeavour to seek any meaning of nationalism beyond that definition.

'Homogenous' Muslims

This category is seen basically as a refinement of the category of 'Majority' Muslims whereby not only the people of a land became Muslim as an overwhelming majority but on top of that they belonged to more or less the same ethnic and linguistic background.

In this context, the lands of Egypt, Sudan and the modern day Central Asian republics fit the bill. The lands of Anatolia (Turkey), Persia (Iran) and Iraq, with a considerable large minority of the Kurdish people, to a lesser degree. And states like Afghanistan and Pakistan do not fit the bill at all.

In fact, immediately we exclude the state of Pakistan from the categorization which would define Afghanistan as a non-homogenous state, for the very reason that this book is assessing the concept of Muslim Nationalism adopted by Pakistan which cannot be divorced from its historical experience as part of the Indian subcontinent, an experience which the state of Afghanistan is not privy to.

The dynamics of Afghanistan and its nationalism translating into its existence as a nation state are different from the dynamics of Pakistan and the Muslim Nationalism it espouses as a nation state. This difference will be discussed in more detail later in the book.

Needless to only state the obvious, the people of lands and countries who would fall in the category of 'Homogenous' Muslims would not perceive nationalism for themselves, and asserted as self-determination, divorced in any way from their centuries old culture or language or customs (not shredded away due to not being in conflict with the monotheistic belief system).

These Muslims too would need no crutch of any concept of nationalism other than the set definition of nationalism in political science as also similarly perceived by the rest of the world, based on ethnicity, culture, language and shared historical experience within, more or less, same territorial boundaries over centuries.

'Voluntary' Muslims

The reader would already have guessed the lands which will be discussed under this category, as these are very popularly quoted as examples to prove that Islam did not spread by the sword.

The lands of Malaysia and the islands in the South Pacific, comprising countries like Indonesia and Brunei, saw the advent of Islam through interaction with Muslim traders and the gradual voluntary conversion of the common population, as well as the conversion of their ruling classes to Islam over a period of centuries. This eventually made them Muslim majority countries.

However, still in the early 21st century, these countries consist of a substantial proportion of non-Muslim population. In Indonesia and Brunei, the non-Muslim population is approximately 20 percent, while in Malaysia, the non-Muslim population is as large as more than 35 percent.

Apart from these countries in Southeast Asia, the country of Nigeria in Africa, with a Muslim population of more than 50 percent, can also be placed in this category, as there too Islam came through trade and migration.

In this backdrop, it is easy to see that due to a gradual, evolutionary, and voluntary conversion to Islam of the indigenous population of these countries, the converted Muslims and their descendants have historically had no qualms or misconceptions about their ethnicity or pre-Islamic historicity. They are very clear about the fact that they and their ancestors have belonged to the land in which they have resided for centuries, before Islam came and also ever since. The same is true for their non-Muslim compatriots, who are either descendants of their same ancestors who did not opt for Islam or who have co-resided with them in their lands since centuries.

In fact, interacting and necessarily coexisting peacefully with their non-Muslim compatriots, who are quite large minorities as well as belonging more or less to the same ethnicities as theirs, added on with the fact that the element of the sword was missing from the conversion to Islam in these lands, makes the Muslims of these lands more tolerant and more secure with themselves on being Muslim as a voluntary adoption of a faith, just as a faith and nothing else.

In other words, they have complete clarity about the fact that their patriotism and nationalism emanate not from their faith but from the land in which they live, and the ethnicity and language to which they belong from pre-Islamic times.

Indeed, some pre-Islamic superstitions, gestures, and small rituals which did not imply overtly polytheistic angles, and therefore were not deemed important to be shredded away, can still be seen in the daily lives of these Muslims. This is also explained to a sufficient degree of detail in the works of Nobel laureate writer V. S. Naipaul, such as *Among the Believers* and *Beyond Belief.*

To a certain degree, this categorization could also include the Muslims of South India. They demonstrate similar historical facts pertaining to the advent of Islam in their areas, in which the element of the sword, conquest, and forced conversion is minimal, if not nonexistent. By and large, they too first experienced conversion to Islam due to interaction with Arab Muslim traders, and their conversions were also more or less voluntary.

However, they never became a majority in their lands and hence, due to insecurities for their faith caused by an overwhelming Hindu majority surrounding them, often fell and even now do fall into the trap of Islamic Dogmatic Fundamentalism.

On the other hand, including the atrocities committed during the Moplah Rebellion in 1921, which also had no connection to the Pakistan movement, the involvement of the South Indian Muslims in the Pakistan movement is not at all significant. They also have less pretensions than the North Indian Muslim about being any different ethnically or historically from their non-Muslim compatriots.

At this stage, it is important to reiterate and record what was mentioned earlier in this chapter, that the ongoing assessment of these categorizations is so far excluding analyses of the effect of the 'Islamic dogmatic fundamentalist' movement which pervades across the Muslim world and its adherents. The goal is to first establish the set parameters of these categorizations as defined by objective historical conditions, instead of what the fundamentalist movement is intentionally trying to achieve by consciously striving to make Muslims all over the world think and act alike, with the least attachment and loyalty to the culture and historical heritage from which they spring forth.

However, as we mentioned the South Indian Muslims, who though 'voluntary' Muslims but are a minority in their lands, and as we progress into looking at the next category of 'Minority' Muslims, in all fairness, it will become progressively difficult to avoid discussing to some length the effect of Islamic Dogmatic Fundamentalism and the matter of 'Identity Politics,' which we have seen intensively in countries where Muslims are a minority in the country of their citizenship.

As we will see in the next category, this will also include the Black Muslims of the USA, the old and new Muslim immigrants in Western countries, and even Muslims in China.

Maybe it is only logical and an opportune juncture to do so, because it may help better in our understanding of the mindset of the 'Minority' Muslim, which, when gifted by history with political power, promotes itself to the mantle of the 'Conquistador Minority' Muslim. This is the final category that will be analyzed after the next one, and which leads us to the main subject of the book, i.e., the Pakistani Muslim and his / her nationalism.

'Minority' Muslims

On the 9th day of the Islamic month of Dhul Hajj in the 10th year of the Hijra (Prophet Muhammad (pbuh)'s migration from Mecca to Medina), the 6th of March 632 A.D., the Prophet of Islam delivered his famous last sermon on the occasion of the annual Hajj. If Islam was to be summed up in a nutshell, this historic sermon can easily and safely be considered to serve that purpose. If Muslims need quick and easy reference as to what they should be believing and practicing as the articles and tenets of their faith, this would be it.

A true Muslim at heart, living in any part of the world, loyally and surely ascribes, at the very least, to as much as is contained in this last sermon. And of that sermon, the following statement of the Prophet constitutes one of the various core principles of what any believing Muslim considers to be the raison d'être of why he or she chooses to be a Muslim:

"… an Arab has no superiority over a non-Arab nor a non-Arab has any superiority over an Arab; also, a White has no superiority over a Black nor a Black has any superiority over a White except by piety and good action."

Indeed, it may be observed that, in the mind of Muslims living in countries where they are not in a majority, this message resonates much more sharply than among those Muslims who are a majority in their countries.

Before this core belief is protracted to see how it affects the mindset of Muslims who are recent immigrants to countries where they are not the majority and are not the original native or indigenous people of that country, we confine this observation to those Muslims who ethnically and culturally belong to the country of their residence since centuries because of conversion to Islam or ancient migration or relocation of their ancestors in that land.

For such 'Minority' Muslims, growing up in their land, their faith and their nationalism are not intertwined, but loyalty to their country and flag, even though being a minority as a religion, does not pose any question or doubt in their minds. There is complete clarity in their minds as to what patriotism means, and their love for their land, its history, its language or languages, its heritage, its culture, and their compatriots is genuine and unremitting.

If they were to feel most comfortable anywhere in the world, it would be in the country to which they have belonged for centuries, and with the language or languages of that country, one of which is also their own language. It is easy for them to rationalize in their minds that they follow a faith different than their compatriots for reasons of accepting certain different personal moral values or belief about the concept of God than their compatriots, but other than that, they are the same people.

Excluding the Muslim minorities who are recent immigrants to the West and other non-Muslim majority countries in the 20th and 21st century A.D., as well as the influence of recent post-colonial Islamic Dogmatic Fundamentalist movements on such minorities, historically, the Slavic, Tatar, and Chechen Muslims in Eastern Europe (including the former Austro-Hungarian Empire and then Yugoslavia) and Russia, indigenous Japanese Muslims, the Han Chinese (Hui) Muslims, the non-Arab African Muslims, and the South Indian Muslims would foremost fit the bill for this category.

If this book was being written in the middle of the 20th century A.D. or before, the identification and bracketing of this category of Muslims, i.e., the 'Minority' Muslims, would have ended here with the examples given above.

However, from the mid-20th century onwards, two accelerating trends emerged anew, that is, never before seen in the world, which had both quantitative as well as qualitative demographic implications on the category of Muslims who are now found as a minority in the countries of their residence and nationality, indigenous or adopted.

One was the rise of the Muslim fundamentalist movement, strengthened, aided, and abetted by the Western capitalist world in its strife against their newly emerged formidable foe of Soviet communism. The second was the huge wave of human migration and immigration from the Muslim world into Western capitalist countries.

Both these trends had far-reaching implications on the psyche of the Muslim populations living as minorities in their countries. Both eventually struck in tandem at the Muslim imagination in general, and that of the 'Minority' Muslim in particular, and 'killed one bird with two stones'. The bird was nonpolitical Islam. And the phoenix that then arose carried the outcomes of these two trends on each of its wings, 'Political Islam' on one and 'Identity Politics' on the other.

Both these outcomes strove, and even now strive, to outstrip the Muslim individual of their national culture which would organically tie them with their non-Muslim compatriots and attempt to alienate the Muslim individual from the secular collective.

Indeed, the Islamic Dogmatic Fundamentalist trend seeks to straitjacket Muslims into one uniform 'culture' across the world, specially encouraging non-Arab Muslims to abandon the culture, colloquialism, and traditions of their homelands and adopt singular ways of behavior, expression, and interaction which would make it impossible to discern a Muslim coming from one land from a Muslim coming from another.

This trend struck a chord and found immediate popularity with 'Minority' Muslims, specially those who had immigrated to Western lands and felt difficulty and alienation in adopting cultural ways vastly different from the countries of their origin, and a reaction at realizing that the advanced West into which they had moved was the result of epic scientific and technological achievements of people who had been Jews or Christians, while the Muslims had nothing to have contributed to the progress of mankind since more than a thousand years.

It is therefore no coincidence that 'Identity Politics' in the West has found strong allies in Islamic Dogmatic Fundamentalist organizations, who in turn befriend and promote those indulging in 'Identity Politics' as under their cover they find ample social and political room to thrive and grow.

The irony for those who indulge in 'Identity Politics,' rather than politics of national cohesion, and defend or fail to critically analyze the often unspoken but socially asserted political agenda of Islamic Dogmatic Fundamentalist organizations in the West, is that the Muslim fundamentalist worldview eventually recognizes no identity other than the straitjacketed version it itself is promoting.

The fact is that currently, as the world has become smaller and smaller with the technological revolution in communication, the ease of traveling across the world, and the en masse immigration from the Muslim world into the Western world, the influence of political fundamentalist Islam has gradually encroached, by interactive resonance, on the social psychology of even Muslim majority countries.

That is, in other words, the immigrants who come to the West, even from the Muslim majority countries categorized above in this book, become 'Minority' Muslims in the destination countries. Subsequently, they are immediately taken in by the already existing and well-entrenched social organizations run and influenced by lobbies involved in making political capital out of the alliance between 'Identity Politics' and 'Political Islam,' as explained above.

The ripple effect of this, in turn, translates and travels all the way back to their families and social circles who have remained behind in their countries of origin. The population back home too starts looking at society and religion in a context and identity contrasted against, and constantly compared with, Western societies as if there was a competition between the two.

So, at present, even the Muslims in 'Majority' Muslim countries have gradually started thinking like 'Minority' Muslims influenced by identity politics. In a way, now the predominant way of thinking has become, for example, a close to two billion minority of Muslims on a planet inhabited by a total of more than seven billion human beings.

The truth is that it is not possible to incisively analyze the complexity of this global tendency among Muslims by divorcing it, or closing eyes, from the 'elephant in the room'. The 'elephant in the room' is, in fact, the state of Israel, created by the World Powers and the United Nations in 1948, contraposed to the plight and the disenfranchisement of the Palestinian people and the occupation of their lands.

Since the main focus of this book is the country of Pakistan and the social psyche of the Muslims comprising that country, there is a risk of digressing if the analysis of 'Minority' Muslims is carried on any further in this chapter. However, before closing on this category and moving on to the next, that is, the 'Conquistador Minority' Muslims, it would be pertinent to mention the particular historical context in regard to the creation of Israel, as that would ease explaining the success of fundamentalist 'Political Islam' in capturing the imagination of Muslims and which also has a bearing on the mode of creation of the state of Pakistan. Therefore, there is a historical link between the two phenomena.

While it is true that the real ascendancy of fundamentalist 'Political Islam' gained strength from the mid-20th century A.D. onwards, after the end of World War 2 with the commencement of the Cold War, the seeds of this tendency had already been sown and watered by British colonialism almost two decades before that as a policy matter, their hands forced by political expediency due to certain turns of events in that period.

From their point of view, this spadework proved to be very handy, as it was sufficiently advanced when the time came to also take on the new foe of Soviet communism, as the need arose for that.

At the beginning of the 20th century A.D., the British Empire was the most powerful and advanced colonial force on the planet, its tentacles gripping countries across the globe. It was in competition with other Western colonial empires and had outwitted all of them to be the foremost European power. However, on the European continent itself, it had also entered into various treaties with some of them.

The real game for colonialization was in the non-Christian world, and one of the low-lying fruits among that was the Ottoman Empire, the 'Sick Man of Europe'. The British had identified since long, in fact as early as the 18th century A.D., the seismic political fault line which existed between the Turks as masters and the Arabs as the colonized people, and had been trying since as early as that to make inroads with the Arabs.

As the Great War (World War 1) commenced, with the Ottoman Empire as an adversary of the British, the latter explored and struck at this fault line and succeeded in arranging an effective Arab uprising against the Turks.

During the course of the war, two epoch-creating events also occurred:

(i) The Sykes-Picot Agreement in 1916 between European colonial powers, mutually allied on one side of the war, to carve up and distribute among themselves the Arabian lands which would break away from the Ottoman Empire, and

(ii) The Balfour Declaration in 1917, which was an achievement for the Zionist lobbies in the British echelons of power to secure a guarantee from the powerful British Empire for the return of international Jewry to their historical homeland in Palestine and the establishment of a 'national home'[1] for them in that region.

When the war ended, the Arabian Peninsula was majorly given over to the Sharif of Mecca, but the Arab lands excluding the peninsula were divided and distributed among the colonial powers along the lines of the Sykes-Picot Agreement.

Thus, historically, it can be seen that the interests of the most powerful colonial empires and the Zionist lobby, which exerted great influence among the ruling circles of the British Empire, coincided in the early 20th century A.D.

The Sharif of Mecca, whose two sons respectively became the kings of Transjordan and Iraq, was not happy at the outcome of the colonial domination of these lands. However, he was soon defeated by the combined alliance of Ibn Saud and the Ikhwan, the Wahabi revivalists of Islam.

The period between the two world wars continued with the Arabian Peninsula preoccupied with its own internal strife, in which the Sharif of Mecca was defeated by Ibn Saud, who consolidated his power in the peninsula by also defeating the Rashidi Emirate, which had historically been inclined to cooperate and collude with the Ottomans.

In this respect, Ibn Saud did receive assistance and support from the British as well, while his ideological allies, the Ikhwan, were also wary of the decadence and the religious digressions, in their view, of the ruling classes among the Muslims.

---

[1] In the letter written on 2nd November 1917 by the British Foreign Secretary, Arthur Balfour to Lord Rothschild, the former informs the latter about the declaration which reads as follows: "*His Majesty's Government view with favour the establishment in Palestine of a national home for the Jewish people, and will use their best endeavours to facilitate the achievement of this object, it being clearly understood that nothing shall be done which may prejudice the civil and religious rights of existing non-Jewish communities in Palestine, or the rights and political status enjoyed by Jews in any other country*".

Meanwhile, during this period, the consolidation of colonial power over the other Arab lands, as protectorates of the colonial empires controlling them, continued. So did the steady — though more of a trickle and not a flood of — migration of Jews from mostly the European world into the land of Palestine, which was under the British mandate.

Since the Balfour Declaration in 1917, Jews had also been buying land from the Arabs in Palestine. Thus, we see that there was a further coinciding of the vested interests of the dominant and victorious forces in the region, which facilitated the return and rehabilitation of Jews to their ancient homeland in the land of Palestine.

The occurrence of the Holocaust under Nazism came as the final blow to any anti-Semitic reservation that may have remained in the home societies of the European colonialist empires. As a catharsis, they, including the consent of the Left and socialist parties of these countries, overwhelmingly voted in favor of the establishment of the state of Israel in the land of Palestine.

The irony in this catharsis was that, in their humanistic, conscientious intention to atone for the atrocities committed on the Jews in their own lands, they were artificially implanting a new state on a land which was now also, and still is, inhabited by the indigenous people of that land since centuries. The prognosis thus provided by the colonizing powers was that of a colonizing mindset. That is, establishing another colonial project in one of their colonies, without giving any consideration to the indivisibility of a historically evolved land and the collective democratic will of all people living in that land at that time.

To not recognize the realities of the present and peoples living in the present, and to destroy the present because of justifications derived from ancient theological scriptures, are in themselves retrogressive and anti-human actions and behavior.

The colonial project of Israel cannot be simplified by justifying it as an atonement for the historical persecution and massacre of the Jewish people. In fact, it becomes more complicated by two more aspects.

One is the abandonment by the European powers and their progressive intellectuals of their creed of secular enlightenment, through which they had separated the 'church,' that is, the theological, from state affairs and politics, by creating a state based on religion and justification for it drawn from religious scriptures.

Second is the abandonment by the European powers and their progressive intellectuals of their creed of democracy, by not asking the democratic will of the people living in the land at that time and condoning the forced displacement—the 'Nakba'—of the indigenous Palestinian people from their homes and towns, which happened as a result of the establishment of the state of Israel.

Ironically, we see contemporary political forces of the Right in Europe, whose political stances would ascribe more to the fascist perspectives of pre-World War 2 Europe, coming forth as the foremost champions of the state of Israel.

This is nothing but the transferring of an anti-Semitic and colonial perspective onto another Semitic colonized third world people in the Middle East. That is, the solution has been reached, and the solution has been transferred out of the borders of Europe. Two Semitic people fight and kill each other, and Europe is also absolved of the guilt of anti-Semitism. Hypocrisy par perfection.

If we are today to challenge the retrogressive force of Islamic Dogmatic Fundamentalism and advocate for democracy in the Muslim world, the task becomes next to impossible in view of the hypocrisy shown by Western democracies when it comes to the question about the state of Israel and the treatment and plight of the Palestinian people.

To justify the state of Israel and its actions based on theology, and its legitimacy sought from religious scriptures, plus carving up and dividing countries and lands without asking for the majority will of the inhabitants of those lands, amounts to sheer negation of both concepts of secularism as well as democracy. These concepts are the pillars on which modern human civilization rests today and which prevent it from falling back into the pits of barbarism from which it has raised itself over centuries with help from the thoughts and works of intellectual giants.

The story of Pakistan and the implied power which fundamentalist 'Political Islam' exerts over it is intellectually linked with the story of Israel.

Notwithstanding genuinely debatable concerns and much defendable rationale of the communities in those lands who too were advocating the creation of these states, the fact appears to be that both states were created as part of neocolonial projects left over by a departing colonial power. Both were formed by carving up and dividing a historically and organically evolved land and forcefully or inadvertently displacing indigenous peoples. Both were formed playing on the sense of insecurity of a minority from a majority rule of the colonialized country which was being divided[2] Both were formed on the basis of theology and legitimacy sought from religious scriptures. Both were formed on the notion that people of different religions cannot live together and cannot be one nation.

On those parameters, if the creation of Pakistan was historically right, then the creation of the state of Israel can also be justified and if the creation of the state of Israel was wrong, then the concept behind the creation of Pakistan can also be challenged. The one difference however, between the two is that in the case of Pakistan, electoral exercise was conducted in almost all provinces which were to be part of the new country[3]. This had provided strong substance to the argument for its existence while in British mandated Palestine no such electoral exercise was conducted to create Israel by the colonial masters and it was brought

---

[2] There is a point of view put forward, mostly by quarters who want to downplay the degree of national integration and social cohesion that existed pre-partition between peoples on an all-India level in British India, that partition and its repercussions were faced only by Punjab and Bengal and not the rest of India. However, while it is true that the brunt of the atrocities committed during the partition of India were faced by the people of Punjab and Bengal, the ramifications which were felt across the entire Indian sub-continent due to this event as far as up to Peshawar in the North West Frontier Province and the state of Hyderabad towards the south of India and in the partitioning of state institutions, departments including the armed forces, treasury and resources functioning de facto as one state for almost a century up to that moment cannot be downplayed or disregarded either by a serious scholastic study in nation building.

[3] 1946 Indian provincial elections, although these too were contested under the system of separate electorate due to which the competition in the constituencies was entirely between Muslim candidates and it was not an exercise in unadulterated democracy.

into existence by a resolution in the United Nations[4], the very birthing body whose later resolutions for itself Israel always violated. Moreover, since that time, the illegal occupation of Palestinian mandated lands by Israel has further weakened the moral case for Israel.

This is the penny that has to drop in the minds of not only Pakistanis and Israelis, as well as the Hindu hardliners in India who have made their country do a volte face on the Palestinian issue and now cheer the Zionists, but also in the minds of all those who want to reach a just solution for the Israeli as well as the Palestinian people, and those who want to achieve equal rights for all living in the state of Pakistan regardless of religion and ethnicity, and end the state of perpetual war and hostility which Pakistan finds itself in with its mother country, India.

And as an added benefit, the unlocking of this political enigma related to Israel (as was another neocolonial project of apartheid unlocked in South Africa[5]) will also break the grip of retrogressive fundamentalist anti science 'Political Islam' over the minds of the 'Minority' Muslims. Whereas, the 'Minority' as explained before now becoming the premise of the predominant thinking process among the Muslims of the world in general.

'Conquistador Minority' Muslims

Although it was mentioned earlier while listing out the categorizations of the peoples of the world converted to Islam, that there is only one country or land which fits the entire criteria of Category F, the 'Conquistador Minority' Muslims, and this is the category in which the Muslims of India fall, the reader too may have reached the same

---

[4] United Nations Resolution 181 passed on 29th November 1947

[5] The creation of the Zionist state on Palestinian land has stark similarities with the Apartheid state of South Africa created on South African soil. That is why there have been increasing voices among the intelligentsia over the years, from Edward Said to Gideon Levy and Ilan Pappe, that the just solution would be a one secular democratic state ensuring the equal rights of all citizens in the eyes of the state. Indeed, with the Israeli 'Knesset' having passed the resolution in July 2024 rejecting the two-state solution the basic premise of the creation of Israel, which stood on the pivotal principle that there would be two states on that land, has been flung out of the window thus bringing back into question the right of Israel to continue as an exclusive Jewish state on Palestinian land.

conclusion by now after having gone through above with the traits presented of the other categories.

Utilizing the theory of elimination, and after finding that all other countries where Muslims reside, one by one, fall into one category or the other from Category A to Category E as defined and described above, the only Muslim-inhabiting country, which is also a sovereign state, left in the bag and which has not been used as an example is the country of Pakistan, officially known as the Islamic Republic of Pakistan.

Some would be inclined to think and say that while Pakistan is certainly not an Arab country or a country where the population is ethnically and linguistically homogenous, it is also not a 'Minority' Muslim country and could at least be bracketed under the Category B of the 'Majority' Muslims.

This line of thinking could hold fast and withstand interrogation if history could demonstrate that there was a territorial state having more or less the boundaries which present-day Pakistan has, before the lands that now comprise Pakistan faced invasions and conquests from outside, specially from Muslim conquerors whose conquests introduced and injected Islam into these societies.

However, history shows that before Muslim conquests started in the lands comprising present-day Pakistan, these lands were organically and civilizationally linked at least with the northern half of present-day India. And prior to the Muslim conquests, these lands were politically combined in often expanding and often contracting kingdoms and empires over the course of centuries[6]. Thus, the historical experience, the cultures, the religions, the languages, and the organic make-up of races were all intrinsically linked or related with one another across the expanse of the northern half of the Indian subcontinent.

---

[6] The Nanda Empire (345 – 322 B.C.), Maurya Empire (322 – 185 B.C.), Gupta Empire (240 – 550 A.D.), Delhi Sultanates (1206 – 1526 A.D.), Moghul Empire (1526 – 1706 A.D. up to the death of Aurangzeb), Maratha Empire (1758 in present day Pakistani areas – 1818 A.D.) and eventually British India (1843 takeover of Sind / 1849 takeover of Punjab / 1880 takeover of areas after 2nd Anglo Afghan war of present day major areas of present day Khyber Pakhtunkhwa and Balochistan – 1947 A.D.).

This is why the country of Pakistan, its existence counted in decades, and the mindset of the Muslims residing in it cannot be analyzed by divorcing it from the millennia of combined historical experience its lands and peoples have shared, including their DNA, with the lands and peoples comprising present-day India.

Of course, the very plea of Pakistan is the plea of a minority religion pleading its case of its sense of insecurity from a majority religion. The existence of Pakistan rests on that plea, which, despite getting the Muslim majority provinces of India as its constituents, gives its Muslim majority citizens a mentality of constantly being under siege from an overwhelmingly non-Muslim majority who until a short time ago were their compatriots.

So, despite being a majority in their own present country, the thinking is that of a minority, and this mindset is, as stated, an ever-continuing existential premise to justify Pakistani statehood. So, the irony is that however much the ultra-Pakistanis wish to demonstrate that they are not Indian (culturally or ethnically), the existential argument that the new state was created just because of difference of religion immediately announces in an unspoken way that otherwise they were one people and could have lived as one country.

This is the inherent contradiction in the logic of justifying the existence of Pakistan, which keeps alive the 'under siege' minority mindset of the Muslims living in Pakistan. Till this self-contradicting logic is not abandoned, and the justification for the continued existence of Pakistan is not sought based on logic of federalism and the benefits of the self-determination and autonomy of peoples living in a decentralized federation, which is the secular logic of political science, the Muslims of Pakistan will not be able to have the thought process of a majority mindset comfortable and at ease with their religion.

They will continue to possess an under-siege mentality, self-denial of their shared Indian history and heritage of thousands of years, and the paranoia of 'Islam is in danger' providing fodder for religious obscurantism and fundamentalism.

But though the mindset is that of an under-siege minority, this mindset is not of self-defense. This mindset is hostile. This minority mindset is not overawed or overwhelmed by the majority, nor does it have an otherwise cultural respect of co-existence for the majority. In fact, this mindset seeks to ridicule and belittle 'the majority' at every opportunity, secretly wishes for its downfall, and cheers any defeats or losses that 'the majority' may face.

This mindset does not recognize the sovereignty of this 'majority' and hopes for a return of the subjugation of this 'majority' as it was subjugated by the minority Muslim conquerors and rulers prior to its eventual colonialization by the British.

This hostile and minority supremacist mindset owes its existence to the historical fact of Muslim conquests of India, where Muslims, though being in a minority, remained used to being, or among the contest for being, the rulers and never just the subjects of the land till British colonialism took over.

Therefore, to understand the official as well as the sociopsychological narrative of Pakistan which has always dominated discourse in the country, it is essential that one takes a step back from assessing the country per se and first look at the historical backdrop from which it came into existence. And there, one would find that the rationale for its creation is intrinsically linked with the centuries-old experience of Muslims, generation after generation, living in the land of India in which they were a minority and not a majority.

The advent of Islam in North India almost entirely owes itself to Muslim conquests from outside India. These start from the first conquest in Sind in 711 by the Arab general Mohammad Bin Qasim, resuming through the Muslim conquests from Central Asia and Afghanistan (the first being in the early 11th century A.D. by Mahmud Ghaznavi), resulting in the Sultanate dynasties of Delhi (from the late 12th century A.D. to 1526), culminating in the establishment of the Moghul Empire starting in 1526 with the conquest by the first Moghul Emperor Babar from Uzbekistan, a descendant of another conqueror of India in the 14th century A.D., Timur.

The Moghul Empire remained at its zenith until 1707, when the last great Moghul Emperor Aurangzeb died. By this time, European powers had already entered India and gained a foothold in Indian economy and politics. In just 50 years after Aurangzeb's death, the British were able to secure their first great victory in 1757 by defeating Sirajudaulah, the Muslim ruler of Bengal, and capturing the nerve centre of Indian economy at the time.

After that, the Indian states fell to the British one after the other, almost like dominos: Mysore in 1797, the Maratha Empire by 1818, Sind in 1843, Punjab in 1849, Oudh in 1856. In a matter of 150 years after the death of Aurangzeb, subsequent to victory in the war of 1857, the British Crown had become the de facto sovereign ruler of India.

The Afghan and Baloch areas of present-day Pakistan were ceded to the British by 1880 after the Second Anglo-Afghan War, and the Durand Line between British India and Afghanistan was drawn up and agreed upon between 1893 and 1894.

All through the above period, the Muslim polity in North India, produced through conversions of the conquered and settlements of the conquerors and the intermixing of the two through marriages and procreation, emerged as an entity used to being associated with the ruling classes rather than belonging to the subservient masses being ruled. Even the conversions that took place through Sufis, coming on the trail of the conquerors, had the advantage of awe among the conquered for the conquerors' religion.

The entire social and psychological makeup of this polity emanated from the dynamics of being courtiers, government officials, and aristocratic landowners, and of the social offshoots serving the same.

As for the vast non-Muslim majority of the Indian subcontinent, the overwhelmingly biggest component of which were the Hindus, but also other indigenous religious entities like Jains, Sikhs, and Buddhists, although they had had great kingdoms and empires prior to the Muslim invasions, throughout this period they remained subjected and the ruled masses of the land. Their religions and culture were assigned to being the religions and culture of the ruled, that is, inferior to that of the rulers.

Their only saving grace during this period can be said to be the brief period of the Sikh Empire in Punjab and the northwest of India, established by the great ruler Ranjit Singh in 1799, which lasted up to 1849, and the

Maratha Empire from 1674, engulfing the majority areas of west, northwest, and central India, up to 1818.

Why the non-Muslim majority of India and their kingdoms succumbed to Muslim conquests and were unable to overpower them for most of that period, yet were not converted en masse to Islam and remained a demographic majority, can be the dedicated subject of a different book.

However, it can be argued that the Sikh and Maratha empires were assertions of self-determination by the indigenous cultures, as organic sons of the soil of the land, the ones who had been conquered, and were not conquerors from outside.

An entirely puritan secular argument would state that the religious hue of any kingdom or empire should not be bracketed or associated with a political case for self-determination. But it is difficult to discard the wars fought for the establishment of the Sikh or Maratha empires as being assertions of self-determination when the culture and religion of these empires were the culture and religion of the conquered indigenous people of the land. For centuries during this period since the Muslim conquest from outside, these were looked down upon as such and considered inferior to the culture and religion of the dominant Muslim rulers.

How this factor of looking down upon these religions plays into the mindset of the 'conquistador', resulting in the demand for a separate state for Muslims, will also be further interrogated later.

It is in this historical backdrop, when the last vestige of Muslim rule in India was routed with their defeat in the War of Independence of 1857, which the British called 'Mutiny', that thinkers and ideologues for the salvation of Muslim culture and privilege emerged from the ashes of their lost empire in India.

The first and most forward-looking agile thinker in this context was the 'Shakespeare' of the Urdu language, which was the evolved language of the ruling Muslim classes at the time, Mirza Ghalib, who had understood that the Muslim social and intellectual structure in India had become decadent and archaic, which is why its power had withered away over time and eventually been defeated by the scientifically advanced Britishers.

31

Indeed, it was Mirza Ghalib who influenced and qualitatively changed the thought process of another intellectual of Muslim salvation, Syed Ahmed Khan, commonly known as Sir Syed Ahmed Khan after receiving knighthood for having saved thousands of British lives during the war of 1857, who presented the case of pardon for the Muslims in front of the British after the war was over.

In 1855, Syed Ahmed Khan was still indulged in working on documents of the bygone era of Muslim rule in India and had produced a new edition of 'Ai'n-e Akbari', an account of the administration of the Moghul emperor Akbar written by Akbar's court historian Abul Fazl. After completing this edition, Syed Ahmed Khan sent it to Mirza Ghalib asking him to write a foreword for it.

Following account is reproduced here of the response which Syed Ahmed Khan received from Mirza Ghalib[7]:

"In 1855, when he finished his highly scholarly, very well-researched and illustrated edition of Abul Fazl's Ai'n-e Akbari, itself an extraordinarily difficult book, and having finished the work to his satisfaction, and believing that Mirza Asadullah Khan Ghalib was a person who would appreciate his labours, Syed Ahmad approached the great Ghalib to write a taqriz (in the convention of the times, a laudatory foreword) for it. Ghalib obliged, but what he did produce was a short Persian poem castigating the Ai'n-e Akbari, and by implication, the imperial, sumptuous, literate, and learned Mughal culture of which it was a product. The least that could be said against it was that the book had little value even as an antique document. Ghalib practically reprimanded Syed Ahmad Khan for wasting his talents and time on dead things. Worse, he praised the English, who at that time held all the keys to all the a'ins in this world.

This poem is often referred to but has never translated in English. Shamsur Rahman Faruqi wrote an English translation.

---

[7] (references:
https:// farzana.wordpress.com/urdu-ghazal/welcome/anthology/sir-syed-ahmed-khan-سرسیداحمدخان/
'From Antiquary to Social Revolutionary: Syed Ahmad Khan and the Colonial Experience' by Shamsur Rehman Faruqi).

The translation is accurate, if lacking the felicity of the original:

"Good news my friends, this ancient book's door

Is now open, because of the Syed's grace and fortune,

The eye began to see, the arm found strength

That which was wrapped in ancient clothes, now put on a new dress.

And this idea of his, to establish its text and edit the A'in

Puts to shame his exalted capability and potential,

He put his heart to a task and pleased himself And made himself an auspicious, free servant.

One who isn't capable of admiring his quality Would no doubt praise him for this task,

For such a task, of which this book is the basis Only a hypocrite can offer praise.

I, who am the enemy of pretence And have a sense of my own truthfulness,

If I don't give him praise for this task It's proper that I find occasion to praise.

I have nothing to say to the perverse None know what I know of arts and letters,

In the whole world, this merchandise has no buyer. What profit could my Master hope from it?

It should be said, it's an excellent inventory So what's there to see that's worth seeing?

And if you talk with me of Laws and Rules Open your eyes, and in this ancient halting-place

Look at the Sahibs of England. Look at the style and practice of these, See what Laws and Rules they have made for all to see What none ever saw, they have produced."

Mirza Ghalib then produced this poem

"Science and skills grew at the hands of these skilled ones
Their efforts overtook the efforts of the forebears.
This is the people that owns the right to Laws and Rules
None knows to rule a land better than they,
Justice and Wisdom, they've made as one
They have given hundreds of laws to India.
The fire that one brought out of stone
How well these skilled ones bring out from straw!
What spell have they struck on water
That a vapour drives the boat in water!
Sometimes the vapour takes the boat down the sea
Sometimes the vapour brings down the sky to the plains.
Vapour makes the sky-wheel go round and round
Vapour is now like bullocks, or horses.
Vapour makes the ship speed
Making wind and wave redundant.
Their instruments make music without the bow
They make words fly high like birds
Oh don't you see that these wise people
Get news from thousands of miles in a couple of breaths?
They inject fire into air and the air glows like embers,
Go to London, for in that shining garden
The city is bright in the night, without candles.
Look at the businesses of the knowledgeable ones:
In every discipline, a hundred innovators!
Before the Laws and Rules that the times now have
All others have become things of yesteryears,
Wise and sensitive and prudent one, does your book have such good
and elegant Laws?
When one sees such a treasure house of gems
Why should one glean corn from that other harvest?

Well, if you speak of its style, it's good
No, it's much better than all else that you seek
But every good always has a better too
If there's a head, there's also a crown for it.
Don't regard that Generous Source as niggardly
It's a Date-Palm which drops sweet light, like dates.
Worshipping the Dead is not an auspicious thing
And wouldn't you too think that it's no more than just words?
The Rule of silence pleases my heart, Ghalib
You spoke well doubtless, not speaking is well too.
Here in this world your creed is to worship all the Prophet's children,
Go past praising, your Law asks you to pray
For Syed Ahmad Khan-e Arif Jang
Who is made up entirely of wisdom and splendour
Let there be from God all that he might wish for
Let an auspicious star lead all his affairs.

The poem was unexpected, but it came at the time when Syed Ahmad Khan's thought and feelings themselves were inclining toward change. Ghalib seemed to be acutely aware of a European (English)-sponsored change in world polity, specially Indian polity. Syed Ahmad might well have been piqued at Ghalib's admonitions, but he would also have realized that Ghalib's reading of the situation, though not nuanced enough, was basically accurate. Syed Ahmad Khan may also have felt that he, being better informed about the English and the outside world, should have himself seen the change that now seemed to be just round the corner. Sir Syed Ahmad Khan never again wrote a word in praise of the Ai'n-e Akbari and, in fact, gave up taking active interest in history and archaeology and became a social reformer."

Truly, the revision of the thought process of Sir Syed Ahmad Khan from that point onward can be considered a turning point and a cornerstone for the destiny of the Indian Muslims in British India. From this point on, Sir Syed Ahmed Khan produced a body of work, including writings and journals, which introduced a rational way of thinking to the Muslim polity of India.

His works advocated utilizing scientific reasoning in addressing matters of history, ideas, and the present world. For example, he considered that Christ had died a natural death and was neither crucified nor taken up to the skies alive by the divine and replaced by a body double to be crucified, as believed by Muslims. He questioned the existence of 'jinns' and embraced Darwin's theory of evolution while remaining a theistic evolutionist, that is, believing that God creates using the laws of nature[8]. Socially, he reasoned that the Islamic concept of no 'interest' in money lending applied only for the poor and not on the rich and saw it as a necessary element for moving the engine of modern economy.

He went on in 1875 to establish the Mohammedan Anglo Oriental College in Aligarh, found with the objective of imparting modern western education to the Muslims along the same lines of rational thought process, which later advanced to be more famously known as the Aligarh Muslim University. It is this university which is historically considered to be the intellectual hotbed for the genesis of the Pakistan Movement in British India.

In essence, his biggest contribution to the salvation of the Indian Muslims was twofold. He succeeded in achieving a break from the conservatism in the Muslim mind, which had become introvert after defeat to the British and rested on a hatred of everything Western, continuing with the orthodox, outdated, superstitious way of thinking, devoid of any ability for scientific reasoning. He convinced it to rethink and question matters by considering the discoveries of science and rationalism.

---

[8] As a side note, Surah Nuh (Noah) verses 13 to 20 from the Quran are quoted below for the reader's reflection:
"What is the matter with you? Why will you not fear God's majesty, WHEN HE HAS CREATED YOU STAGE BY STAGE? Have you ever wondered how God created seven heavens, one above the other, placed the moon as a light in them and the sun as a lamp, HOW GOD MADE YOU SPRING FORTH FROM THE EARTH LIKE A PLANT, how He will return you into it and then bring you out again, and how He has spread the Earth out for you, to walk along its spacious paths?"

Secondly, he succeeded in bringing the intelligentsia of the Muslims to acquire Western education, not be averse or insular toward the new British rulers of the land, and to take part in the new state structures being introduced by the British to run the colonized Indian state and economy.

However, throughout this great endeavor taken up by him, his loyalty and priority were clear to himself. He had taken up this endeavor solely to serve the Indian Muslim and not the whole of native India. He was very clear that he was working for the renaissance of the Indian Muslim, and the Indian Muslim had to remain aloof and separate, in fact detached, from any collective aspirations for the whole of native India including other religions of the country.

Here one has to take a pause, and before any overarching judgment is passed on him as having been the sole source or prime instigator of communalism that later fermented vehemently in the land, it would be fair to observe that after the advent of the British, the renaissance emerging among the native populations in India was somehow already evolving with a religious hue.

During the same period in the 1800s, India had seen the emergence of the Shuddhi movement started by Dayananda Saraswati and the founding of the Arya Samaj, which sought to reclaim India for Hinduism and the reconversion of the Muslims of India back to Hinduism. A reform movement among Hindus had also been brought to the fore of Indian polity by the likes of great intellectuals like Swami Vivekananda.

The fact that the case for the creation of Pakistan can never be objectively discarded or ticked off with over simplistic explanations—such as being the result of the British policy of "divide and rule," or the British strategy of creating a buffer state against communism, or communalism generated only by Muslims, or Jinnah's 'personal ambition for acquiring political power' (despite being an individual who at one time was called the "ambassador of Hindu-Muslim unity")—shows that the continuation of this case owes its existence to the reality of intense religiosity that pervades, to date, very deeply in the society and psychological makeup of the people of the Indian subcontinent.

Whoever was and is in denial of this reality runs the risk of always erring in resolving the antagonistic and, with the introduction of nuclear weapons into the equation, potentially fatal contradictions which exist in the subcontinent.

As mentioned earlier, it was probably inevitable that the cultural aspect of active resistance to conquests from the outside could not avoid being colored by the native religions of the land, as symbols of defiance and self-determination by local populations. This was all the more inevitable in a society where industrial revolution and scientific and intellectual enlightenment had never occurred when the alien conquests happened. Local culture, intertwined with the local religions, was the only means available to the conquered to intellectually sustain and survive themselves against the conquerors.

Therefore, the divide with heavy religious coloring had already occurred in society before the arrival of the secular and scientifically equipped Western conquerors into India. The religion of the conquerors and rulers from outside for almost a millennium was one—the religion, as well as the rulers, descending from outside India—while the religion of the conquered was another. Those who converted from the conquered to the religion of the conquerors were promoted in society, while those who did not convert were kept assigned to the subdued strata of society.

When it is said that Muslims and Hindus had lived in peace together before the British arrived and that there was no rioting or fratricide prior to the advent of the British, it is an erroneous inference, because before, the two religions were not existing in an equivalent equation, and one religion was dominating the other. There was no rioting as equals, but there were plenty of incidents of one-sided religious suppression and massacres, and eventual apparent peace achieved with the victory of one religion over the other and the bowing to defeat by the other.

The true test for reformers among both the Muslims and Hindus of India after the ultimate victory of the British Crown over India and the Western colonialization of the country was to grasp the truth of science and rational thought and rise above the religious bent in their renaissance.

The test required reviewing and shedding the unscientific elements in their religions, recognizing the premise of their colonialization and disenfranchisement from political power by the British in their mutual unity as Indians, and reaching out to each other with a conscious resolve that the contest between the two religions that had occurred prior to the advent of the British was over. And that it was no longer important for one to claim superiority over the other on the social and political level.

The creation of Pakistan, and the fact that it could not eventually be avoided, historically shows that the reformers may have succeeded in some aspects of the test but did not pass this test overall. The responsibility for failing this test lies with the reformers on both sides. On both sides, while the reformers were ready to revisit their respective religions internally from a scientific and rational viewpoint and adapt to the new world, they were unable to bring themselves to rise above the religious bent in politics and let go of centuries of prejudice and reaction against the other religion.

While the reformer on the Muslim side continued to suffer from a sense of supremacy over the Hindu and local religions, the reformer on the Hindu side could not overcome the bitterness and resentment against Islam, which had subdued Hinduism politically, converted Hindus, and left some of its influences on those who did not convert.

By the time leaders like Jinnah, Gandhi, and Nehru came to the fore in the Indian National Congress (INC), who initially did try to bridge the divide and rise above the religious bent, it was already too late. The die had been cast, and it ran deep in society.

The All India Muslim League had already been formed in 1906, and the Hindu Mahasabha had already placed itself as a powerful pressure group inside the INC since 1915. Jinnah and Gandhi both wavered toward the Muslim League and the Hindu Mahasabha respectively due to this on-ground reality.

Historically, it is only Nehru, the idealist, who emerges steadfast and unwavering against the pull of religion in politics. But his influence was not powerful enough to prevent the politics of communalism and partition from dominating and eventually becoming the decisive factor in the actions taken by the British in 1947 when departing from India.

Still, it is to the credit of Nehru, and Gandhi who eventually chose him to lead India, that the politics of religion was kept at bay long enough in India to establish strong foundations of secularism and enlightenment in India, including but not limited to the constitution. It is due to these strong foundations that it is still difficult for the powerful political forces of Hindutva in India to overturn the secular constitution of the country.

After recording this historical perspective, we return to the separatist premise of the reform movement of Sir Syed Ahmed Khan and continue to see how this led to the emergence of the 'Minority Muslim' mindset of the Pakistan movement and the foundational premise of the Pakistani mindset. Both of these need to be challenged, bettered, and replaced by a more advanced and sophisticated secular worldview and logic of political science, which in turn is the only way through which Pakistan will be able to survive and continue as a viable federal state.

By now, we have established that the foundational premise of the Pakistani mindset is the 'Minority Muslim' mindset, but of an escalated version which encapsulates in itself an addition of two elements: the baggage of being the 'Conquistador' in the land of the majority, and secondly, as a result, feeling threatened by the majority in a democracy, that is, a sense of insecurity.

That is why, in this book, the Pakistani Muslims, as well as those in northern India who participated in the Pakistan movement and are still sympathetic to it, are categorized as 'Conquistador Minority' Muslims. This 'Conquistador Minority' Muslim mindset has carried over as a foundational premise in the very formative root of Pakistan, which is why, despite becoming a Muslim majority country, it is this mindset which persisted and prevailed and was complemented by permanently having Hindu majority India as a giant neighbor on its borders.

As the above mindset captured the imagination of the political consciousness steering the formation of Pakistan and eventually was beget with the task of ruling Pakistan, the ruling politicians as well as the civil-military bureaucracy, who were the physical carriers of this political consciousness, consistently demonstrated some behavioral peculiarities since the inception of the state.

These consistent peculiarities were as listed below:

1. <u>A cynical attitude toward majority rule and subconsciously always associating it with chaos or anarchy, which would upset the stability of the country.</u> The majority population being poor and illiterate or uneducated was viewed with scorn and as if less human, incapable of knowing what

was best for them. Their choice was considered to be driven by the material or coercive influence of the politicians leading them, rather than as an intelligent choice.

The famous Italian Marxist intellectual Antonio Gramsci, in his book *The Modern Prince*, pointed out that whereas it is the educated middle classes in a society who have the ability to influence public opinion and sway elections in a way far greater than the influence of an individual vote, the poor people, i.e., the dispossessed strata of society have only one way of affecting elections, and that is through their vote in the elections. And the fascists want to take even that one power away from people[9].

This attitude of scorn toward the will of the people literally stunted the capacity of these classes in Pakistan to grasp the dynamism and complexity of pluralism, political compromise, alignments, and the very palpable material interests of the masses at play, interests, of which it is the masses who are most cognizant. This dynamism, complexity and cognizance of the interests of the masses are part and parcel of a

---

[9] "What is measured is precisely the effectiveness, and the expansive and persuasive capacity, of the opinions of a few individuals, the active minorities, the elites, the avant-gardes, etc. – i.e. their rationality, historicity, or concrete functionality. Which means it is untrue that all individual opinions have 'exactly' equal weight. Ideas and opinions are not spontaneously 'born' in each individual brain: they have had a center of formation, or irradiation, of dissemination, of persuasion --- a group of men, or a single individual even, which has developed them and presented them in the form of current reality. The counting of 'votes' is the final ceremony of a long process, in which it is precisely those who devote their best energies to the State and the nation (when such they are) who carry the greatest weight. If this hypothetical group of worthy men, notwithstanding the boundless material power which they possess, do not have the consent of the majority, they must be judged as either inept, or as not representative of 'national' interests --- which cannot help being decisive in inflecting the national will in one direction rather than in another. 'Unfortunately' everyone tends to confound his own 'private interest' it may be with that of the nation, and hence find it 'dreadful', etc. that it should be the 'law of numbers' which decides; it is better of course to become an elite by decree. Thus, it is not a question of the people who 'have the brains' feeling that they are being reduced to the level of the lowest illiterate, but rather one of people who think they are the ones with the brains wanting to take away from the 'man in the street' even that tiniest fraction of power of decision over the course of national life which he possesses." – Antonio Gramsci (Modern Prince, Chapter 13 'Number and Quality in Representative Systems of Government').

sophisticated, functioning democracy. In this way, being imbued with such cynicism since childhood, this mental faculty of the 'educated middle classes' never received intellectual nourishment, and adulthood was reached with this faculty in a retarded state.

2. A disparaging and ridiculing attitude toward all cultures and languages other than the culture and language of the court and courtiers of the last Muslim rulers in India. This manifested in policy and behavior by considering the advancement of the local languages and cultures of the lands that now physically constituted the country of Pakistan as somehow a treasonous or anti-state activity, and branding those local politicians as traitors who advocated for the advancement of local languages and the autonomy of the provinces forming the federation of Pakistan.

This attitude was more rampant among the middle classes of Urdu-speaking migrants from India and the majority Punjabis, who were the dominant ethnic groups in the bureaucracy of the newly born state. Their loyalty to the cause of Pakistan was more consciousness-driven rather than based on material pragmatism, as was the case with those feudal lords who opted for Pakistan in fear of the anti-feudal manifesto of the Indian National Congress.

In fact, the Punjabi middle classes went so far as to disown their mother tongue and preferred to speak Urdu with their children, who grew up without knowing how to speak their mother tongues. Speaking Punjabi was considered by Punjabis themselves as uncouth and was assigned to being used only when required to abuse someone or express dirty humor.

It was only much later, when the Punjabi middle classes sought to overtake the Urdu-speaking middle classes in the civil and military bureaucracy and generally in the upper strata of society, that they began to use Punjabi more frequently, but only colloquially, as a mechanism of asserting identity and grouping themselves. In the formal realm of government administration and education, the Punjabi language still remained an outcast.

This alienation among Punjabis mutated to the extent that they began to consider themselves as the standard for measuring how purely Pakistani any ethnic group could be. Non-Punjabis rooting for their own languages were seen as less Pakistani or less enthusiastic about being Pakistani.

Meanwhile, the Urdu-speaking community, whom the Punjabis had overtaken in the bureaucracy, came to be somehow perceived as being Indian agents by the latter, since it was present day India where the former's elders had come from.

Naming children, landmarks, and missiles after outside Muslim conquerors of India or Arab Muslims, rather than preferring to choose names from local languages and folklore, is another manifestation of this mindset. Many Pakistanis keep surnames that associate them with ancestral genealogy external to the Indian subcontinent and take pride in doing so, as if being descendants of races originating in lands outside of the Indian subcontinent, specially from Arabia or Central Asia, somehow makes them superior to the local races.

It becomes even more amusing to observe that there is no cultural or linguistic remnant among them which would in any way identify them to the outside world as belonging to the races which they claim to be descendants of, and even the present-day same ethnicities and races in those lands would not own them or seriously accept them as their own. Even the authenticity of the claim of such Pakistanis as being descendants of those races is sometimes suspect.

But the attitude, of considering one having a family name that links the person to outside races, as being somehow racially superior to a person who is clearly a descendant only of local races, persists in the subconscious mind even if not explicitly acknowledged.

3. A tendency to succumb easily to Islamic Dogmatic Fundamentalism and viewing the world through the lens of religious communalism.

This was first manifested very soon after independence and the demise of the founding father, the Quaid e Azam (Great Leader) Mohammad Ali Jinnah, that despite having the famous speech of the Quaid e Azam delivered on 11 August 1947 to the Constituent Assembly which said that religion would have nothing to do with the state, an Objectives Resolution was passed by the Constituent Assembly on 12th March 1949 with Islamic dogmatic fundamentalist caveats which politically Islamicised the state and eased the way in the future for implementation of fundamentalist sharia on the state and the people of Pakistan.

This caveating was done entirely with the purposes of divorcing Pakistan completely from its Indian heritage and ethos and keeping check on and persecuting those political forces inside Pakistan who wanted to solve the controversial issues of the country through the rational precepts of secular political science and democracy.

Similarly, in all international events, the foreign policy choice of Pakistan to side in an event was driven by viewing who was Muslim in the event rather than by reflecting as to what was just as per international law. That is not to state that the foreign policy stances of Pakistan were not on the just side most of the times but to point out that the criteria in taking sides was communal and/or fundamentalistic.

For instance, the reason why Pakistan and Pakistanis support the Palestinian cause is not just because the land of the Palestinians has been taken away from them unjustly but also because the Palestinians are mostly Muslims. Then on top of the communal comes the fundamentalist angle whereby the religion driven desire, for the reconquest of Jerusalem and the Dome of the Rock and the hatred of the Jews, pools in. This prevents the Pakistanis from understanding that there are another people in that land too who have a legitimate right for a homeland or equal rights in a secular state in that same land.

The Serb Bosnian conflict, the Greek Turkish dispute over Cyprus, the support of the Taliban state in Afghanistan and the conflict between Azerbaijan and Armenia are some other examples where communalism and fundamentalism were manifested as important factors in the state's foreign policy criteria.

During military rules, with the backdrop of the Soviet invasion of Afghanistan, this tendency mutated further into policies of the deep state harboring and hosting foreign jihadists and militants who later became the source of launching terror across the globe, which were rolled back with great difficulty and sacrifice by successive civil democratic governments.

4. Viewing India as the perpetual and the worst enemy of Pakistan. After the partition of India and the creation of Pakistan, the dominant narrative on the Indian side regarding this historical event was that Pakistanis were basically our own people and 'brothers' who had chosen to make a separate country due to the dividing influence of the British and misplaced concern about the rights and status of the Muslims in a Hindu majority country. And would it not be better if we were one again?

That a line had been drawn between two peoples who were basically the same and that lines could be drawn on lands but not in the people's hearts. This narrative in India remained dominant till the late 1980s, i.e., up to the time that militancy and unbridled terrorism had not reared its head in Indian Kashmir, and the early 1990s which saw the rise of the Hindu Right with the destruction of the Babri mosque in Ayodhya and the demand for the reclamation of that land for the Ram mandir (temple).

In fact, Gandhi paid the price with his life for fasting and standing up for Pakistan's right to receive its due share of the national treasury on the departure of the British. It was on the basis of this narrative that India was always reluctant to cede any more territory than necessary, which was also the rationale of its actions in Kashmir once the Maharaja there had signed the treaty of accession to India. While in the princely states of Junagadh and Manavadar and Hyderabad, its actions ran counter to the intentions of the princely rulers of these states.

However, on the Pakistani side, the dominant narrative was always of exclusion and being 'not Indian.' Here again, we see a post-Pakistan, more secular reflection of the Quaid e Azam on the nature of relations with India, versus a more jingoistic and belligerent view of the country adopted by the civil-military bureaucracy which was running Pakistan.

In early 1948, the Quaid had told the then US Ambassador to Pakistan, Paul Alling, that he foresaw the relation between India and Pakistan to be more along the lines of the association between the United States and Canada[10]. Similarly, addressing the All India Muslim League Council meeting in Karachi in December 1947 he had stated that *"I tell you that I still consider myself to be an Indian. For the moment I have accepted the Governor-Generalship of Pakistan. But I am looking forward to a time when I would return to India and take my place as a citizen of my country."* [11] When Sri Prakasa, the first high commissioner of India to Pakistan visited the Quaid and told him that Nehru wanted to know what to do with

---

[10] 'The United States and Pakistan (1947 – 2000)' by Dennis Kux.
[11] https://muslimmirror.com/eng/the-truth-about-indias-partition-and-its-sole-architect/

the Quaid's personal mansion at Malabar Hill in Bombay, 'Jinnah's voice turned to a tremor and he said *"you do not know how much I love Bombay. I still look forward to returning to it one day. Tell Nehru not to break my heart. I have built it brick by brick".'* [12]Contrary to these views and the vision expressed by the Quaid, the attitude of Pakistan's civil military bureaucracy became increasingly hostile towards India, specially after the armed conflict over Kashmir in 1948, which the Quaid also condoned, and with the consolidation of 'minority Muslim' migrants from India, both from the Urdu-speaking northern India as well as eastern Punjab, in government positions. The power of the military officers who were still more under the influence of the British high command grew greater than the politicians comprising the Muslim League, who were devoid of the necessary spadework and grassroots involvement of the masses to establish the supremacy of a democratic constitution over the state.

Acquisition by migrants of India of the properties left behind by the fleeing Hindus and Sikhs during the 1947 partition further contributed towards the hardening of the stance towards India on a social level, to preempt any reclamation of these properties by the original owners. Indeed, as time progressed further away from the year of the partition, the vision and influence of the founding father, the Quaid, receded and that of more anti-India narratives and outlooks gained dominance.

Considerable material has been written elsewhere generally about the fading influence of the Quaid immediately after 1947. Indeed, the Rawalpindi conspiracy case of 1951 also indicates how a General discontented with the political government's and the army's Commander-in-Chief's approach on dealing with the Kashmir issue was also supported by a middle class Left which had already bought the political rationale of partition under the Adhikari thesis of the Indian Communist Party.

Regarding the attitude towards India, it does not require an expert economist to see that continuing of strong economic ties and free trade with India would be the cheapest and best formula for the prosperity of the common people of Pakistan. But after the creation of Pakistan, as the social classes who were psychologically as well as economically more

---

[12] 'Pakistan: Birth and Early Days' by Sri Prakasa.

motivated to propound an India-hating narrative along with the feudal classes grew stronger inside the country, this was coupled with the phenomenon of new alignments of states being formed in the backdrop of the start of the Cold War between the capitalist West and the socialist USSR.

The dominant social classes running Pakistan suddenly saw the promise of considerable monetary windfall resulting from aligning with the West in this Cold War and chose to not opt for continuing trade and economic ties with India. Needless to elaborate on the fact that this windfall mostly benefitted the ruling social classes of Pakistan and did not trickle down to reach and benefit the bottom most classes of the country.

Neither were the lower classes of the society free to interact economically on their own with India under this anti-India and minus-India policy implemented by the ruling social classes of Pakistan. However, the inertia of less stringent border control and free cultural exchange between the two countries continued till it ended with the war of 1965, which again was the result of Operation Gibraltar[13], a project of the predominantly anti India narrative and lobby.

5. Difficulty in seeing non-Muslim compatriots as equals. There is no one more indigenous or 'son of the soil' to the land which constitutes the country of Pakistan than the Hindus, Sikhs, or the Christians of Pakistan.

For the Hindus and Sikhs, as is obvious, are those people residing on this land since millennia or centuries who did not convert to Islam, and the Christians are mostly those indigenous lower classes of the land who converted to Christianity after the advent of the British, to escape the local caste system.

However, the Pakistani Muslims, who constitute almost 97 percent of the population, consciously or subconsciously, view these religious minorities as if they are being given extra favour by being accepted as Pakistanis. As if they have come from somewhere else, or that a good

---

[13] 'Operation Gibraltar' was the code name of the military incursion into Indian Jammu and Kashmir by the Pakistan Army in August 1965 which eventually led to Indian attack on mainland Pakistan on 6th September 1965 and the start of the 1965 war between India and Pakistan.

Pakistani (read 'good Pakistani' for Muslim Pakistani in their minds) shows generosity or magnanimity by being hospitable to these religious minorities, as if they have newly arrived or are guests in the land. Absent this generosity or magnanimity, the true place of these religious minorities is a place of less status than the Muslim Pakistani, a place subservient to the Muslim Pakistani. Indeed, it is a fact that positions of sweepers and cleaners, even as advertised by the government or companies, are assigned in the mind of the Pakistani Muslim to be the forte of Pakistani Christians. The patriotism of Hindus and Sikhs is subconsciously mistrusted or suspect in the Pakistani Muslim mind, with the Sikhs recently having become an agent and a pragmatic tool to be used for the breakup of India through the creation of Khalistan.

The Ahmadis too are completely of the indigenous stock of the country, the true sons of the soil being entirely Punjabis by descent, in fact a community which was part of the spearhead of the Pakistan movement.

The national poet of Pakistan, Iqbal, had for a brief period of time been an Ahmadi[14] and the Quaid is on record as having said *Who am I to declare a person as non-Muslim who calls himself a Muslim,*" answering a question of whether the Ahmadis could join the Muslim Conference in Kashmir[15].

Pakistan's first foreign minister Sir Zafarullah Khan, the first Chief of Pakistan Air Force Zafar Chaudhry, the Generals and heroes of the 1965 war Akhtar Hussain Malik, Iftikhar Khan Janjua and Abdul Ali Malik and the first Nobel Laureate from Pakistan Dr. Abdus Salam are all Ahmadis. But Pakistanis (Pakistani Muslims), even after having the Ahmadis been declared constitutionally as non-Muslims, have trouble viewing Ahmadis as patriotic and loyal to the country and worthy of being acknowledged and celebrated as equal Pakistanis.

---

[14] 'The Ahmadiyya Betrayal' by Kunwar Khuldune Shahid (https://www.nation.com.pk/12-Nov-2015/the-ahmadiyya-betrayal).
[15] 'Tahrik Huriyyat Kashmir (History of Independence Movements in Kashmir), volume 2, 1936 – 1945', 'Jinnah, The Muslim League And the Ahmadi issue' by Yasser Latif Hamdani (https://thefridaytimes.com/08-Jul-2024/jinnah-the-muslim-league-and-the-ahmadi-issue).

The famous 11th August 1947 speech of the Quaid, which states, *"You are free; you are free to go to your temples. You are free to go to your mosques or to any other places of worship in this State of Pakistan. You may belong to any religion, caste or creed, that has nothing to do with the business of the state."* is quoted to prove the greatness of the Quaid but conveniently ignored for all practical purposes while running the affairs of government and state and on private business and social levels.

The constitution of Pakistan requires that the positions of the Prime Minister and the President of the country can be occupied by only Muslim citizens of the country. In this way, the Conquistador Minority mindset, wary of a non-Muslim population it conquered and subdued and mistrustful and insecure about Islam and the practice and tenets of Islam being in danger from those who are not Muslims, is ingrained in the subconscious mind of the average Pakistani Muslim from the very outset of childhood.

There is a sense of guilt and insecurity running deep in the mentality of the average Pakistani Muslim that by going the extra mile in sympathizing with the minorities when they are persecuted or accused of blasphemy or by mentioning and acknowledging the religion of their ancestors, they would somehow betray Islam and risk the wrath of Allah.

This behavioural peculiarity became more intensified and accelerated after the ascent to power of the fundamentalist General Zia ul Haq and the domination of militant low intellectual Mullahs in society thereafter, to such low levels of detail that, as an example, in recent decades the common farewell statement among Pakistanis became 'Allah Haafiz' (may Allah be the protector) from the centuries-old 'Khuda Haafiz' (may God be the protector), the word 'Khuda' being the generic Persian word for 'God' and which had been adopted over centuries as an inclusive effort in united India among people of different religions so as to liberate themselves from any religion-specific God while bidding farewell to each other. This insecurity and religion-based superstition of the average Pakistani Muslim dumbed down to the extent of considering it risky for salvation to use any word other than the word 'Allah' used in the Quran for God, thus falling for the supremacist and narrow exclusivist outlook that the Islamic Dogmatic Fundamentalists and the Mullahs want to imbue among the

Muslims, while ignoring that etymologically the word 'Allah' is pre-Islamic as are the Arabic names of persons who were born before the advent of Islam but converted to Islam. This sense of insecurity and superstitious dumbing down of the fear for salvation are also reflected on very trifle levels when Muslims started making it a point to write 'mashaAllah' and 'inshaAllah' with capital A(s) in the middle of these words, as if Allah is a human entity who would take offence if the word 'Allah' was not written with capital A.

So it is, after summing up and reflecting on these analytical observations of the 'Conquistador Minority' Muslim mindset, that we understand the sociopsychological drivers pressing on the demand for Pakistan and thereafter governing the state of Pakistan with an under-siege mentality, feeling more insecure than was warranted, hence taking some policy decisions and actions which were innately flawed for statecraft and nation-building.

These flawed decisions and actions, resulting from a flawed thinking process, were taken in the very first years of the newly born state, indeed in the first decade, which eventually culminated in strengthening and enabling the military to successfully launch the first military coup in 1958.

And since then, the state became entangled in a vicious circle of a perpetual tussle between the advocates of military rule, always raising the bogey of insecurity and anarchy playing to this very mindset, and the proponents of constitutional supremacy of a democratic federal civil society organically led by the traditional as well as rising civil economic ruling classes of the country.

In this tussle, the foremost educated middle classes of the country, mostly urban or becoming urban or 'urbane', having been seeded with the mindset traits explained above, chose to jump in the team of the former, i.e. the advocates of military rule.

It is this choice of these middle classes which the book will further explore, because this choice would seem surprising to an onlooker belonging to an organically evolved democratic society who would expect a progressive educated middle class to oppose any form of military rule or dictatorship and work for the prevalence of the rule of law under a democratically constituted constitution.

In other words, an onlooker from a historically evolved democratic society would expect a progressive educated middle class of a country to be working on a grassroot level with the people, siding with their right to cast votes and choose their leaders, having a studious grasp of the economic stage of development of their country and opposing any adventurer from the military who sets aside the constitution of the country at gunpoint, thus enrooting the ideas in the country of 'might is right' and 'constitution is just a piece of paper which can be thrown anytime in the dustbin.'

But before we delve in this direction and enter the specific realm of the post-1947 state of Pakistan created by the 'Conquistador Minority' Muslim, we first have to tie up some loose ends still remaining which keep some basic questions still open.

The questions which ask, "So, was the creation of Pakistan correct?", "Should Pakistan remain as a state?", "Should Pakistan be an Islamic state theocratically ruled by sharia?", and "Should Pakistan shed off its Muslim identity?"

Therefore, before we move on to the next chapter, we have to see as to what the answers to these questions should be and what should be the verdict on Muslim Nationalism.

Verdict on Muslim Nationalism

It is abundantly clear from the studies and findings of Political Science and the lessons of history, including the experience of Europe and the Westphalian concept of the nation-state, which lead the study of the most modern concept of nationhood, that religion alone cannot hold fast as a viable premise for nationhood. This book also attempts to reiterate the same, and the entire discourse in this chapter also supports the same stance.

Indeed, the breakup of Pakistan in 1971 has already defeated and buried forever the concept of a nation based solely on religion. So, on what premise does the remaining Pakistan trudge on in the modern community of nation states? What is its raison d'être? What are the present and future generations of Pakistan to be told about this?

It is not deniable what we saw, when discussing the categories of the 'Minority' Muslim and the 'Conquistador Minority' Muslim, that in face of alienation in Western societies and later the backdrop of the Israeli Palestinian issue, which affected all Muslims internationally, and in pre-independence India with the rise of the Hindu identity movements, later consolidated and expanded in post-independence India, that the emergence of a Muslim Identity consciousness does carry genuinely justifiable weight.

However, this Muslim Identity can never mature to a degree to qualify as a principle of political science to replace the concept of nationhood. It would need more than just this religion-based identity to enable a people to qualify as a nation.

The ethos of the Indian Muslim (read as well 'Pakistani Muslim') is much different from the ethos of an Arab or a Turkish Muslim living as a minority in the West or the Black American Muslim. All are struck by the politics of Muslim Identity, but they cannot constitute as a separate nation together.

But the ethos is a start. It alone, like religion, cannot mature the Muslim of the subcontinent to be called as a separate nation for just being a Muslim, but it is a start. Because the ethos of the Northwestern Indian Muslim is different from the ethos of the North Indian Muslim, it is different from the ethos of the South Indian Muslim, and it is different from the ethos of the Bengali Muslim.

But looking inward, this ethos is again not enough. Inside Northwest India, i.e. the territory which now constitutes the state of Pakistan, there are majorly four federating units or provinces which historically have existed as separate states, kingdoms, or 'governorates' in different time periods of considerably long durations and possess distinct culture and languages different from one another, despite some similarities due to geographical contiguity. This inner distinction prevents from qualifying Pakistan to be called as one nation. In fact, it is a federal state majorly comprising of four nationalities.

But what about the Westphalian concept of the nation-state? Can Pakistan be called a nation-state like there was once a nation-state called Yugoslavia or like India today is convincingly called a nation-state, which it really is, rather than one nation as Indian nationalists would like it to be called?

In fact, herein lies our answer for Pakistan. India is not one nation but a nation-state, a federation of multiple nationalities each possessing their own distinct histories, culture, and languages, and so is Pakistan.

The creation of Pakistan is a historical reality. This reality, though it cannot be justified by the claimed premise of the two-nation theory based on religion, which already met its demise in 1971, is still a de facto reality. And in Political Science, a de facto reality is never viewed as devoid of valid historical reasons, even though this de facto reality came about overstepping the set definitions of the latest civilized and humanely acceptable political models for organizing and governing human society.

The truth is that though the people who would comprise the new state of Pakistan were not one nation, those rooting for it historically had a civilizational ethos different from the civilizational ethos of the people who would religiously be a majority in post-British India. It was a sad fact, but it was true.

Also, the combined people of post-British India were in no way one nation as the intellectuals of the Indian National Congress (INC) wanted it to be accepted. India was, and still is, a multinational state. And at the time of the departure of the British, it was a multinational state with different areas and different cultural national identities being at different stages of economic development.

It is true that the political solution being offered by the INC, despite making the mistake of calling India as one nation, was more secular and humane with acceptance and room for federalism in the independent state of India. But the concerns of the Muslim ethos, concentrated in the northwest and northeast of India, which could not relate with the centralist plans and ambitions of the INC for a post-British India, as well as the Hindu identity politics lurking in the shadows of the future despite the good intentions of the leaders of the INC, were also genuine historical concerns.

Maybe they were retrogressive concerns, of a feudal past of glory and rule in India, but the INC had been unable to diffuse these concerns in the minds of the Muslim middle classes and masses who eventually joined the movement of the All-India Muslim League and voted for them.

True, the two-nation theory was a stilted and dumbed-down, obnoxious, and inflammatory potion created to represent these concerns, but it did become a rallying cry for all those northwestern and northeastern Indians who were feeling uneasy about the abolition of feudalism, the rise of Hindu identity politics, a strong unitary state center, and losing the cultural ethos of the court and courtiers of Muslim rule over India.

Those Pashtun, Baloch, or Sindhi nationalists who today attempt to disown the state of Pakistan cannot point to nationalist mass movements inside their provinces at the time of the departure of the British which were stronger and more popular than the movements of the All-India Muslim League or the INC. In fact, the leading political forces of these provinces at the time threw their weight behind either the Muslim League (G.M. Syed supporting the Muslim League in 1947) or the INC (Khan Abdul Ghaffar Khan supporting the INC, which was ironically a proponent of a unitary state with a strong center) rather than being able to raise a more popular movement for national independence of their respective provinces or states.

Therefore, we can say that Muslim Nationalism was a flawed political concept, but it was successfully used at the time to bring together the interests and concerns of northwestern, northern, and northeastern Indian Muslims, and the result that ensued was the formation of a political arrangement out of post-British India which was called the state of Pakistan.

Pakistan thus is a territorial political arrangement but not a nation, and if it is to stand the test of time, it will have to look at itself as such and run itself as a federal, secular, democratic state, free from the notion of only Muslim nationhood, although it may remain a conservator of Indian Muslim cultural and linguistic heritage, and instead call itself a Westphalian Pakistani nation-state.

But any attempt to keep the concept of Pakistan limited to only Muslim nationhood would always be a retarding force in Pakistan's quest to become a successful nation-state instead of a failed state, and the proponents of such an attempt will always be found standing on the wrong side of history.

The ethos of Pakistan and Pakistanis, post-independence, has also been unique since 1947, as we shall see in the book, and particularly after 1971 has further matured away from the Indian ethos, enough to historically obtain a uniquely Pakistani ethos, including political, in which the different nationalities living inside Pakistan now look and feel and speak and read and write more like each other than people of their ethnicities living in countries other than Pakistan. That is a sign of hope for the viability of Pakistan to continue as a nation-state in the future.

When the two-nation theory was defeated and sunk in the Bay of Bengal, as stated by Indira Gandhi in 1971, Zulfiqar Ali Bhutto came up with an advanced version of the two-nation theory based not on religion but on the basis of the Indus Valley civilization being different from the rest of India.

This version also is not entirely true and cannot withstand the interrogation of history, as the civilization of India is too interconnected with and enrooted in the Indus Valley civilization to be ignored or hidden. However, presenting this version of a two-nation theory to justify the existence of Pakistan does come across as a valiant and secular attempt by Bhutto against the concept of a strong unitary state with a strong center for India.

It helps in working toward a more democratized, decentralized, and deregulated federal constitution for not only Pakistan but any federal state, including India, which in the end would be good for the prosperity and the empowerment of the people living in these federations.

However, in the final summing up, the correct way forward for Pakistan as a viable state would be to neither continue with the two-nation theory based on Muslim Nationalism nor try to cheat history by denying the historical, intrinsic, and intimate link which the rest of India has with the Indus Valley civilization, but to acknowledge that Pakistan was created as a federal state at a certain juncture in history when the ethos of the North Indian Muslim and the North Indian Hindu were unable to find the grace in themselves to acknowledge the ethos of the other and still live in one state, and thus a political arrangement was made creating two multinational federations.

Once created, there is no reason why these two federations should be antagonistic to each other. And while recognizing that there are more things which make the people of these federations similar to each other than to any other people of the world, there is also no need now, having once tasted the flavor of decentralization, to go back to becoming one country again.

In fact, the correct way forward for both federations is maximum decentralization, maximum democracy, and maximum deregulation internally; and maximum trade, maximum communication, and maximum ease of travel between one another, to the extent that the societies in both countries reach the level of maturity we see in the United Kingdom (UK), where the people of Scotland or Northern Ireland can talk about staying in or exiting the UK without the societies there melting down into a bloodbath.

Strictly speaking, there may be very few states which would qualify to be called completely absolved of religious coloring, constitutionally or socially. Many European countries, including the United Kingdom, carry the Christian Cross in their flags. In fact, England cannot be termed a secular country constitutionally, where the ruling sovereign is also the head of the Church.

But if there did exist any notion of nationhood based on the Christian religion, it was killed and buried in history as a dead idea after the downfall of the Holy Roman Empire, the Napoleonic wars, and finally, most convincingly, by the two World Wars of the 20th century where one Christian nation slaughtered another. Still, the Christian Cross continues to be maintained in the national flags of many European countries.

In the United States and India, the constitutions explicitly separate religion from the affairs of the state, but at the grassroots level, religion is constantly invoked politically to garner votes and affect policy. Therefore, it is not necessary that a state completely shun the religious sentiments or aspirations of its people to become a nation-state.

But the basic principle for a nation-state to succeed in its existence and its continuity is that the laws which are made in that state treat its citizens equally, without partiality in favor of or against any particular religious, ethnic, or linguistic community living in its territory, with no citizen of that state stripped of the opportunity to serve in the highest office, if chosen or elected via the prevalent and legally incorporated political procedures.

In that sense, Pakistan too can survive as a nation-state, while not discarding any of its historical baggage of being the conservator of Indian Muslim cultural and linguistic heritage, if moving forward that basic principle is the political compass for its rulers and legislators while making laws and enforcing them.

The Problem with Islamic 'Dogmatic' Fundamentalism

Although, if once the penny has dropped in one's mind about the fundamentals of political science which irrefutably demonstrate the objective premises and requirements for the successful formation of a nation state, one would never falter in rejecting any proposition of nationhood based solely on religion or, for that matter, any ideological, i.e. cerebral, premise, there still remains and will remain a question specially in the Muslim mind which needs to be answered with a bit more specific elaboration, if the Muslim mind is ever to move forward towards a rational understanding of nationhood.

The question which can keep arising and does keep arising is as follows: What is wrong with the international Islamic Dogmatic Fundamentalist movement's attempt to consciously strive to make Muslims all over the world to think and act alike with the least attachment and loyalty to the culture and historical heritage from which they spring forth?

And the corollary questions: What is wrong with all of humankind eventually thinking, looking, and behaving alike? Is it not a good idea which will create equality among all humans and also finally defeat racism and national chauvinism / 'feat' narrow nationalism?

In fact, this is a question not just limited to Islamic Dogmatic Fundamentalism or the Muslim mind, but this was an intellectual dilemma also for almost all ideological trends and movements in human history including international communism and before that Christian fundamentalism in the 'dark ages' of the Inquisition and religious wars prior to the advent of the age of enlightenment and the emergence of the Westphalian concept of nation state.

The key concept to note in understanding the problem with this question or, so to say, challenge to a rational, scientific, and secular understanding of nationhood as defined and refined to date by the study of political science, is the concept of any desire to 'think, look, and behave alike'.

Because human beings are not sheep. Each human is an individual, with characteristics and aspirations diverse from the other. It is the essence of the human spirit to be free, first as an individual before finding oneself as part of a family, community, territory, and nation to assert freedom for those collective identities too against any attempt to deny that freedom.

Human beings can never be straitjacketed into thinking, looking, and behaving in the same way. Historically all such attempts have always failed and in fact such attempts in their very content are reactionary and retrogressive. Human creativity is ensured only by an assertion against such stifling of the human spirit and has occurred only through the possibilities of non-uniformity and non-conformance.

Uniformity has already been attempted by communist states like Mao's China, Pol Pot's Cambodia, Stalinist Russia, North Korea, by militarist states like Nazi Germany, Fascist Italy and Baathist Iraq and Syria, and by 'Islamic Dogmatic Fundamentalist' ideological states like the Islamic Republic of Iran and the Taliban in Afghanistan. Whatever technological impetus is seen there, if any, is always borrowed and not indigenous and such states eventually and invariably face social and economic stagnation and life in these states comes to a grinding halt of monotone, with the state then surviving only by lashing out externally at other states through war or terrorism or looking for external sources of financial and or technological support and information to keep itself propped up.

Uniformity can be useful only for short term mission oriented projects like playing sports matches or going into battle with the national enemy. In those instances, it provides impetus and fervor as a reminder of unity, team spirit and fraternity but it cannot be prolonged to become the permanent way of life as then it would become anti natural. Posing this concept in another way, the whole society cannot be converted into the army or the police.

Equality does not mean uniformity. Uniformity is impossible, if only one were to understand that if equality meant uniformity and racism was to be defeated based on that concept then all whites should either be made black or all blacks should be made white, none of which is possible. Equality means active recognition of equal opportunities and rights for all and recognition of the existence of diversity in the other. It never means overriding the cultural legacy and constituent of the other, or the individuality of each human being.

More so, is the conflict with cultural legacy dangerous and anti-human because it tends to adopt a denialist attitude towards the historical reality of an individual and a people which is unhealthy not only for a correct diagnosis of a human predicament at any given time and progressive understanding of each people's own unique civilizational history of survival and development, but also for the possibility of natural human continuity and creativity.

The origin of Islamic Dogmatic Fundamentalism also lies in this very denial of human reality and attempt to impose by force and coercion a uniform straitjacket on all Muslims thus stifling the possibility of query, critique, research, and creativity among them.

The wiser of the established source scholars of Islamic jurisprudence like Imam Abu Hanifa (note: the majority of the Muslims of India and Pakistan have historically been Hanafi Sunnis) have shown flexibility towards local customs and traditions of non-Arab territories which do not conflict with the core principles of Islam, being understood as mainly being monotheism and abstention from consuming or doing what is categorically identified in Islam as "haraam".

The main retrogression, in fact crime, contained in Islamic Dogmatic Fundamentalism is its curbing and crushing of intellectual freedom and the spirit of query and criticism.

All those Muslims who buy into or succumb to the ideological propositions of current Islamic Dogmatic Fundamentalism should ask the following question. Why is it that after the advent of Islam, the world not only saw successful conquests of the existing superpowers of the day by Muslims, but also a spurt of intellectual and scientific advancement under Muslims culminating in what is famously known as the Islamic Golden Age, but since then nothing for centuries up to date, to further contribute to the newer and newer knowledge database of humankind?

It was not because of the Mongol invasion and the rape and pillage of Baghdad but something else had happened by that time, changing the course of the Islamic intellectual thought process.

The roots of current Islamic Dogmatic Fundamentalism, which is dogmatic, nurture on the intellectual work of Imam Al Ghazali, who secured the final victory over Islamic polity in the intellectual battle between the Mutazilites and the Asharites. The Mutazilites were the carriers and conservators of ancient Greek philosophy and way of thinking by logic and believed in the freedom of human thought and disputed the eternality of the Quran, rather considering the Quran as the creation of God, i.e. God preceded the Quran, whereas the Asharites stood for orthodoxy based on the literal interpretation of scriptural authority.

For instance, it is famously known that Al Ghazali did not recognize the scientific material causes leading to a material effect and considered that whatever occurred in the material world was because God willed it at that time. The intellectual success of the Asharites and Al Ghazali was also made possible by the existence of genuine resentment and reaction against the repressive measures through which the Mutazilite thought process had been imposed during the Golden Age by Islamic Caliphs, specially Caliph Maamoun, under whom and whose successors Imam Hanbal, a source scholar of Islamic jurisprudence and an opponent of the Mutazilite way of thinking, was persecuted and imprisoned.

Al Ghazali wrote his famous book *The Incoherence of Philosophers*, which was later refuted by the book *The Incoherence of Incoherence* written by the great and enlightened scholar Ibn e Rushd (known in the West as Averroes). However, the thought process of Al Ghazali had gained predominance over Islamic polity, specially after adoption, sanctification, and patronage of this thought process by subsequent Islamic Caliphs, and the die was cast for the defeat of the Mutazilite thought process and the identification of Islamic Sharia as somehow being a bastion against scientific thought process and advancement.

This identification and misplacement of Islam as being an opponent of science is what causes Islamic Dogmatic Fundamentalists to deny the science of human psychology and the significance of human culture and come up with dictatorial political and social structures always opposing raw democracy, pluralism, freedom of inquiry, freedom to criticize existing theological concepts, and the indigenous and / or genuine cultural aspirations of peoples around the world.

In fact, the reason why eventually Islamic Caliphs chose to patronize the intolerant and dogmatic thought process of Imam Ghazali was that it suited their class interest and the dictatorial and absolutist method of rule over people.

The initial progressive mindset of those Caliphs who had supported the Mutazilites had emanated in the backdrop of the consolidation of the Islamic empire over cosmopolitan societies and interacting with them, as the Arabs moved from being a tribal people towards a more advanced feudal agrarian society which warranted this mindset for the success of this consolidation and the technological prerequisites needed for organizing society in this qualitative transformation. However, since the gap between the ruling Arab dynasties and the people of the lands they ruled could not be fully crossed over even after the passing of centuries, this progressive mindset did not sustain and, as mentioned, it became inevitable that the Caliphs eventually chose the intolerant and dogmatic school of thought over a rational one to crush the thought process of query and critique.

In Pakistan too, over the course of decades, a zeitgeist has emerged whereby it seems as if Islam and Islamic Dogmatic Fundamentalism are one and the same thing. However, it was not so during the Pakistan movement prior to 1947, and in fact, intellectuals from sects and schools of thought like Shias, Ahmadis, and Ismailis, who are now anathema to hard core Sunni fundamentalists ruling the roost over national narrative in present-day Pakistan and de facto considered as politically incorrect in the country, were at the forefront of the Pakistan movement and close comrades of the Quaid e Azam, who himself belonged to a Shia sect.

Subsequently, even up to the '60s and '70s, intellectual ideas like *rabubiyat* propounded by the Quranist scholar Ghulam Ahmed Parvez were well tolerated and heeded and referred to in national discourse.

In recent times, the situation became so dire that even mainstream Islamic Fundamentalist scholars were persecuted. Ghulam Murtaza Malik was assassinated, and Javed Ghamdi had to flee the country because their attempts to explain Islam rationally and diversely were not tolerated by the zeitgeist.

Therefore, if the intolerant and anti-progress zeitgeist has to be changed to become a more tolerant and rational one, it needs to be understood how this happened and what are the fallacies on which the incumbent zeitgeist is built.

Religious fundamentalism is not something new or unique to Pakistan. It has emerged following close on the heels of the emergence of religion in human society. It starts with a religious group thinking that the ideas and principles of their religion, which were conferred on their prophet or messenger or avatar by deity, are superior to those of other religions and that these ideas and principles can be implemented in each society in any era as they were implemented in the earliest days of their religion.

In short, they think that their religion is free from the context of time and space (land), and it can be implemented without adjustment in any society and in any era. To do this, they consider as their prime religious duty and preach the same.

Moving from this generic identification to the specific case of Islam, we interrogate how it made its way there.

Islam emerged in the desert of Arabia. What was the land of Arabia like, more than fourteen centuries ago?

Before Islam, there were two superpowers in the world. In the mid-East, the Sassanids ruled the lands of Iran and Iraq, while the lands of Syria, Egypt, Palestine, North Africa, etc. were ruled by the Romans. These empires stood on the pillars of advanced slave societies. The agrarian and industrial production in these societies relied on the labor of slaves.

In contrast, Arabia was home to a less developed Bedouin tribal society. These tribals were nomadic and moved around searching for oases. They used to fight each other over grazing grounds, streams of water, and livestock. The victor tribe would execute the men of the defeated tribe and enslave their women. Few Arab lands were agrarian. The city of Medina and coastal areas like Oman, Hadhramaut, and Yemen had converted into trading towns.

Arabia had a tribal system. Grazing grounds and water streams were the collective property of a tribe. In some tribes, even livestock would be collective property. For household chores and basic labor like rowing on ships, Arabs also indulged in the buying and selling of slaves. So, it was primarily a tribal society with the embryo of a slave society.

So, it can be said that in that era, the Sassanids and the Romans existed as superpowers in the world through an advanced slave-owning system of production and would fight each other for world domination, while the Bedouins of Arabia were living a life of intellectual backwardness and disunity in a less advanced tribal system. There was no concept of unity among Arabs. Numerous tribes had numerous gods. Idol worship, looting and rape, violence and murder were commonplace.

In that context, the greatest feat accomplished by Prophet Muhammad (pbuh) was that through the concept of one God, he succeeded in imparting the consciousness of unity and organization under one Arab state to the Arabs. Through the establishment of this state, a more advanced system of living came into being, and in order to meet the growing economic needs of Arab society, the tribes of this state struck externally at the war-weary Sassanids and Romans and, because of possessing a superior version of strict, non-decadent discipline imbued by the Islamic messages of Prophet Muhammad (pbuh), succeeded in defeating these superpowers.

Historically, the victories of the early Arab Muslims over the Sassanid and Roman empires are a unique case study for socio-political intellectuals whereby the subjective emerges victorious over the objective without any change in the objective economic conditions of the subjective, i.e. 'mind over matter,' and empirically defeats all deterministic reading of philosophy which lays greater emphasis on the material over the ideal (the eternal debate between Aristotelian and Platonist schools of philosophy).

Thus, the Arab tribes became successful in becoming masters of huge tracts of agrarian lands, and during the period of the Rashidun Caliphate (the first four 'righteous' caliphs), the Arabs started transiting from a tribal system into a feudal system. The Rashidun Caliphate was actually a transitory period between tribal system and feudal system. It was different from the tribal system in the sense that it was enrooted not in blood and race but in religion, which was actually the face of Arab nationalism at that time. Therefore, the Rashidun Caliphate was the need of that time.

In this period, the leader of the state was chosen in a tribal way but using the language of religion, not tribal superiority. Caliph Abu Bakr (ra) was chosen in this way, and then, on the advice of the 'Sahaba,' Abu Bakr (ra) nominated Umar (ra) as the next Caliph. Umar (ra) had constituted a committee of six 'Sahaba' to decide on who would be the next Caliph, the result of which was that Usman (ra) became the next Caliph after the assassination of Umar (ra).

During the time of Usman (ra), the nepotism of the Banu Umayya grew in strength. Umayyad governors were nominated, and vast tracts of agricultural lands were awarded to Umayyad princes. After Usman (ra), Ali (ra) became the Caliph, and his supporters were those who were opposed to the Umayyads.

The caliphate of Ali (ra) was first challenged by Talha (ra), Zubair (ra), and Ayesha (ra) (the wife of Prophet Muhammad (pbuh)). The 'Battle of Camel' ('Jang e Jamal') took place near Basra, in which Talha (ra) and Zubair (ra) were killed. As Ali (ra) concluded this battle, he faced rebellions from Umayyad governors, including Ameer Muawiya (son of Abu Sufyan, the die-hard critic and opponent of Prophet Muhammad (pbuh) who accepted Islam at the very end when Prophet Muhammad (pbuh) entered Mecca as the victor). A stalemate was reached between them whereby, effectively, there were two Caliphs even during the period when Ali (ra) was alive as Caliph, in which the lands of Hejaz, Iraq, Iran, and territories extending to Central Asia were under the rule of Ali (ra), and the lands of Syria, Levant, and Egypt were under the rule of Ameer Muawiya.

Ali (ra) was assassinated by Kharijites, disgruntled and resentful of Ali (ra) for having made truce with Ameer Muawiya, and after the assassination of Ali (ra), Ameer Muawiya made a treaty with Ali (ra)'s elder son Hasan to become the sole Caliph of the whole Islamic empire.

Thereafter, the Umayyads, starting with Ameer Muawiya, took complete control over the government and established dynastic rule, i.e., Kingship, struggling against which the second son of Ali (ra), (Imam) Hussein, gave away his life in the epic and tragic battle at Karbala.

All this history has nothing to do with theology. It is completely political history, not in any sense an integral component of the religion of Islam, because according to Islam the blood of one Muslim, i.e., taking the life of a Muslim, is haraam for another Muslim, and here we see Muslims killing other Muslims. However, fundamentalists on both sides, Shias and Sunnis, consider this political history too as religious history and view where they stand in this political divide as integral articles of their faith.

The Umayyads established and consolidated the feudal system, which was a superior and more efficient system than the tribal system and the slave-owning system in the context of economic growth. And in human history, the political manifestation of feudalism is invariably Kingship and dynastic rule.

In the early period of the ascent of the feudal system, when this system was the accelerator and the best-known superior social organizer for human economic and technological growth and advancement, the tribal and slave-owning basis of organizing society became primitive and weakened, and serfs and settled family units strengthened. The same happened under Umayyad rule. The farmers of Iraq, Syria, Egypt, etc., who had been 'liberated' from the shackles of the Sassanid and Roman rulers by the Arab victories, were turned into serfs for Arab feudal lords.

Secondly, the Umayyads considered Arabs, Arabic language, and Arabic culture as superior to other languages and cultures and thus suppressed the latter. The reaction to this manifested in the form of rebellions, and in just ninety years, the Abbasids overthrew the Umayyads and came to power with the help of the Iraqis and the Sassanids. The Abbasids included the non-Arabs with the Arabs in the award of agricultural lands and included them too in the ruling class.

After almost five centuries, as the Abbasid Caliphate withered away, the Ottoman Caliphate emerged from the land of Turkey as its successor dynasty.

The Muslim empire remained under feudalism while the European nations were leaving feudalism behind and adopting the Capitalist system with the advancement of science, technological breakthroughs, the successes of Reformation in Christianity, weakening of the hold of Church, and emergence of ideas of rational thought and the Age of Enlightenment. Anyone who will study just a little bit deep will come to know that the Muslim empire had stagnated due to the predominance of the Imam Ghazali thought process of rejection of the rational way of thinking, while scientific advancement and the Age of Enlightenment had occurred in Europe due to the European thinkers having picked up the works and thoughts of rational Muslim thinkers like Averroes (Ibn e Rushd) and Ibn e Khuldun and running away with them as their own and themselves becoming the intellectual successors of those great thinkers.

It is famously known that even though the printing press was invented in the first half of the fifteenth century AD, resulting in a revolution in the spread of information and ideas in the Western world, the Muslim world under the Ottomans took a full three centuries before they finally adopted this mode for the publication of books, as it was considered as a tool of the devil by Islamic scholars under the Ottomans. This provides a kind of gauge to measure the amount of lost time by which the Muslim world fell behind the Western European civilization.

In the process of replacing their moribund feudal systems with the more advanced capitalist system for running their economies and adjusting to the needs of mass industrial production effected by newer and newer scientific discoveries and technological breakthroughs, the European nations underwent democratic revolutions, initially even without full adult franchise. The monopoly of religion over the state and science was broken and secularism established. Kingdoms gave way to ever more powerful parliaments.

Eventually, these advanced European nations conquered the world and laid the foundations of international colonialism, which eventually outlived any progressive value it had and was defeated in the 20th century

AD to be replaced by constitutionally sovereign nation-states the world over, following the capitalist or socialist models of production and with universal recognition in principle of the one person one vote concept of democracy.

In this historical context, it needs to be understood how practical and applicable in the modern capitalist era is the point of view of Islamic Dogmatic Fundamentalists that they will bring a system like that of the Rashidun Caliphate in Pakistan.

If the belief of the Muslims is that the Quran and Islam are for all times, past, present, and the future, then they have to understand that this cannot be so if the manifestations of the core principles of their faith lack the ability to be different in different eras and different societies. This is the theological work which has not been done in Islam, while it has been done to a vast degree in the other prescriptive Abrahamic religions like Christianity and Judaism. And any attempt in Islam to do such theological work is considered as heresy or the work of Satan by Islamic Dogmatic Fundamentalists and is shot down the moment it is started by the dogmatic and intolerant thought process of the intellectual legacy started by the Asharites and Imam Ghazali.

There are two main reasons why fundamentalism is so successful in the Muslim world in general, and in Pakistan in particular.

The first reason has to do with the fact that historically new religions initially become popular with the common folk or people before they were owned and taken over by the ruling classes when they saw that this popularity had become irreversible. Initially, a religion emerged as a spiritual panacea and beam of hope for the deprived or oppressed classes of society, but when it gained momentum and the ruling classes of society felt it as a threat to their rule, they adopted it as their own and became its prime flag bearers.

Rulers have used religion to strengthen their rule. In order to prolong their rule, they garnered the support of the leaders of the religious group, and in return for that support, rewarded those leaders with land and wealth. In this way, the religion, which was initially representative of the aspirations of the common people, became a tool for keeping the people suppressed and enabling the rulers to continue their rule.

The ruling classes and the religious group made an alliance to rule over the common people. The rulers made a system under which all kinds of help were provided to the religious group to increase their influence over the common people. The religious group became the authority over religion. It became the prerogative of the religious group to decide what was in accordance with religion and what was not.

The ruling classes had control over the religious group, and in order to carry out all their legitimate or illegitimate, pro-people or anti-people actions, would get the religious group to provide them with the required justification and permission, whether in fact those actions went against the core principles of that religion or not. The name of religion was used to usurp the rights of the people and to guard against freedom of thought and progressive ideas.

The case of Christianity is considered in this context. When the Christian religion emerged, it was in the era and the land under the rule of the Roman Empire and the slave-owning system. Christianity gained popularity among the farmers, slaves, and other deprived classes because it spoke of their equality and for the alleviation of their sufferings.

Initially, the Roman rulers stuck to their paganism and idol worship, but they realized over the years that this creed of theirs and their priests had lost the trust of the people. Therefore, the Roman emperor Constantine I converted to Christianity in 312 AD. Thereafter, the common people in the realm of the Western world were ruled by Christian rulers and the papacy. This period in history is known as the 'Dark Ages' of medieval times.

Fundamentalist thought was produced by the ruling classes in cahoots with their religious cohorts because this thought protected their political power in society. Fundamentalist thought declares a de facto exploitative system (can be economic, political or social) of an age to be in accordance with religion and considers it justified to eliminate the people who speak against it.

The conversion to Islam by the ruling wealthy tribal families of Banu Umayya among the Quraysh in Arabia, and Islamic scholars justifying the dynastic rule of the Umayyads, is the example in Islam where rulers and leaders of the religious group in their realm worked in alliance to maintain the political power of the ruling classes.

There was no positive role of the Islamic Dogmatic Fundamentalists in the Pakistan movement. At the time, their foremost leaders opposed the creation of Pakistan. They declared this movement to be against Islam. They called the Quaid e Azam as 'Kaafir e Azam.' But when Pakistan did come into being, these same people started the propaganda that Pakistan was created for the establishment of the Islamic system (read: their version of Islamic system, descending from the Al Ghazali mode of thought through the works and thinking of the likes of Ibn e Taymiyyah, Hassan Al Banna, Sayyid Qutb, and Abul A'la Maudoodi).

Much can be debated about the founder of Pakistan, Jinnah the Quaid e Azam's vision for the kind of Islamic system he meant when he said that we have the principles of Islam and the Prophet (pbuh) to guide us in running the new state ("We have got the great message in the Quran for our guidance and enlightenment," circa April 1943). But in the absence of any explicit approval by him for any specific Islamic Dogmatic Fundamentalist manifesto, how could that be any different from the aspirations of the founding fathers of the United States of America when they pledged to be guided by their faith?

It is one thing to be inspired by one's faith in the manifestation of one's actions and what one stands for in public life, and entirely another to implement an elaborately codified version of a theocratic state on one's society. What is certainly known is that there was no alliance in political action between the Quaid e Azam and the Islamic Dogmatic Fundamentalists, that the Quaid e Azam was a firm believer and adherent of the political modus operandi inherited from the British parliamentary system of government, that he himself was on a personal level as far as possible from the kind of leader that Islamic Dogmatic Fundamentalists have in mind, that he definitely said in February 1948 that "In any case, Pakistan is not going to be a theocratic State to be ruled by priests with a divine mission"[16], and that he definitely stated in his famous speech of 11th August 1947 that "You are free; you are free to go to your temples. You

---

[16] 'Jinnah's Vision of Pakistan' by Sharif al Mujahid
(https://www.tni.org/en/article/jinnahs-vision-of-pakistan)

are free to go to your mosques or any other places of worship in this State of Pakistan. You may belong to any region or caste or creed — that has nothing to do with the business of the State".

However, after Jinnah, an alliance developed between the rulers of the state and the Islamic Dogmatic Fundamentalists. In the backdrop of the Cold War between the godless communist Soviet Union and the West, it was becoming increasingly convenient for the West to see a strengthening of the unelected national security and bureaucratic apparatus of the nascent state as well as of the anti-communist Islamic Dogmatic Fundamentalist forces and thought process in society, and an alliance between the two.

The ruling feudal classes within the new state of Pakistan too, who had trembled earlier at the anti-feudal manifesto of the Indian National Congress and now continued to tremble at the prospect of a propertyless communist manifesto taking over through Soviet backing, had no problem with this strategy. Hence, in 1949, the Objectives Resolution was passed, sealing the foundation of Pakistan as an Islamic ideological state.

That the power of the Islamic priests, the Mullahs, and political parties of the Islamic Dogmatic Fundamentalists in society in setting up the basic parameters of a national narrative would automatically flow seamlessly after such a resolution was inevitable.

Indeed, it is not beyond reasonable "what if" comprehension that had Jinnah naturally lived on for just a few more years, he may very likely have met the same fate as the founder of the new state at the hands of the unelected national security apparatus, as did Mujib ur Rehman of Bangladesh and even Zulfiqar Ali Bhutto of the post-1971 newly democratically constitutionalized state of Pakistan. Already the stories of how he had been abandoned to die, and the famous ambulance story, point in that direction with many unanswered questions.

Religious parties became a tool for the unelected rulers of Pakistan. These parties provided open and sometimes tacit support to dictators and even called these rulers "Ameer ul Momineen" (Leader of the Faithful). For example, on 8 December 1969, while addressing party workers, the leader of Pakistan's Jamaat e Islami, Mian Tufail, stated that:

"I have strong hope that the legacy of the Islamic form of government, which had been discontinued after the martyrdom of Hazrat Ali (r.a.), will start to be restored by one of the adorers ('aashiqaan') of Hazrat Ali (r.a.) in the land of Pakistan. I pray to Allah that He gives Mr. Yahya Khan (the then decadent and drunkard military dictator) the chance to restore the Islamic democratic system in Pakistan with the courage and sense of purpose and sincerity which he has repeatedly mentioned in his speeches, Amen". [17] In this way, these religious political parties attempted to strengthen the rule of usurper generals and dictators in return for a financial windfall, which flowed their way emanating from the coffers of the West against Soviet communism.

The second reason for the deep entrenchment of fundamentalism in the Muslim world in general, and in Pakistan, in particular, is the reaction of Muslims towards the colonialist system.

After their defeat and conquest by Western colonialism, as the Muslims delved into introspection to figure out the reasons for their downfall, the hatred of all things Western blinded them from recognizing and realizing that those reasons could be found in the superior scientific and technological advancement of their Western colonizers and the colonizers' superior socio-legal systems achieved after undergoing the age of enlightenment and renaissance.

Instead, the Muslims succumbed to the reactionary point of view emerging after their defeat, that the reason for their downfall was that the Muslims had stopped following the footsteps of their ancestors. In other words, instead of looking at the present and forward from there, they intellectually turned around and started looking backwards as the basis of moving forward, which was a contradiction between intent and action.

There is a famous fairytale in the East in which a prince goes on a quest to rescue a princess abducted by an evil magician. In the last leg of that quest, the prince comes across a field he must cross, and the sage guiding him shows him a plethora of stone statues standing in that field and tells him that these were the prince's predecessors who were turned into stone when they looked back after hearing luring voices from behind

---

[17] The phenomenon also alluded to in 'The Vangaurd of the Islamic Revolution - The Jama'at-i Islami of Pakistan' by Seyed Vali Reza Nasr (Chapter 7 – 'The Secular State, 1958–1971;The Regime of Yahya Khan, 1969–1971') published Berkeley: University of California Press, 1994. http://ark.cdlib.org/ark:/13030/ft9j49p32d/

as they started to cross the field. The sage advises the prince that as he too will start to cross the field, he will hear voices from behind so luring, so seductive, so sweet that he will be immensely tempted to turn around to look where those voices are coming from. "But never turn to look back, otherwise you too will turn into stone," advises the sage.

So, it has happened with the Muslims. The voices of the past, of the glory and conquest and empire of the Muslims, are so sweet, so soothing, so ego-boosting and self-satisfactory, that it is easier and lazier to dwell in them, telling the world that we are no less than you because once we were the greatest. However, the past is gone and was built on premises qualitatively different from those on which the present is built and those on which the future will be built.

The Muslims thought that they could restore their greatness by bringing back the era and system of the Rashidun caliphate. Whereas, in fact, the reason for their backwardness was that the economic and political class among them which had to struggle against feudalism and the orthodox and archaic ideas and way of thinking which went with it, was weak. The class which had to take society towards the higher societal form of capitalism, industrialization, technological advancement and education and their applications in society, urbanization, end of serfdom, and emergence of a free class of working people independent in the choice of serving or leaving their employers, and the enrooting, establishment and social expansion of democracy and secularism. Just as the European nations did. The cultural manifestations of that struggle could be different for the Muslim societies from those of the Europeans, but that was the only road to take to go forward.

There is no mention of statecraft in the Quran, only guiding principles for personal conduct and for interacting with other people and society. It forbids usury and hoarding, but there is no mention of or partiality in favor of any particular economic system. However, to date, Muslim clerics and orthodox ideologues dominating the religion have termed, sometimes the tribal system and sometimes the feudal system, as systems "natural" to human nature ("deen e fitrat" or "fitri nizam"). This is because, as we have seen, the feudal system prevailed at the zenith of Muslim domination in the world.

No system is permanent in history. Human society has constantly evolved and will keep evolving. Therefore, the feudal system too is not a permanent system. The feudal system did not exist among the Arabs when Prophet Muhammad (pbuh) started preaching Islam. The prevalent system was tribal. Arab society shifted from tribal to the feudal system and values when the Arabs conquered fertile lands in the Levant, Egypt and Persia. But due to being mentally stuck in that past, Islamic Dogmatic Fundamentalists have almost always opposed land reforms abolishing feudalism in Muslim societies and have considered any such attempts as overstepping the limits of Islamic laws.

Islamic Dogmatic Fundamentalists condemn both the capitalist as well as the socialist system and state that a system somewhere in between is the Islamic system. They think that by teaching moralism to capitalists, or those with control over capital in society, they will eliminate poverty.

A person of any class can become a fundamentalist, but majorly it is the middle class which is most prone to succumbing to fundamentalism. The upper classes already are in possession of great wealth and control over resources in society and thus more driven by profit and continuation of the protection of their vested interests, whereas the working classes, in their intense economic struggle for survival, are mostly more pragmatic than ideological.

It is the middle class which is considerably more well-off than the lower classes to aspire more than just bare survival, but at the same time, is not in personal possession and control of the resources in society. The middle class is, for all practical purposes, the servant and executor of the upper class. It is the class which constitutes the bureaucracy running a state. The middle class is the wage-earning protector of the interests of the upper class in a non-socialist society. The middle-class traders and entrepreneurs are also more of a supply chain for the upper classes than being the dominating class in society controlling the resources.

The middle-class individual strengthens the rule of the upper classes but nurtures a wish that one day he too will become part of the upper or ruling class. But this wish is seldom fulfilled in a system of big capital or big landlordism. Therefore, the middle class, while serving the upper class, is at the same time also jealous, envious, and in the extreme case, hateful of the upper class[18]. Ironically, it is also jealous and resentful of fellow middle-class individuals who do make it to the upper classes and is

---

[18] In his book 'Escape from Freedom', Eric Fromm declares in the chapter 'Freedom in the Age of Reformation' that it was Martin Luther's reformation movement which was the social face of the advent of capitalism and the departure of feudalism as a dying system and quotes Max Weber as having termed the emerging middle class as the backbone of the new capitalist system. But he elaborates in great detail about the inherent contradictions with which the middle-class mindset was ridden, including Luther himself, as follows: *"... ... ...the old order was breaking down. The individual had lost the security of certainty and was threatened by new economic forces, by capitalists and monopolies; the corporative principle was being replaced by competition; the lower classes felt the pressure of growing exploitation. The appeal of Lutheranism to the lower classes differed from its appeal to the middle class. The poor in the cities, and even more the peasants, were in a desperate situation. They were ruthlessly exploited and deprived of traditional rights and privileges. They were in a revolutionary mood which found expression in peasant uprisings and in revolutionary movements in the cities. The Gospel articulated their hopes and expectations as it had done for the slaves and labourers of early Christianity and led the poor to seek for freedom and justice. In so far as Luther attacked authority and made the word of the Gospel the centre of his teachings, he appealed to these restive masses as other religious movements of an evangelical character had done before him. Although Luther accepted their allegiance to him and supported them, he could do so only up to a certain point; he had to break the alliance when the peasants went further than attacking the authority of the Church and merely making minor demands for the betterment of their lot. They proceeded to become a revolutionary class which threatened to overthrow all authority and to destroy the foundations of a social order in whose maintenance the middle class was vitally interested. For, in spite of all the difficulties we earlier described, the middle class, even its lower stratum, had privileges to defend against the demands of the poor; and therefore, it was intensely hostile to revolutionary movements which aimed to destroy not only the privileges of the aristocracy, the Church, and the monopolies, but their own privileges as well. The position of the middle class between the very rich and the very poor made its reaction complex and in many ways contradictory. They wanted to uphold law and order, and yet they were themselves vitally threatened by rising capitalism. Even the more successful members of the middle class were not wealthy and powerful as the small group of big capitalists was. They had to fight hard to survive and make progress. The luxury of the moneyed class increased their feeling of smallness and filled them with envy and indignation. As a whole, the middle class was more endangered by the collapse of the feudal order and by rising capitalism than it was helped.*
... ...
Thus, while Luther freed people from the authority of the Church, he made them submit to a much more tyrannical authority, that of a God who insisted on complete submission of man and annihilation of the individual self as the essential condition to his salvation. Luther's "faith" was the conviction of being loved upon the condition of surrender, a solution which has much in common with the principle of complete submission of the individual to the state and the "leader".
Luther's awe of authority and his love for it appears also in his political convictions. Although he fought against the authority of the Church, although he was filled with indignation against the new moneyed class--part of which was the upper strata of the clerical hierarchy--and although he supported the revolutionary tendencies of the peasants

inclined to drag down its fellow man if it can before he makes it to the top. In fact, more often than not, it can be more atrocious in the suppression of members of its own class or lower classes than would be a member coming from the actual ruling upper class towards them (in fact middle class and lower middle class individuals often succumbed to fascist hatred of another ethnic or religious group of their own class as that hatred gives them a sense of empowerment over the lives of others, which in normal circumstances they would not possess, examples of Jew hatred in Europe and hatred of Ahmadis in Pakistan, in both cases full of mind boggling viciousness and vitriol, being cases in point. This hatred was very well depicted in the famous 1961 movie 'Judgement at Nuremberg' wherein a maid, sympathetic to the Nazi cause, is shown to have testified against an elderly Jew man to have him condemned to death for the crime of 'Aryan defilement' under the Nuremberg Laws of 1935. The middle class forms moralism as the basis of its envy or hatred. It considers itself to be in possession of a higher moralism than that of the upper class and the upper class devoid of moralism[19]. 'So, what' it says, 'if the upper class has all

---

up to a certain point, yet he postulated submission to worldly authorities, the princes, in the most drastic fashion. Even if those in authority are evil or without faith, nevertheless the authority and its power is good and from God.... Therefore, where there is power and where it flourishes, there it is and there it remains because God has ordained it.' Or he says: God would prefer to suffer the government to exist, no matter how evil, rather than allow the rabble to riot, no matter how justified they are in doing so.,. A prince should remain a prince, no matter how tyrannical he may be. He beheads necessarily only a few since he must have subjects in order to be a ruler. The other aspect of his attachment to and awe of authority becomes visible in his hatred and contempt for the powerless masses, the "rabble", specially when they went beyond certain limits in their revolutionary attempts.

… … … … ..

But while his thinking on economic matters was the traditional one, his emphasis on the nothingness of the individual was in contrast to, and paved the way for, a development in which man not only was to obey secular authorities but had to subordinate his life to the ends of economic achievements. In our day this trend has reached a peak in the Fascist emphasis that it is the aim of life to be sacrificed for "higher" powers, for the leader or the racial community."

[19] *"While this class was actually envious of those who had wealth and power and could enjoy life, they rationalized this resentment and envy of life in terms of moral indignation and in the conviction that these superior people would be punished by eternal suffering."* (Eric Fromm in his book 'Escape of Freedom' chapter 3 'Freedom in the Age of Reformation' and refers to S. Ranulf's book 'Moral Indignation and Middle Class

the wealth and can do whatever it likes, it is I the middle-class individual who has a higher sense of moralism than the upper class and will not do certain things even if I had the power or ability to do it but which the upper class does without scruples. Therefore, I possess a higher moralism than the upper class'. It ignores the fact that the moment it is in possession of the same wealth or power which the upper class possesses, it will almost invariably do the same things without scruples, even maybe with a vengeance (as we see in the case of the nouveau rich or middle class individuals becoming dictators), which it claimed it will not do even if it had the power to do so. This moralism is not limited to Islamic Dogmatic Fundamentalists. It can also be found to be a driving perspective even in examples such as the Nazis, the conservative Catholicism in Franco's Spain, the Arab and African dictators of the twentieth century, and the middle classes supporting the Hindutva narrative in India[20]. Another aspect of this moralism is that since the middle class is mostly comprised of wage-earning individuals, i.e., their worth is established primarily by the skill sets, education, and capabilities of which only they are in possession as individuals and not from any preexisting wealth, property, or influence thereof, therefore it considers itself as 'self-made' and hence again superior to an individual born in the propertied upper classes.

In this way, the middle-class individual considers itself superior to the upper class. That it considers itself morally superior to the upper class is also one of the reasons why it has little respect for the constitution of the country, passed majorly by political parties representative of the ruling class interests of the country, or those loyal to the monarch in case of a monarchy, and harbors in a corner of its heart the attitude of 'anything goes' if it rocks or topples the boat of the ruling classes and has a tendency to celebrate illegal unconstitutional coups with not much scruples

---

Psychology' as being "*a study which is an important contribution to the thesis that moral indignation is a trait typical of the middle class, specially the lower middle class*".

[20] Even in the 1930s elements among American Democrats like the Kennedys were enamoured of the successes achieved in those years by Hitler and Mussolini in their countries (https://www.bbc.com/news/world-us-canada-39371715, John F. Kennedy's Hidden Diary, Europe 1937, The Travel Journals of JFK and Kirk LeMoyne Billings (https://www.berghahnbooks.com/title/KennedyJohn), 'The Ambassador: Joseph P. Kennedy at the Court of St. James 1938–1940' by Susan Ronald (https://kirkcenter.org/reviews/joseph-kennedy-american-fascist/).

considering that "it serves them right" (them being the upper class), but more about that later.

In the case of religious fundamentalists, specially Islamic Dogmatic Fundamentalists, the source and manifestation of this moralism is the dogmatic fundamentalist form of religion according to which the moralism of today has to be the same as the moralism of fourteen hundred years ago.

The result of this approach is that in the event of a political takeover by Islamic Dogmatic Fundamentalists, society and economy tend to become more state-run by a one-party in power than by the mechanics of a free market and political pluralism, and if this political takeover continues for some decades, then stagnation sets in, with the state and the governing party becoming more and more brutal towards dissenting trends and tendencies.

In other words, Islamic Dogmatic Fundamentalism is politically no different in essence than fascism or the communist totalitarian system. One reason for the historic failure of the state-run Soviet-styled socialist systems, or more frankly defined, the 'state capitalist' systems, was this stagnation, brought about over more than seven decades by the one-party rule of communists who, in fact, were in their genesis, middle-class individuals. We see the same in the case of Iran and pre–Deng Xiaopeng's China and North Korea.

The salvation for such societies can only come when these revert to free market mechanisms and deregulation of big capital, maintaining and protecting the freedom of big capital and possibilities thus ensued. Economies can only move forward when the concentration of big capital for investment purposes is not looked at as politically incorrect, although maintaining the rights of the working people and consumers through pro-democratic and equal opportunities legislation.

But we are now digressing from the main subject of theocratic fundamentalism.

Looking at the social aspect of Islamic Dogmatic Fundamentalism, here too we see that it does not discern between the requirements of different eras and different societies.

We take the example of slavery. The slave-owning system existed at the time of Prophet Muhammad (pbuh), before and after the advent of

Islam. It existed in all societies and continued to exist as late as the nineteenth and even twentieth centuries.

Islam allowed the continuity of the slave-owning system but preached for the good treatment of slaves in its edicts. It encouraged the freeing of slaves at times of celebration, or as a mode of atonement, or as expression of gratitude to the Almighty, or when a non-Muslim slave converted to Islam, thus earning the right to never be a slave, thus inherently encouraging the spirit of abolishing slavery.

So, the eventual target can be interpreted to be the abolition of slavery, although gradual (which is not very different from the outlook on slavery of the founding fathers of the United States of America, who were inherently abolitionists but could only end slavery approximately eight decades after laying the foundations of the new state and writing the Bill of Rights).

However, the Islamic Dogmatic Fundamentalists do not choose to interpret it that way and consider slavery to be a system to be remained upheld in the edicts, as if it was an inherent principle of Islam, even in modern times.

Both in the case of the Afghan Jihad against Soviet occupation and the Afghan communists' army, and by 'ISIS' in Iraq and Syria, the Jihadists would enslave and rape the women they captured using the allowance of slavery in Islam as a pretext.

Another case is that of the rights of women. Islam was the first religion which recognized and codified the rights of women in business, property inheritance, and legal and marital matters in a way which was progressive at the time in which it emerged. But that does not mean that those rights cannot be expanded through theological rationalization when the social and technological context has changed and advanced.

For instance, the proportion of inheritance of a daughter as being half that of the son can be considered as the very basic right of the daughter if the father dies without a will, but can be increased by the will of the father or if the sons do not contest a bigger share for their sister, and religion can thus remain silent on a bigger share for the daughter. But Islamic Dogmatic Fundamentalists tend to keep the share of the daughter definitely half of the sons.

Similarly, in the case of being a witness, the responsibility of bearing witness by a woman being half that of a man can be considered as a very basic concession for the woman as having less responsibility and liability, but not a lesser right than that of a man. In modern times, when women can be as educated and as independent in their affairs as a man, the witness of one woman can be recognized as equal to one man.

Another case is that of producing four witnesses for proving the rape of a woman. The requirement of producing four witnesses of the actual act of intercourse in extramarital sex is not for rape in the Quran but rather more as a deterrent to the easy implementation of the harsh punishment prescribed for extramarital sex in Islam. For what are the probabilities that four witnesses together will get the chance in most cases of having actually witnessed at the same time the occurrence of the actual act of intercourse (not foreplay) between two unmarried individuals?

For rape, in modern scientific times, the crime can easily be evidenced through DNA testing and even through other forensic means. That should be recognized in court to punish the rapist. However, Islamic Dogmatic Fundamentalists shirk from giving such rights to women and want to treat them in the same way as fourteen hundred years ago or even a few centuries ago, when they were not as literate, educated, or economically empowered and independent as they are now in today's modern scientifically advanced society, and were reduced to being at home only producing and raising children and carrying out domestic chores.

The fundamentalists want to keep women backward and want to prevent them from becoming fully empowered citizens in a society capable of contributing as much as men or even more.

Then we come to the issue of polygamy. Polygamy, and the keeping of concubines, was common in ancient times in all civilizations. In Christianity, polygamy practiced by societies where Christianity spread met its demise around the 4th century AD. However, in the rest of the world, polygamy was commonplace. So too it was in Arabia when Islam emerged.

Islam put a limit on the number of wives in the patriarchal society. In fact, the Quran verses related to the limit of four wives discourage men from marrying more than one at a time and state that "if you are afraid you will fail to maintain justice, then ˹content yourselves with˺ one or those ˹bondwomen˺ in your possession. This way you are less likely to commit injustice" (Surah Nisa verse 3).

Moreover, the allowance in the Quranic verses for marrying more than one is not without context. In fact, the context is the intention of supporting orphans. This means that the allowance is not based on a desire to marry based on love or physical attraction but in the context of supporting orphans.

The exact verses of the Surah Nisa from the Quran, related to polygamy and the context in which the issue comes up and is addressed, are reproduced below to see exactly what we are talking about when we talk about polygamy in Islam:

Surah Nisa (Quran, the 4th Sura) [https://myislam.org/surah-an-nisa/]

"4:1 O mankind, fear your Lord, who created you from one soul and created from it its mate and dispersed from both of them many men and women. And fear Allah, through whom you ask one another, and the wombs. Indeed, Allah is ever, over you, an Observer. 4:2-And give to the orphans their properties and do not substitute the defective [of your own] for the good [of theirs]. And do not consume their properties into your own. Indeed, that is ever a great sin. 4:3-And if you fear that you will not deal justly with the orphan girls, then marry those that please you of [other] women, two or three or four. But if you fear that you will not be just, then [marry only] one or those your right hand possesses. That is more suitable that you may not incline [to injustice]."

Here it is Allah, advising Man that "That is more suitable". However, Islamic Dogmatic Fundamentalists are found advocating for and encouraging more than one marriage for men, and that too just out of a desire to do so without the context specifically quoted in the Quran, as if this was a better thing than being monogamous in an advanced society of equal men and women.

Regarding the issue of a woman as a ruler, the Islamic Dogmatic Fundamentalists, as a religious principle, reject this idea. It was the same with Maudoodi's Jamaat-e-Islami in Pakistan. But when they fell out with the military dictator General Ayub Khan, they supported Fatima Jinnah, the sister of the Quaid e Azam, against him. Then, in the 1973 constitution, when seats were allocated in the parliament for women and the same in the case of the 'Majlis e Shura' formed by the military dictator General Zia ul Haq, the Jamaat e Islami sent its women members to sit there. But when in 1988, Benazir Bhutto ran for election as the Prime Minister of the country, these Islamic Dogmatic Fundamentalists opposed her with the propaganda that a woman cannot be the leader of a state.

A similar issue is related to the time value of money. It is one thing to charge interest on a borrower who cannot pay it and then exploit him and strip him of all belongings because of that, and another to not take cognizance of the devaluation of money over time as the forces of demand and supply fluctuate and inflation occurs. A very valid question in the modern economy is whether it is fair for a borrower to borrow 'x' amount of money for a period of several years, or even months or weeks, and then after the loan period return only 'x' when the purchasing power of that 'x' has reduced? In that context, it is encouraging to see that Islamic modes of banking and finance have been developed to reconcile this question with the core value of Islam related to this subject. There is a positive way forward for Muslims if intellect and rationale are used in addressing questions of modern times rather than being a rejectionist and trying to revert society towards a barter economy, thus becoming a force of regression against the advancement of human society as it grows more and more complex. Society only moves forward, and any attempts to run it through ways in which it was run centuries ago are signs of primitiveness and retrogression. Such attempts will look as if a caveman from prehistoric times is suddenly placed on the roads of a bustling modern city.

When it is said among Muslims that the Quran and Islam are for all times to come and it is the last message from God, there are two ways in which this proposition can be looked at.

Islamic Dogmatic Fundamentalists look at this proposition and say that it means two things. One, that everything that came before Islam stands rejected, and two, that after the completion of the Quran, everything in human society will be run in the way it was run in the times when the Quran was completed. This fundamentalist interpretation isolates the Muslims from the rest of humanity in a bubble of rejection and traps them in a bubble of time that never moves forward.

A progressive thought in Muslims which rejects this fundamentalism will look at this proposition and understand that, one, the completion of the Quran is a link in the continuity of the beliefs on which Islam was built and consolidated and, that continuity is an inherent part of the Islamic heritage, and two, that the completion of the message from God is not the closing of the door to the future but rather an opening of the door to the future and embracing the ever changing and ever advancing objective future with the guiding principles advocated by the Quran and knowing how to flex and continue using these principles in changing times and changing circumstances.

In that sense, on a lighter note, such a thought process among Muslims could be equated to the stance of many Marxists who say that although the communist system as interpreted and implemented in the 20th century has been historically and objectively defeated, they can still use the dialectical materialist principles of Marxism to analyze that defeat, as well as to analyze and steer the future in the changed and changing world after that defeat. As an example, when looked into deeply, the neoconservative movement in the United States will be found to be standing on the shoulders of the anti-Stalinist Left and intellectuals like Irving Kristol. But we digress again.

As implied earlier, it is easy to see that the wording and imagery used in the Quran are found to be very relevant and meaningful to a mind belonging to humans existing in the Arabia of the 7th century, where and when the Quran was revealed to them. A rational and intellectual Muslim mind would recognize that and would prefer to capture the essence of the message being conveyed in the Quran rather than become stuck with a literal reading and interpretation, without historical context, of the messages, imagery, and symbolism written in the Quran. This actually brings one back to the fundamental debate between the Mutazilites and the Asharites of whether God precedes the Quran or whether the Quran is eternal (and literal). Surely, a rational but religious mind would be more convinced by the premise that it is God who precedes the Quran, and the Quran is but a creation of God in a certain historical period of mankind, and it is God who is eternal.

The fact that Islamic Dogmatic Fundamentalism became the dominant narrative in Pakistan is not proof that it is the narrative of the future for Pakistan or that a major part of Pakistani society is its natural ally. Islamic Dogmatic Fundamentalists are not progressive. They are not the face of progress for Pakistan. They and their thinking will always pull Pakistani society backwards. They seem strong because, historically, the national security state provided them with state patronage for decades.

Although they had been gaining force after the passing of the 1949 Objectives Resolution, the anti-Ahmadi rioting in the 1950s and the 'Tehreek e Nizam e Mustafa' of 1977, they became a superpower inside Pakistan after General Zia ul Haq, a Jamaat e Islami sympathizer and 'Maudoodiite', became the ruler of Pakistan in July 1977. To consolidate his rule, he strengthened and stacked Islamic Dogmatic Fundamentalists all across the military, the bureaucracy, the secret services, the media, and educational boards and institutions. On the other hand, a crackdown was imposed, and humiliation and ridicule were heaped on progressive forces and ideas in society. With the occurrence of the communist Saur revolution in Afghanistan in April 1978 and the entry of Soviet military forces in Afghanistan in December 1979, the Islamic Dogmatic Fundamentalist forces in the region were brought to the forefront by General Zia ul Haq as well as by the capitalist West to fail the Afghan communist government and their Soviet backers.

The United States and the then Saudi state poured dollars into the coffers of Islamic Dogmatic Fundamentalist parties. They were supplied with a hoard of modern weaponry to fight against communists in Afghanistan and to terrorize any sympathizing or neutral progressive force within Pakistan. The Islamic Dogmatic Fundamentalist parties made their militant wings, which were used to assassinate their opponents. To finance the armed effort against the Afghan communist regime, the smuggling of drugs and arms in the region and from the region was encouraged. Arms and heroin dealers were at the back of Islamic Dogmatic Fundamentalists and in bed with them. This is the time when even foreign Islamic militants, including a one Osama Bin Laden, joined this ongoing rave party of Islamic Dogmatic Fundamentalists in Pakistan in huge numbers.

It was these forces who were used in the resurgence of terrorism in Indian Kashmir from 1989 onwards after the departure of Soviet troops from Afghanistan. It was them who, and whose money, were used inside Pakistan to destabilize elected governments formed after the demise of General Zia ul Haq. It was from this fountain that international terrorism was eventually carried out across the globe, leading up to the emergence of the post 9/11 world of 'War on Terror,' which ironically suited also their ex-backers in the West with global designs for reassertion of power, the reverberations of all of which are faced by the world to this day and the struggle to eradicate which, from the planet, is still not over.

Islamic Dogmatic Fundamentalism as it exists, organized on the thought process of dogmatism and literalism, is a force of backwardness not only for Pakistan but for the entire Muslim polity across the world. If Muslims choose to adopt it as being the way forward, it will be as if they have applied reverse thrust on an airplane in midair. The plane will invariably lose control and crash. Their societies will become unstable, face chaos and internal repression and stagnation, and become failed, stagnant, decaying states, just like a plane crash. This will lead to their societies being prone to being taken over and/or controlled by societies more scientific and in tune with the requirements of changing times and technology.

There are two points worth mentioning before the subject of 'the problem with Islamic Dogmatic Fundamentalism' is concluded in this book.

Firstly, Islamic Dogmatic Fundamentalism is not a trend limited to any particular sect in Islam, as some mostly identify it, understandably, with Sunni Wahabi or Salafi sects. This mode of thinking can exist in any sect of Islam, if the Muslim mind starts thinking like an Asharite and not a Mutazilite. The theocratic Shia rule in Iran is evidence of this. Similarly, although the Ahmadis are now considered outside the fold of Islam, they trace their origin in Islam. And for all said about the persecution and murder they have faced just for being Ahmadis, even they are mostly found succumbed to a dogmatic fundamentalist way of thinking in their theology.

Indeed, when legislation was being passed in 1974 in Pakistan to constitutionally declare them as non-Muslims, and their leader, Mirza Nasir Ahmad, was asked to defend their position, he is on record as having stated, and this interpretation was also contained in their defense document the 'Mahzarnama,' that for Ahmadis, all non-Ahmadis were non-Muslims[21].

The second pertinent point to mention about the subject of 'the problem with Islamic dogmatic fundamentalism' is regarding the word 'dogmatic' in the title 'the problem with Islamic dogmatic fundamentalism' itself. Why I choose to write the title as 'The problem with Islamic dogmatic fundamentalism' and not just 'The problem with Islamic Fundamentalism'?

Because fundamentals, and fundamentalism based on those fundamentals, are not the problem. The problem is when one makes those fundamentals into dogmatism, i.e., rigidity in belief or conviction, or when evidence clearly does not support a proposition which was being considered as fundamental.

Dogmatic fundamentalism can even occur in science. The fundamentals of Newtonian physics are different from the fundamentals of Einsteinian physics. The fundamentals of Newtonian physics are valid in a certain frame of reference, but as soon as discovery moves out of the bounds of that frame of reference, those fundamentals become unusable.

Similar is the case with Islamic Fundamentalism. When it becomes dogmatic and fails to recognize that it has entered a realm where the frame of reference has changed, it is then when it becomes problematic.

---

[21] https://www.alhakam.org/mahzarnama-the-memorandum/, https://www.alislam.org/library/books/Mahzarnama.pdf, 'The 1974 ouster of the 'heretics': What really happened?' by Nadeem F. Paracha (https://www.dawn.com/news/1057427)

About Anti-Islam and Anti-Pakistan Narratives

Following is a quote from the ex-Soviet journalist and dissident, Yuri Bezmenov (died 1993): "A person who is demoralized is unable to assess true information. The facts tell him nothing, even if I shower him with information, with authentic proof, with documents and pictures. ... he will refuse to believe it... That's the tragedy of the situation of demoralization."[22]

Bezmenov wrote, lectured, and talked extensively in the West, after his defection, about how a society can easily be destabilized and subsequently controlled, once demoralization sets in among the majority of the populace. He identified four steps in this process: Subversion or Demoralization, Destabilization, Crisis, and Normalization. In the first step the seeds of doubt are sowed in the populace about the foundations and the pillars of the social and political constitution on which their state stands, in the second step the seeds grow into plants of action hitting out at the social and political structures of society, in the third step the crisis occurs as a result of the destabilizing action resulting in the collapse of what existed before to be replaced by what has to brought in anew, and in the last step the new is normalized and the perpetrators of the new no longer want more revolution and the revolutionaries become opposers of revolution.

The prime context of this discourse by Bezmenov was the self-hate which was being promoted inside the United States, in particular, and the capitalist West in general, by the pro-Soviet agencies and the Left. *"The theory of subversion goes all the way back 2,500 years ago. The first human being who formulated the tactics of subversion was a Chinese philosopher by the name of Sun Tzu. Twenty-five hundred years B.C. He was an adviser for several imperial courts in ancient China, and he said, after long meditation, that to implement state policy in a warlike manner is the most counterproductive, barbaric and inefficient to fight on the battlefield. You know that war is continuation of state policy, right? So, if you want successfully to implement your state policy and you start fighting, this is the most idiotic way to do it. The highest art of warfare is*

---

[22] https://bezmenov.neocities.org/lecture/

not to fight at all, but to subvert anything of value in the country of your enemy until such time that the perception of reality of your enemy is screwed up to such an extent that he does not perceive you as an enemy. And that your system, your civilization, and your ambitions look to your enemy as an alternative, if not desirable than at least visible. "Better red than dead." That's the ultimate purpose, the final stage of subversion after which you can simply take your enemy without a single shot being fired — if subversion is successful."

When societies and countries are living under different political and economic systems, different religious discourses influencing their peoples' imagination, different cultures and traditions, and different historical legacies and heritage, would it be correct to say that only one of each of those would be the correct one for mankind and all others are wrong and evil?

Humankind residing in different lands have had different historical experiences which have brought each of them to the stage in which each of them currently exists. However, now, after the advent and predominance of scientific progress and the rationalization of the human thought process, certain human values and rights are recognized by all societies as universal human values and rights.

These include the values of anti-colonialism, anti-racism, democracy and freedom of expression, rule of law, right to food, health, education and shelter, gender equality in opportunities, and secularism, i.e., no preferential or discriminatory treatment by the state for any religion.

Those societies and states which do not uphold all these universal values are implicitly considered as deficient by the intellectual wisdom guiding those at the helm of the United Nations, which is to date the most humane international body created by humankind where it is possible for the diverse societies we talk about to come together and interact with each other without physical antagonism.

But any deficiency identified in a state or society in the context of these universal values does not qualify it to be labeled as evil or to be destabilized and terminated. For we can see in history that even in the most repressive of systems, there is possibility of reform, correction, and advancement from within, without destabilization and without demoralization and self-hate.

As long as it is humans we are talking about, humanity will surface inevitably. Soviet society de-Stalinized and had become much less brutal long before Mikhail Gorbachev came along. The Chinese communist-run state abandoned its extreme Left policies after the death of Mao Tse Tung and gradually waded almost completely into the realm of the free market economy. The monarchies of Europe gradually transformed into constitutional monarchies with executive powers completely shifted to pluralist democracies (and chaos and repression followed where monarchies were not maintained and sought to be ended abruptly). Even the theocratic state of Iran, run by clerics, became more urbane and relatively tolerant of pluralist and critical voices.

As human civilization advances scientifically, as scientific education makes inroads in societies, as economies succeed in finding the possibility to flourish, as bellies are filled and life becomes more comfortable, the possibility of the intellectual and cultural level of a people to rise and become more mature and more tolerant of newer ideas increases.

Of course, the fact that a state remains deficient in any of the mentioned universal values points to the fact that there is still predominance of the retrogressive element in its society, which keeps it deficient with respect to that value. But it can also mean that those running that society may realize that, although they are deficient in that regard, due to the internal stage of historical development of their society and certain external factors which could cause destabilization rather than advancement, that deficiency would be done away with in good time, but not abruptly right now.

Indeed, a credible argument can be made that Arab countries where monarchies, which have the organic sanctity of tribalism and tribal codes of hierarchy behind them, were abandoned through military coups, ran aground into brutal dictatorships, economic and social stagnation, and wars and civil wars. And those Arab countries where monarchies and naturally evolved balance in society were maintained through the sanctity of tribal code and respect of tribal hierarchy, there their people enjoyed the dividends of stability and economic prosperity.

Post 9/11, the anti-Islam trend in the world has gained strength by leaps and bounds to the extent that now some very influential quarters including political parties and leaders coming to power and intellectuals, are bent on getting the entire religion of Islam labelled as an evil religion or the religion of Satan to become the universally accepted truth, the whole truth and nothing but the truth. They want to depict the clash with Islam as a clash of civilizations, as if it is all things good in human civilization on one side and Islam on the other. They forget, or intentionally close their eyes to the fact, that Islam is an inherent part of the human civilizational story as we saw earlier, the Arabs and Muslims building on the intellectual legacy of Greek philosophers and the renaissance of Europe picking on the thoughts of Averroes and Ibn e Khuldun, and the scientific work left by Arab and Muslim scientists of the Golden Age of Islam.

In fact, the narrative of the clash of civilizations with Islam on one side and the rest of the world suits and is propounded by political parties and leaders, and intellectuals of another quarter. Yes, the Islamic Dogmatic Fundamentalists. They, too, are eager for this clash of civilizations. In fact, the Anti-Islam advocates and the Islamic Dogmatic Fundamentalists could be friends, allies, and bedfellows in the launch and success of this 'clash of civilizations' project if they wanted to (and maybe many times they are and may be found to be so in various instances).

In recent times, the anti-Islam advocates and debaters have come up with findings and claims through which a new narrative is put forth. It is proposed that the existence of the Prophet of Islam, in the context of the land and his personal life story in which it is quoted, as well as the development of the Quran, stands refuted, and the genesis of the message of Islam is traced to the reign of the Umayyad Caliph Abdul Maalik in the year 685 AD[23].

The theory states that while it is true that the Arabs rose as a potent force, conquering lands from the Romans and the Persians, it was only in Abdul Maalik's time, when, as a ruling empire, they needed their own

---

[23] *The book 'In the Shadow of the Sword' by Tom Holland is one of the authentic books on the subject. Although the author himself cannot be placed in the category of anti-Islam advocates and debaters but the latter do rely on such books to provide strength to their endeavour of refuting Islam.*

religion to replace the religion of the Romans and the Persians as a codified constitution of their own empire. This was because, in those times, religion was the constitution providing legitimacy to rulers.

Thus, the first available physical copy of the Quran cannot be found before the year 685 AD, and that it is a fact that the hadith and the 'Seerah' (the life of the Prophet) were not written before the 8th and the 9th century AD, almost two centuries after the passing away of the Prophet, accepted universally to have happened in 632 AD. As per this theory, the Arab rulers who had conquered the Levant created Islam retrospectively based on a legendary figure in their history by the name of Muhammad.

However, after quoting these findings, the Anti-Islam advocates go into a tirade against the Prophet of Islam quoting from the hadith, which they themselves state was written retrospectively, to demonstrate that he committed excesses and since Muslims follow him and consider him to be the ideal man to emulate therefore Muslims are on the wrong path and should be shunned. And the world should do away with Islam (the strategy is of 'Subversion or Demoralization, Destabilization, Crisis...').

They do not see the inherent flaw in the logic of this two-pronged strategy they adopt. If the story of the genesis of Islam and its Prophet is not as quoted in the hadith and 'Seerah', then how can they quote from these to prove that the Prophet committed the excesses they allude to? But on the other hand, any rational mind would acknowledge that the Arabs did rise from Arabia and defeat economically much superior powers of the era and conquered their lands, and, unlike the Mongols, succeeded in establishing a sophisticated empire which also gave humankind the era known as the 'Golden Age of Islam'. This could not have been made possible by people abiding by a code containing nothing good in it.

A rational mind would analyze the Islamic civilization in a historical context based on the social, economic, and cultural drivers which presented Islamic civilization to the world as the dominant force of advancement for a certain period of time.

To oversimplify Arabian life of those times based on the values and morality of today would be infantile and reactionary, and lead to persecutory behavior towards almost 1.5 billion population of the world, which in itself would be an anti-human trend, reversing the universal human values we referred to, even in the societies where these have been achieved.

Human history and the organic development of human societies and the way they organized themselves over centuries and moved forward cannot be ticked off with frivolity. As is human life not a matter of frivolity, so is the study of human history a serious matter. It is childish, and in fact callous if done by adults, to make mockery of the religion, culture, and history of a people.

If it seems easy for those bent on demonizing Islam to refer to examples of behavior which in modern times would be considered abhorrent or frowned upon, so it is easy to pick from any religion or historical legacy instances of similar behavior. If violence against enemies has been allowed in Islam, so is it encouraged in the Old Testament[24], and the history of the Judeo-Christian legacy is full of violent wars waged in the name of their religions, drawing legitimacy from their scriptures. Slavery was advocated for by Christians using quotations from the Bible[25], and as we are well aware, was not abolished by them till the 19th century AD. The sexual liaison of Thomas Jefferson, a giant among the United States' founding fathers and the strongest pillar of American enlightenment, with Sally Hemmings is a vivid example of abuse of power in a society where slavery had still not been abolished. Even the sexual liaison of George Washington, the father of the nation of Americans, with the slave woman Venus is not discounted as impossible by historians. Of course, taking sexual advantage of slave women by American slave owners will not be found to be a rarity if a focused study is conducted of this subject particularly. And then, as already mentioned before, the abolition of slavery was postponed by the founding fathers of the United States although they did not believe in it and had written the Declaration of Independence with the vision which excluded the possibility of slavery in the mutual relations between citizens coexisting in their state. It is well known that Thomas Jefferson's anti-slavery passage was removed from the final version of the declaration and the abolition of slavery postponed

---

[24] *Deuteronomy 12, 13*

[25] *Genesis 9:18-27, Ephesians 6:5, Leveticus 25:44-46, Timothy 6:1-2, Colossians 3:22 are some verses that provide justification to pro-slavery Christians.*

for the reason that the states coming into the fold of the newly constituted country relied extensively on slave labor for production in the agricultural fields, and the new state needed bumper production of cotton and tobacco to export to Europe and earn much-needed revenue to sustain their state.

So, we now return to Islam. As stated before, first those who seek to demonize Islam should decide whether the story of Prophet Muhammad (pbuh) is, as narrated by hadith and *seerah*, a retrospective story. And if so, then is it worthy of being used to demonize Islam and Muslims? Or is it a true story, and if so, then should the first research proclaiming it to be a retrospective story stand discredited? But can it really be discredited if it stands on scientific grounds?

But for all practical purposes, it seems that those bent on demonizing Islam want to go down the path of taking it as a true story and pick on the narrative of this true story with the intention of demonizing it and demoralizing the Muslims in particular, and the world in general, with respect to this narrative.

Therefore, it is important to see whether this attempt at demoralization is the right way forward and will it create more confrontation and reaction rather than reform and advancement in the world?

The above question is a very relevant question for the advanced Western world, which leads human civilization at present and from where it matters what policies and strategies are made to deal and interact with the Muslim world. It matters immensely, not just because the governments of Western states have to interact internationally with around 50 Muslim-majority countries, but also because Muslims now constitute a big proportion of their own citizenry.

Although the governments of Western countries have been wise in seeking ways of avoiding direct confrontation with Muslims, specially with ones who belong to their own citizenry, on ground they seriously lack in formulating the correct intellectual narrative which would replace their existing mode of dialogue and engagement with the Muslim population. The on-ground intellectual narrative has largely been dominated by the anti-Islam voices, the result of which is that this manifests in demands for policies which would be more hardline against immigration and immigrants, and make laws that would impose regulations from the top on

Muslims without having a dialogue with them, resulting in the Muslims interpreting those laws as anti-Muslim laws.

The basic problem with Western governments and intellectuals who seek a positive resolution of issues with Muslims is that the former consider themselves as outsiders and hope and wait for the Muslims to reform themselves. They are 'waiting for Godot'[26]. They consider that since they themselves are not Muslims so it would not be a nicety to engage with the Muslims in an intellectual debate which could restart and advance the theological work stopped centuries ago with the last 'Imam' of Islamic jurisprudence (Fiqh) and make it possible for the Muslim mind to join the rational and scientific fold of the modern world and its prerequisites.

Any commentary on Islam or the Muslim world that is made by non-Muslims in the West is made as an outsider. It is as if, although Muslims have become their fellow citizens since decades now, they still see them as "the other," as recent immigrants or guests. They are kept at arm's length.

Of course, such policy by Islam haters and anti-Islam intellectuals is understandable, but not from those who seek a positive resolution to the lack of integration of Muslims in their society. To keep Muslims at arm's length and not engage with them as their own is the same as the stance of those among the Western Muslim apologists who hold that primitive practices which are considered as illegal among non-Muslims (like forced marriages, polygamy, female circumcision, wife beating, praying in non-designated public spaces, etc.) may be tolerated if found to be practiced among Muslims because it is part of their culture.

It has been called the patronizing and condescending attitude of "racism of lower expectations." It is because of this abandonment of the task of critical engagement by the Left, Liberal, and Centrist elements in the Western political spectrum that the Right and the historically traditional religious denominations of the West have taken up the task of defending the realm of their own civilization in their own particular way.

---

[26] *'Waiting for Godot' is a play by Samuel Beckett in which the characters in the play are waiting for a figure called Godot who never comes.*

The correct way is to stop "waiting for Godot" and start conversing with Muslims as they would converse with a fellow citizen and fellow human being of their own civilizational (ethnic or religious) heritage. And this conversation has to constitute not asking Muslims what is in their religion, but knowing their religion in the proper historical context and suggesting to Muslims, not through confrontation or ridicule but through serious and sincere dialogue as a compatriot respecting and acknowledging the historical context in which Islam arose as the most potent civilizational force, how theological work in their religion needs to be advanced to bring it up to par with the requirements of modern times.

As a side remark in this context, even from a pragmatic objective of seeking cultural integration of the Muslims within the West while at the same time liberating them from orthodox rigidity, it is bemusing and self-defeatist on the part of proponents of national integration when they seek to ban the use of "hijab" or "burkinis." In both cases, where women do not cover their face and only wear hijab, and when they acquiesce to mixed swimming wearing a burkini, these are radical progressive breakaways from the edicts of reactionary fundamentalists imposed in their home countries which seek to obliviate women from social and practical life. In fact, by imposing a ban on hijab, the state could lose the effectiveness of differentiating between women of less and more religious leanings and all advantages that having this knowledge can bring.

It is true, and it is also the big reason why the well-intentioned Western intellectuals hesitate to go down this road of conversing with Muslims of advancing their theological work, that there is risk of violent reaction from orthodox and fundamentalist hardliners among Muslims if this mode of conversation is pursued. But this is the more humane way forward rather than the antagonistic, xenophobic, and rejectionist way of Islam haters and proponents of the anti-Islam narrative who want entire sections of populations to be marginalized and be seen with contempt in the societies where they reside, and pose an entire religion, which is a source of succor for almost 1.5 billion people on the planet, as an enemy.

So, to assess the Islamic context in a serious, not frivolous, and more humane manner, to challenge the imagination and intellect of the Muslim mind, and to allay the concerns of the non-Muslim mind influenced by the demonization of Islam propagated by haters of Islam and Muslims, we will go with the proposition that the story of the Prophet of Islam as considered authentic by Islamic scholars, and which is the one firmly embedded in the perception of the world in general and the Muslim mind in particular, is a true story.

What then are the elements which are used to demonize Islam and demoralize the Muslims and the world about Islam which need to be interrogated in a rational manner and sought to be superseded or advanced by a more progressive interpretation than the traditional and coarse one preferred by both Islamic hardliners as well as Islam haters (as we saw, they are one in preferring the coarser interpretation)?

We have already dealt with the interrogation of polygamy, slavery, and violence in Islamic edicts. However, the one big slander which Islam haters use is the life of the Prophet (pbuh) with respect to his many marriages including the one with the young Aisha (ra). Another is the alleged indiscriminate massacre of Jews after the battle of Banu Qurayza. We will deal with interrogation of these before we conclude on the futility of demonizing Islam and of choosing to adopt a strategy of demoralization for it.

So, if the story of Prophet Muhammad (pbuh) is true, then it is also true that before prophethood he was a person respected by all tribes residing in Mecca. It was he who was asked to be the arbiter among them when the question arose as to which clan would put back the Black Stone into the Kaaba after its renovation, five years before he claimed prophethood. Then it is also true that he was an ascetic devoted to spiritual meditation in the cave of Mount Hira and a man of upright character, a devoted husband to his only wife Khadija (ra), who remained so till she died a quarter of a century after their marriage.

And then, it is also true that he was so reliable by all as a man who always spoke the truth that when after three years of preaching secretly, he stood on the hill of Safa and asked the tribes of Mecca that if he told them that there was an enemy army on the other side of the hill ready to attack them, would they believe him, the spokespeople of the tribes stated that as they knew him to be a person who never told a lie, they would. It was then that he told them that they should know that he brought the message of Allah about the oneness of God and that no one should be worshipped except Him.

When those who slander the Prophet (pbuh) for his numerous wives and snigger like imbeciles at this fact in established history, do they choose to look at this fact on the criteria of present-day societies? And are they saying that a person who was an ascetic individual of high character and known for his truthfulness, given the titles of 'Al Ameen' and 'Al Saadiq' by the Meccans before the advent of Islam, who is not known in his entire youth to have indulged in any kind of decadence or sexual liaisons or multiple marriages which were common and acceptable at that time, suddenly turned into an individual only focused on sex?

A serious reader or student of history and socio-political changes in human history would never interpret these facts in that oversimplified manner. In fact, such a reductionist reading of these facts should be considered infantile and an insult to intellectually honest historical analysis.

The entire discourse of Islamic values with respect to the sexual relations between man and woman rests on the pivot of marriage and family life. It is very well known how harsh and rigidly strict Islamic edicts are about promiscuity and extramarital sex. A true Muslim is expected to never enter a sexual liaison except through marriage. Period. So was the discipline taught to the Arabs of that time with the message of Islam.

The concept of marriage as espoused in Islam, specially at that time when it emerged, was and is a mode of control and restraint of promiscuous behavior rather than being a mandate for unlimited indulgence. The Surah Nisa of the Quran is replete with detail about how the matters in a marriage should be conducted, always highlighting the responsibilities and liabilities of men towards their wives. We have already seen how the verse 4:3 of Surah Nisa, related to more than one marriage, can clearly be progressively read to discourage the practice of polygamy.

The other aspect of marriages in the time of 7th-century Arabia is their significance as transactions of trust and brotherhood between clans and individuals. In that respect, the marrying away of daughters or sisters to a man was seen as an expression and commitment of loyalty and camaraderie with that man. It was a transaction of socio-political nature in that society.

It was Islam which emphasized and added the pre-requisite of consent of at least the guardian (in most cases the father, and if not the father, the next elder or the brother) and, in extended interpretation, that of the marrying female individual, to formalize the marriage contract. In that sense, the woman in those times was also a transactional commodity carrying socio-political significance.

That this was so, just like slavery existed at that time, are truths of those times. If these are not truths of the present times, it is unfair to perceive and analyze the modus operandi of socio-political leaders of those times on the criteria of present times. It is the same as understanding that although women got voting rights for the first time only in the 20th century and slavery was abolished only by the 19th century, these facts do not discredit the progressiveness of leaders and their actions before that time who did not grant voting rights to women or abolish slavery in their lifetime.

In the context of these two aspects, we now look at the marriages of Prophet Muhammad (pbuh).

His first wife was Khadija (ra), whom he married when he was 25 and she remained his only wife till she died when he was 49. Slanderers of the Prophet choose not to appreciate this fact, that till the age of 49 the Prophet was a monogamous man. Similarly, those Islamic Dogmatic Fundamentalists who advocate polygamy, while harping on the need for Muslims to always follow 'Sunnat' (i.e. the personal behavior and minute personal conduct of the Prophet) to the minutest detail, are dumb in saying to the Muslims that this too is a 'Sunnat' that one should not marry more till the first wife is alive.

The second wife of the Prophet was Sawdah (ra), who was the widow of As-Sakran ibn Amr (ra), one of the early converts to Islam. The Prophet married her after he had become a widower and needed companionship. Sawdah (ra) was advanced in her years and already mother to six children. Could the Prophet not have chosen a younger woman without children to marry after becoming a widower if the intent was sexual pleasure?

The third wife of the Prophet was Aisha (ra), who was the daughter of Abu Bakr (ra), the Prophet's best friend. Much has been said and written, including by the slanderers of the Prophet, about the fact that Aisha is proclaimed by most sources to have been a child when she was married off to the Prophet. Regardless of the debate that exists about the real age of Aisha being 18 and not 9 when she was married to the Prophet[27], implying that her consent was included considering the emphasis of consenting individuals in a marriage being a re-requisite in Islamic Fiqh, the fact is that the issue of sex is secondary in a transaction which sealed the relation between the Prophet and Abubakr (ra) who in turn belonged to one of the elite families of the Quraysh. Indeed, those Islamic Dogmatic Fundamentalists who in this day and age still advocate child marriages, specially to older men using this 'Sunnat' of the Prophet, choose to overlook the factor of consent by the guardian Abubakr (ra) in this marriage. In this day and age, it will be difficult to find an educated and forward-looking Muslim father or elder who would marry away his child daughter, specially to a grown-up man. This is also chosen to be overlooked by slanderers of the Prophet. Finally, although there is no evidence to prove the nature of the intimate relationship between the Prophet and Aisha (ra), it is difficult to comprehend for me at least, looking at this particular matter in the entire socio-political context, that in this transactional marriage, sex was the primary consideration, and that too sex with a child.

The fourth wife of the Prophet was Hafsa (ra), who was the daughter of Umar (ra). It is well known who Umar (ra) was and what his standing in Meccan society and the significance of his conversion to Islam meant for the overall advancement of Islam. Later, he became the second Caliph of Islam after the demise of Abubakr (ra). Hafsa (ra) had become a widow, and Umar (ra) initially offered her to Usman (ra) and Abubakr (ra), but both refused. We can again see a transactional proposal underway to seal the bonding between men of high standing in Meccan society, all of whom

---

[27] https://guardian.ng/features/aisha-was-18-not-nine-when-she-married-the-prophet/ , https://www.icraa.org/aisha-age-review-traditional-revisionist-perspectives/ , https://yaqeeninstitute.org/read/paper/understanding-aishas-age-an-interdisciplinary-approach

had become early converts to Islam. After both Usman (ra) and Abubakr (ra) had refused, the Prophet agreed to marry Hafsa (ra) when Umar (ra) complained to him about the refusals. In this way, he sealed an eternal bonding and loyalty of Umar (ra), who would be a formidable foe for any adversary, in this case becoming one for the opposers of Islam.

The fifth wife of the Prophet was Zaynab binte Khuzaymah (ra), who belonged to a prestigious non-Quraysh tribe of Mecca and who was a twice-divorced individual before she married Ubayda bin Haaris (ra), a companion of the Prophet. Ubayda (ra) was martyred in the Battle of Badr, after which the Prophet married Zaynab with the stated intent of providing support to a widow who would be otherwise reduced to poverty in times when followers of Islam were struggling against the elite tribes of non-believers, and that those who followed Islam should not get the impression that their families would be left on their own or abandoned if they died fighting for Islam. In addition, the marriage to Zaynab (ra) also sealed the Prophet's commitment to, and won the hearts of, her tribe.

The sixth wife of the Prophet was Umm Salama (ra), original name Hind, whose father also belonged to the elite Quraysh tribe and who was married to Abu Salama (ra), a companion of the Prophet. Abu Salama (ra) was martyred in the Battle of Uhud, and Umm Salama became a widow with three children. These were the times when the Meccan Muslims had migrated to Medina and were refugees in Medina. To support her, both Abubakr (ra) and Umar (ra) proposed to her, but she refused. Finally, the Prophet proposed to her and she agreed, and the marriage took place, almost immediately after which her fourth child from Abu Salama (ra), who was on the way when Abu Salama (ra) died, was born. Does this sound like a man who is marrying for sex, when the woman he is marrying is already pregnant and he knows that he is adding 3 plus 1 stepchildren into the fold of his responsibility? The case of Umm Salama (ra) is similar to the case of Zaynab binte Khuzaymah (ra), whereby the families of those struggling for Islam were provided with the most honorable support in the eyes of the onlookers.

The seventh wife of the Prophet was Zaynab bint Jahsh (ra). She was the first cousin of the Prophet and twenty years younger than him. Being the first cousin of the Prophet means that she was the daughter of the

Prophet's paternal aunt, that is, she belonged to the family of the Quraysh. She was married to a person from the Quraysh who died by the time the Muslims made their 'hijra' (migration) from Mecca to Medina. Zaynab (ra) was already a convert to Islam by this time. She was married off by the Prophet to his adopted son, Zayd (ra), who in turn was an ex-slave freed by the Prophet. The Prophet loved Zayd (ra) as his own son. When the Prophet had proposed Zayd (ra) to Zaynab (ra), she had initially refused on the basis that she was from the Quraysh, whereas Zayd (ra) had been a slave. However, the Prophet, who wanted to elevate the status of freed slaves and espoused the equality of men except on the basis of piety, convinced her to marry Zayd (ra).

As per the historian Montgomery Watt, it is likely that Zaynab (ra) wished to be married to the Prophet[28]. That the marriage of Zaynab (ra) and Zayd (ra) was not smooth is an understatement. The incident of the Prophet's visit to Zayd (ra)'s home in Zayd (ra)'s absence when he coincidentally saw Zaynab (ra) not properly clothed, and thus admiring her, which is used by slanderers of Islam to attempt to reduce the Prophet to a man driven by desire, is rejected by most Muslim scholars as an authentic fact. This also does not withstand logical interpretation of any such incident, because Zaynab (ra) was the Prophet's first cousin, and he had seen her all his life, and it was not the first time that he had become aware of her beauty.

When Zayd (ra) divorced Zaynab (ra), the Prophet decided to marry Zaynab (ra). This should again be seen as providing honor and support to Zaynab (ra), who was a member of the Quraysh family, in fact, his own family, and who had just been divorced by an ex-slave in Medina in the early years of the migration, when the migrants were not well established in their new abode. In those times also, it was considered a taboo among Arabs to marry the widow of their own son, even an adopted one. By marrying Zaynab (ra), the Prophet also sealed a discernment between a biological son and an adopted son in the minds of the Arabs. It is also pertinent to mention here that when the Prophet married Zaynab bint Jahsh (ra), his fifth wife Zaynab bint Khuzaymah (ra) had already passed away

---

[28] *Watt, W. M. (1956). Muhammad at Medina, p. 331. Oxford: The Clarendon Press*

a year before. So, at the time the Prophet married Zaynab bint Jahsh (ra), she effectively became his fifth wife, alive with four existing ones at the same time.

The eighth wife of the Prophet was Juwayriyyah bint al-Harith (ra), who was the daughter of the chief of the Banu Mustaliq tribe. The Banu Mustaliq tribe was constantly conspiring against the Prophet and was the initiator of several assassination attempts against the Prophet. Eventually, the Muslims attacked the Banu Mustaliq, and they were defeated in battle, in which the husband of Juwayriyyah (ra) was also killed. She fell among the booty of the Prophet's companion Thabit bin Qays (ra). However, she went up to the Prophet and pleaded her case, stating that she was the daughter of the chief of her tribe, and it was not becoming of her to become a slave woman. At that, the Prophet proposed to her to marry him and acquire the status of a wife, which she gladly accepted. Subsequently, when her father and other members of her tribe who were held captive were freed, they all converted to Islam. Do we see here a lust for sex, or do we see here a realpolitik maneuver of honoring an entire tribe and gaining their eternal loyalty and being part of a larger strategy of uniting tribe after tribe under the banner of a single religion, religion in those times serving as the basis of a constitution of a single viable state?

The ninth wife of the Prophet was Ramla bint Abu Sufyan (ra), better known as Umm Habiba (ra). Her first husband was Ubaydullah bin Jahsh, who was the brother of Zaynab bint Jahsh (ra), both brother and sister being the first cousins of the Prophet. Ramla (ra) and Ubaydullah were early converts to Islam and were part of the people who made the first migration to Ethiopia. There, Ubaydullah converted to Christianity, but Ramla (ra) stood fast to Islam, and thus they separated. At this time, this was the first year of the 'hijra' (migration) to Medina, the Prophet reached out and proposed to her, and she was married to him in Ethiopia in absentia of the Prophet. It was only six years later, when she arrived in Medina, that she started living with the Prophet. The fact that she was the daughter of Abu Sufyan, the archenemy of the Prophet and one of the foremost elites of Mecca, turns into a no-brainer in understanding why the Prophet himself chose to propose to her once she became alone in an alien land on the conversion of her first husband to Christianity. Later, when the Prophet eventually conquered Mecca, Abu Sufyan and his wife also converted to Islam, and it is famously known that the Prophet announced that whoever took refuge in the house of Abu Sufyan (ra), they would be granted full clemency. To not understand all this in the historical context and continue to indulge in slandering the personality of the Prophet is very plainly, intellectual disingenuousness.

The tenth wife of the Prophet was Safiyya bint Huyayy (ra). She was the daughter of the chief of the Jewish tribe of Banu Nadir. She was a divorcee who was married to Kenana bin Rabi, who was the treasurer of the Banu Nadir tribe. She became a booty after the victory of the Muslims over the Jewish tribes in the Battle of Khaybar. The Battle of Khaybar was fought after the renege of their treaty with the Muslims by the Jewish tribes by joining the Meccan forces besieging Medina in the Battle of the Trench. Once the Meccan forces had turned back and the siege was finished, the Muslim forces attacked the Jewish tribe of Banu Nadir at Khaybar. As stated above, the battle ended in victory for the Muslims. Saffiya (ra)'s father was executed after battle and Safiyya (ra) became booty. She was initially taken by a companion of the Prophet, but the Prophet superseded him and took Saffiya (ra) for himself as his wife. This is a case similar to the case of Juwayriyyah (ra).

The eleventh wife of the Prophet was Maymunah bint al-Harith (ra), whose original name was Barrah. She belonged to the Hilali tribe of Mecca and was a half-sister of Zaynab bint Khuzaymah (ra) and Asma bint Umays (ra), a wife of Abu Bakr (ra). She was widowed, and the Prophet married her in the seventh year of the 'hijra' (migration) just after the performance of the 'Lesser Pilgrimage' which happened during a time of peace treaty (of Hudaibiyya) with the Meccans. She was in her late thirties when she married the Prophet and remained married to him for the last three years of his life. Needless to elaborate on the socio-political significance of this marriage.

Rayhana bint Zayd (ra) and Mariyya Qubtiyya (ra) are two other women who were wives of the Prophet. All sources are not agreed over the fact whether they were wives or only mistresses in the household of the Prophet. The case of Rayhana bint Zayd (ra) is similar to the case of Juwayriyyah (ra) and Saffiya (ra), as Rayhana (ra) was a Jewish woman who became widowed in the siege of Banu Qurayza and was taken as booty and then taken in by the Prophet himself into his household. Mariyya Qubtiyya was a slave woman gifted to the Prophet by the Christian governor of Alexandria, Egypt, in the year 628, and she was freed by the Prophet when she delivered the Prophet's son, Ibrahim (ra). Ibrahim (ra) passed away at the age of two, six months before the demise of the Prophet himself.

Summing up, in the correct perspective, we see the Prophet of Islam, as a celibate and spiritual man till the age of 25 respected by all in Mecca, a monogamous man till the age of 49 with his beloved wife Khadija (ra), and then again a monogamous man for another four years till the age of 53 with his second wife Sawdah (ra), a widow and mother of six when she married the Prophet. All marriages subsequently we have seen started from the year 623 AD; Aisha (ra) 623 AD, Hafsa (ra), Zaynab bint Khuzaymah (ra) and Umm Salama (ra) 625 AD, Zaynab bint Jahsh (ra) and Rayhana (ra) 627 AD, Juwayriyyah (ra), Ramla (ra) and Mariyya (ra) 628 AD, and Safiyya (ra) and Maymunah (ra) 629 AD. From the age of 53 up to the age of 63 when he passed away from this world, these are marriages of building ties and loyalties in a highly fragmented and rough tribal society, unifying them under a strict code of conduct and family life, making them become one strong unitary state, a first in the history of the Arabian desert peninsula.

Any objective scholarly socio-political study would, and so it does whenever it is done, acknowledge this life as a phenomenon of sheer political genius. If the motivation were to build a harem for pleasure or sexual gratification, as was done explicitly by kings and conquerors of all religious backgrounds, including subsequent Muslim ones, then the marriages would without exception or majorly be to young virgin girls. Neither do we see a case of forced marriage of suppressed and submissive women. Instead, we see, except in the case of Aisha (ra), where consent was given by her father (and if, as debated, her actual age at the time of marriage was 19, then it could be argued that her consent was included), mature, headstrong, and self-assertive women being proposed, and their entering the contract of marriage with the Prophet with independent consent. The conduct of the Prophet in the incident of Aisha (ra) having been left behind in a caravan and brought back by Safwan Ibn Muattal (ra) and for which the Quran verses 24:11–15 were revealed, is manifestation of the socially cognizant and tolerant way in which the Prophet led his society rather than from a petty personal perspective. Of course, the Prophet of Islam is different from the Prophets before him, as he did not abstain from or shirk from delving personally into all aspects of material life. He went beyond just preaching and took action, achieving a successful revolution in the minds and administration of his society. Not even trying to understand his life from this perspective would be to knowingly choose to take a reductionist view of history.

We now address the second biggest point of slander used by Islam haters, and again twisted and distorted by Islamic Dogmatic Fundamentalists to achieve their own hateful ambitions, before we conclude eclectically on the subject of anti-Islam narratives.

The case is that of the massacre of Jews conducted after the siege of Banu Qurayza. As we have already seen, during the Battle of the Trench, the Jewish tribes of Banu Nadir and Banu Qurayza had reneged on their agreement with the Prophet not to side with the Meccans against the Muslims in Medina. After the Meccans eventually withdrew, the Muslims besieged these tribes as retribution for their betrayal. When the Banu Qurayza surrendered, it is vital to remember that what happened subsequently to the Banu Qurayza was not the decision of the Prophet. What really happened was that after the surrender of the Banu Qurayza, the Banu Aws, a tribe friendly to Banu Qurayza, approached the Prophet and appealed for leniency[29]. Thereupon, the Prophet nominated Saad bin Muaadh (ra), who was an ex-Jew convert to Islam and a former ally of the tribe, to decide the fate of the Banu Qurayza. The Banu Aws accepted, and it was Saad bin Muaadh (ra) who then decided that "the men should be killed, the property divided, and the women and children taken as slaves". It is important to remember that in those times, it was not uncommon for a whole tribe to be eliminated entirely from existence in acts of retribution. This incident though not at all one to be cheered, as it is done by Islamic Dogmatic Fundamentalist fascists spewing hatred against the Jews and

---

[29] *The Jews of Arab Lands: A History and Source Book (Norman Stillman); William Montgomery Watt (1961), Muhammad, Prophet and Statesman*

calling for their deaths wherever they may be found, it does have to be viewed in the overall context of the political and military machinations taking place in the land at that time in the struggle between the Meccans and the Muslims, the former bent on suppressing and defeating the latter and the latter trying their best to survive and save their new found religion. Adrenalin and infantile reductionism have to be kept in their place, and history ought to be studied with objectivity and with reference to the exact context of the period under the lens. True, it can be critically questioned looking retrospectively that: was that which happened then, the only option to go forward with which would ensure a prevention of such betrayals for good? However, even if an objective answer to that question repeatedly comes out in the negative, although there will likely be at least some analysts of that time who may conclude that it could not have been otherwise, it will not change the fact that the decision for the massacre was not taken by the Prophet himself.

Finally, considering that the premise we are using to understand the life of the Prophet in its context is that the story of the Prophet is true as told through *hadith* and the *Seerah*, it is important for progressive validation and interpretation to always caveat it with the requirement for its corroboration with the Quran.

For Muslims to understand, when they say that the sole objective of the Prophet's life was to deliver the message of God to humanity according to the revelations provided by God and that he did not introduce anything on his own, then the logical conclusion follows that no *hadith* or quote from the *Seerah* should be considered as validated if it cannot be corroborated with any explicit concept, commandment, or edict given in the Quran.

In the end, a Muslim is free in this world to read and understand the Quran and adopt it in his or her personal life by free choice. But for interpretations affecting the collective, it is necessary for Muslims to collectively move forward with the method of *Ijtihad* (independent reasoning), to be taken up by their qualified scholars, to advance Islamic theology to cope and address the new conditions of a modern and scientific world and resume the process of *Fiqh* (jurisprudence), which has stopped and is stagnant since almost 1200 years, with the last such work done by Imam Shaafi.

As against Islam, a similar strategy of demoralization has come forth regarding the state of Pakistan ever since the utility of Pakistan as one of the frontline states, protecting the interests of Western capitalism after World War 2, waned after the collapse of the Soviet Union. This utility did see a short comeback after the 9/11 attacks on the United States, but since that time around the foe of the West was its previous ally against Soviet communism[30], thus having acquired deep entrenchment in numerous corridors and agencies of the Pakistani state, the West gradually became wary of this utilitarian view of Pakistan. In the backdrop of the growing anti Islam narrative globally, which we talked about above, and the growing Hindutva narrative in neighbouring India, a country which provides a much more profitable prospect with its advanced capitalism and a huge viable market, the intellectuals and politicians in the West became more and more amenable to narratives which demonize Pakistan, discredit the raison d'être of its existence, and to the possibility of a world again without a Pakistan.

This strategy of demoralization is reciprocated and helped by political forces within Pakistan too, who are either bent on the dismemberment of the Pakistani state to begin with in their stated or unstated political manifesto, or are those who buy into the idea of doing away with the state of Pakistan and question the historical legitimacy of the creation and continuity of the state of Pakistan, due to frustration caused by the marginalization, and in extreme cases the elimination, of elected political entities and civilian administrative and economic forces by the Pakistan military, including the excesses committed by the latter in doing so, or those who are genuinely intellectually confused.

The case of Pakistan, from the socio-psychological perspective, which is the objective of this book, will be addressed in further detail in the next chapter. But to conclude this chapter, this strategy of demoralization is challenged too, for the state of Pakistan.

---

[30] *Unholy Wars (John K. Cooley), Butcher and Bolt (David Loyn)*

This challenge is made not just because that is what would be expected of one who is a Pakistani by citizenship, but because a case has to be made against a worldview which, just like demonizing a religion of almost 1.5 billion of humanity, sees solutions to problems of international conflict and human rights abuse in carving up and dividing, and breaking up, and then carving up again, old and new countries at its whim and fancy, continuing to behave like the colonial powers of yore, with utter disregard of the human suffering and misery that accompanies such a worldview each time it succeeds in doing that.

True, that a state reacts brutally when an attempt is made to dismember it, specially through violent means, and there is no excuse for that if, in the execution of this state brutality, any recourse to a political solution has been abandoned and crimes against humanity are committed, which delegitimize the state and make it legitimate at that time to go ahead and dismember it.

But regardless of a state's reaction to an attempt at its dismemberment, or in parallel to that, what does fanning a politics of dismemberment or secession entail, specially in third world conditions, where modern political processes are in the nascent stages of institutionalizing? It entails an increase of hatred of each other among people, fratricide, and holocaust.

We have seen enough of that in examples such as the holocaust of the Indian partition in 1947, the Nakba and war on Israel in 1948, the atrocities and crimes against humanity committed after the dissolution of Yugoslavia in the 1990s, the crimes against humanity committed by opponents and proponents of Bangladesh against each other in East Pakistan in 1971, and the despicable excesses committed against humanity by common people against each other in the Syrian civil war which started in 2011.

A truly democratic and humane worldview would never opt for uncompromising secessionism but struggle for decentralized federalism democratized to the grassroots level. There is valid criticism of the risk and existence of supranationalism in projects like the European Union, where people of a certain nation feel disempowered, their self-determination limited. But if this supranationalism is checked and subdued through new legal and administrative measures and reforms, the idea of the European Union is in fact, a visionary and humanist idea and the correct way forward for humanity in other regions as well and the vision of narrow nationalism challenging it, is a reactionary and retrogressive one. The same can be said of bodies and initiatives like the SAARC (South Asian Association for Regional Cooperation), of which Pakistan was and is a member. The potential for progress, prosperity, and friendship among peoples through such initiatives is immense.

Earlier in this chapter, we already saw that the creation of Pakistan owes itself not just to the whim of a departing colonial power[31], but had enough historical seeds of ethos which democratically overpowered all other competing supra and sub-nationalisms and came into being at a certain stage of history as a de facto assertion of self-determination against a unitary center and for the preservation of the civilizational ethos of the Indian Muslim.

Verily, the unfolding of the Hindutva politics in India, striving to establish a Hindu Rashtra (Hindu Nation), can easily be used to demonstrate the historical, if not political, correctness of the Pakistan Movement and an absolution of the vision of its founder, the Quaid e Azam Mohammad Ali Jinnah an ex-member of the Indian National Congress, in choosing to spearhead it. To go forward as a viable state, Pakistan has to become an inclusive and federal state and prevent itself from becoming a theocratic state. But other than fulfilling those essential prerequisites, there is no reason why it has to be browbeaten to consider itself being any different from any other independent and sovereign federation existing in the world, proud of the ancient historical heritage of its people including their linkage with the rest of the Indian subcontinent, as well as with the neighboring states in its west, and the unique internal experience since its creation in 1947, which qualifies it to continue on as a 'Westphalian' nation-state in its own right and the people living within its boundaries to be now considered primarily, Pakistani.

---

[31] *India was partitioned under the 3rd June 1947 Partition Plan, and this partition was given final sanction along with granting independence to India through the Independence of India Act passed by British Parliament enacted 18 July 1947*

Pakistani Zeitgeist

On the midnight of 14th August 1947, within time amounting to more or less a split second, a new country with well-defined and set geographical boundaries came into being on the Indian subcontinent. This territory detached itself from a unified British India, and at that moment, so did it detach itself and the people living within its borders from the collective story of the rest of India. Up to that moment, its internal story had been intrinsically intertwined with the internal collective story of the rest of India, the northern part at least. But from that moment onwards, it flung away on its own like a planet hurtling in space, embarking on an internal story unique to itself, insulated from the rest of India living outside of its international borders. From that moment onwards, the people of Pakistan stopped being intimately privy to the internal sociopolitical dynamics and machinations of the rest of India, as did the people of post-Partition India to those of Pakistan.

Both new countries that formed out of British India embarked on their respective journeys of national discourse, dominated by an overpowering official narrative in each of the two countries.

In India, the basic premise of its official narrative was Indian nationalism, that is, that the only nationalism worth recognizing within India was Indian nationalism, that India was one nation not only now but since the beginning of human civilization on the Indian subcontinent, and that India as a nation had finally achieved independence from British colonialism.

In Pakistan, the basic premise of its official narrative was the Two Nation Theory, that is, that in India there were two major nations, Hindus and Muslims, and therefore after the departure of the British it was essential that this fact be recognized and both nations be given their own country, and that Pakistan had achieved its independence from both British colonialism and the Hindus. And now, all living inside Pakistan could be considered as one nation, the Pakistanis, but primarily this was a country for the self-determination of the Muslims of India, with the existence of other religious minorities recognized and their rights as citizens to be safeguarded, represented by the white band on the national flag of Pakistan.

Both these official narratives were seriously flawed from the intellectual perspective of political science, which eventually led to the domination of retrogressive religious forces in each country.

In the case of Pakistan, we have already discussed at length how the Two-Nation Theory, that is, Muslim Nationalism, does not withstand the interrogation of political science. Because, one, a nation is not defined based on religion, and second, if the only premise for Pakistan is the self-determination of the Muslims of India, then what of the Muslims that remained living in India even after Partition, who currently are close to equal in population to the Muslim population in present-day Pakistan? As we shall see more, this flaw in this official narrative inevitably led to the consolidation of the theocratic case for the state of Pakistan and the inevitable domination of religious fundamentalist forces in the intellectual echelons of power in the Pakistani state, and anyone offering a different narrative than this official one immediately facing the risk of being brandished as a traitor.

In the case of India, its official narrative at inception was flawed because it rested on the inherent concept for such a narrative, of the One Nation Theory, that India had always been one nation before and after colonialism. A One Nation Theory by default will never recognize the sub-nationalism of the culturally and linguistically diverse regions joining its political union, and off and on is likely to consider express assertions of self-determination by these constituent regions as anti-national. Inevitably, the continued stance of India being one nation had to lead to the domination of a religious discourse intertwined with the national, because then the only cultural thread that remained, linking all of India together, was the majority Hindu religion. Thus, for the Indian state to continue with a strong unitary center, it became inevitable that a party that put emphasis on the Hindu identity of India would gain predominance in national politics.

True, that because of wise inclusions in the Indian constitution with respect to the secular and federal nature of the Indian state, it is more difficult in India than in Pakistan to convert the state into a theocratic state.

The state is more tolerant and even encouraging of the diverse cultures and languages in the country, and even when the Hindu nationalist party does come into power, it has to rule more secularly than in an overtly religio-fascist manner.

In Pakistan, however, due to its constitution from the start proclaiming an Islamic republic, even a liberal or secular leader or party finds it repeatedly difficult to rule in a secular manner and succumbs to using Islamic jargon and overtones to justify and make progress on the deliverance of their political agenda, manifesto, and promises to the people. In that sense, the Indian official narrative was a bit less flawed than the Pakistani official narrative, judged from the scholastic criteria of the principles of political science, but for both countries, the progressive way forward would be to continue as more and more democratized and decentralized federal Westphalian nation-states.

However, we would digress if we continued about post-Partition India, as this book is about Pakistan primarily and not India per se, and other elements of international and historical phenomena are discussed on the side when need is felt for elaborating related context.

The story of the Pakistani zeitgeist is not necessarily a negative one. We see, as we go down the path of studying it, that there have been many positives, too, of resilience, resistance, compassion, and heroism. We will discuss all, negatives as well as the positives. But eventually, the objective of this book is to look critically at socio-psychological aspects which prove to act as brakes on the vehicle of progress for the Pakistani state and its people.

There have been many authoritative books written on the political and social evolution of Pakistan by some of the foremost intellectuals of the country, like K. K. Aziz, Khalid Bin Sayeed, Hussain Haqqani, Ayesha Siddiqa Agha, Ayesha Jalal, Khaled Ahmed, Nadeem Farooq Paracha, and Dr. Pervez Hoodbhoy, to name a few. Such works are already available to reflect with facts and figures from the historical, political, and social angles academically on the state of affairs in Pakistan. This book does not seek to emulate those works. This book only attempts to offer an insight from unique socio-psychological angles with its own discourse, bringing to the fore certain psychological or social nuances which may have been overlooked, understated, or considered too petty, politically incorrect, or subjective to be spoken of or written.

The Democratic and Institutional Legacy of the British

The one major saving grace for Pakistan is that it came into being through the ballot, not the bullet.

The movement for the creation of Pakistan was a political, not militant, one. It relied on the modern democratic electoral infrastructure which had been introduced and infused in India by the British colonialists to govern the country in an efficient manner with the collaboration of the colonized natives.

From the time of the formation of the All-India Muslim League in 1906 and the election of Muhammad Ali Jinnah to the Imperial Legislative Council in 1909, the journey of the Pakistan movement was always a political one, never a lapse into armed struggle. Same can be said of the politics of the Indian National Congress. The successful Indian freedom struggle against colonialism was a political struggle unlike many other colonies in the rest of the world which gained independence through armed struggle.

The fact that a successful freedom struggle has not been a violent one which brings immense bloodshed and military confrontation between the forces of freedom and the colonial state, has its own dividends for the independent native state which comes into being after the political defeat and demise of colonialism on that land. The new state is built on an already existing modern infrastructure of political bodies, the legal penal codes do not have to be reinvented but are modified to meet the needs of the new state and while this modification is not done the existing penal codes continue, there is already an administrative bureaucracy full of native employees running the state who do not have to be eliminated or fired, and the bad blood between the departing colonialists and the previously colonized is not to that extent of hatred that technological, educational, and trade ties may not continue between the new underdeveloped independent state and the more advanced departing colonial power.

That the Pakistan movement and the Indian freedom struggle were flagbearers of such a struggle qualifies them to be considered as great freedom struggles, and their foremost leaders, such as Gandhi, Nehru, and Jinnah, as great and wise leaders.

It is the fact that the Pakistan movement was such a struggle[32] and not an armed struggle, and it were the politicians who were creating Pakistan and not the soldiers and officers of the armed forces of the country who later became the armed forces of Pakistan, which is the reason why all military dictatorships in Pakistan eventually failed and were invariably brought down to be replaced by legitimate political constitutional rule. This was unlike many dictatorships in the Middle East, Africa and Latin America where dictators lasted for decades and when they fell, society sank into violence, fratricide or chaos.

The core component of the Pakistani zeitgeist is inherently democratic in nature because the existence of Pakistan is the product of a legacy of political and democratic struggle.

---

[32] HIGH LEVEL RECAP OF MAJOR MILESTONES IN THE PAKISTAN MOVEMENT: *1905 Partition of Bengal -> 1906 Simla Deputation -> 1906 Founding of the All-India Muslim League ->1909 Minto–Morley Reforms -> 1911 Annulment of the Partition of Bengal -> 1914–18 World War I -> 1915 Gandhi arrives (returns) in India -> 1916 Lucknow Pact -> 1916-1918 Jinnah along with Annie Besant, Joseph Baptista, Bal Gangadhar Tilak and Subramania Iyer forms and runs the All India Home Rule League -> 1919 Rowlatt Act and Jallianwala Bagh Massacre. Jinnah resigns from the National council in protest -> 1919 Montagu-Chelmsford Reforms -> 1919–23 Khilafat Movement (Gandhi supports it. Jinnah and Iqbal refrain from supporting it, in fact Jinnah opposes it) -> 1927 Delhi Muslim Proposals -> 1928 Nehru Report -> 1929 Fourteen Points of Jinnah -> 1930 Simon Commission Report -> 1930 Allama Iqbal presidential address to All India Muslim League session -> 1930–32 Round Table Conferences -> 1932 Communal Award (1932) -> 1933 Pakistan Declaration / Now or Never Pamphlet -> 1935 Government of India Act -> 1935 Sind becomes separate province, delinked from Bombay presidency -> 1937 Elections -> 1937–39 Congress Rule in 7 out of 11 Provinces -> 1937 Strong anti congress governments in Punjab and Bengal. Anti congress parties win in Sind -> 1938 A. K. Fazlul Huq of Bengal joined Muslim League -> 1938 Jinah Sikandar pact in Punjab -> 1938 Pirpur Report -> 1939-45 World War II -> 1939 Resignation of congress ministries and non-congress power players got golden chance -> 1940 Pakistan Resolution -> 1942 Quit India Movement by Congress and non-congress players further get space -> 1942 Cripps' mission -> 1944 Gandhi – Jinnah Talks -> 1945 World War II ends. British Empire is bankrupt at the end of the war -> 1946 Elections. Muslim League sweeps in Muslim majority areas -> 1946 The Cabinet Mission the last British effort for united India. Jinnah accepts it, Nehru and Congress reject it -> 1946 Direct Action Day in the aftermath of cabinet mission plan failure -> 1946 Interim Government installed in office -> 1947 June 3 Partition Plan. Independence of India Act passed by British Parliament enacted 18 July 1947 -> August 1947 Creation of Pakistan*

Moreover, the multiethnic and federated nature of the Pakistani state, which is also a modern political concept and a governing legacy of the departing British rule, also makes it essential that democracy prevails. It becomes imperative for any ruler, including military dictators and fascists from the middle classes who are bent on subverting democracy and failing the constitution, to indulge in realpolitik and dialogue rather than only brute force to carry the people of Pakistan with them.

The use of coercion, intelligence services, and military or police action is only fruitful if the ruler, through this realpolitik, is able to gain the dominant consent of the people or of a big majority of influencing voices and lobbies in most provinces. That is the reason why, although atrocities and torture have been committed by dictatorial regimes and state agencies, these are no match for the extent of brutalities committed in Arab, African, and Latin American dictatorships. In Pakistan, there have always been ample possibilities for family and supporters of the victims, as well as human rights organizations and the press, to raise voice against acts of dictatorial suppression and bring these cases in front of the country's higher courts, which too are a legacy of British colonial rule.

The other major saving grace for Pakistan, ironically, is found in the deeply institutionalized professional discipline of its armed forces, who otherwise have been the prime culprits in putting brakes on the progress of Pakistani civil government, economy, and society through their military dictatorships repeatedly imposed on the country and dabbling in business interests to the detriment of the progress of civil economic forces in the country.

The professional discipline—that is, not violating the internal hierarchical command and obedience structure at any time and not overstepping the internal protocol of organizational elevation of its officers—has prevented the armed forces of Pakistan, the Pakistan Army in particular, from descending into an internal breakup with various militias and warlords thus ensuing, spilling each other's blood. This professional discipline and protocol have also prevented the army from becoming the personal property of any Chief of Army Staff or military dictator and subsequently of their offspring(s), as happened sometimes in other third-world countries.

The Pakistan Army, the way it is structured and disciplined, is part of the inheritance left behind by the British Crown. A major reason for this professional discipline remaining intact inside the armed forces of Pakistan can also be attributed to the evolution of the Pakistani state as a national security state in the historical backdrop of the Cold War and subsequently the 'War on Terror,' whereby the Pakistani military continued to work closely with the British and later the U.S. security establishment. A dividend of this collaboration has been that this professional discipline has become a compulsive second nature for Pakistan's military officers.

This saving grace also makes it possible for democratic political forces in the country to create enough policy space for themselves, as this professionalism of the rank and file of the Pakistan Army enables its officers to see impersonally when it has become futile to continue on with their dictatorship (or intervention) and when their dictator's time has run out of steam.

'Muhajir' or 'Settler': The Core Factor of the Migrant in the Rural-Urban Divide

The way the urban centers of Pakistan have evolved since the inception of the state is different from the evolution of urban centers in most countries.

Historically, urban centers, which eventually came to be called cities, in most countries came into being with the concentration of large populations flowing in from contiguous rural areas gathered for the enhancement of modern industrial and commercial activity. The cultural composition and language of those living in the cities was not different from those living in the rural areas. In fact, mostly they were the same people, with those residing in cities having cultural and family roots going back into the rural areas.

In Pakistan, the urban centers did not evolve in this manner. In 1947, when the partition of British India occurred, all urban centers in the territory of the then West Pakistan and current Pakistan were dominated by Hindu and Sikh populations. Karachi, Hyderabad, and Rawalpindi were

Hindu and Sikh majority cities, while cities like Lahore, Lyallpur (later Faisalabad), Sialkot, Sukkur, Quetta, and Peshawar had large Hindu and Sikh populations, not much less than half of the total population in these cities. It was the Hindus and Sikhs who occupied key roles and positions in the economy and the administration of these cities. These non-Muslim populations in these cities were also the indigenous people of the land, carriers of the same culture and language of the land from which these cities had emerged and had organically evolved from and were linked to the adjoining contiguous rural heartland in the backdrop.

As partition occurred, these cities emptied of the Hindu and Sikh populations and were replaced by Muslim migrants in the millions coming over from across the border in post-British India, majorly from areas of East Punjab, the Upper Provinces (Uttar Pradesh), the Central Provinces (Madhya Pradesh), Bihar, the Nizamate of Hyderabad, and the Indian state of Gujrat.

While the migrants pouring in from East Punjab in India settled mostly in West Punjab in Pakistan and had less alienation with the local population in terms of culture and language, the migrants coming from areas other than East Punjab in India possessed a social culture and language completely different from the local population.

Therefore, it can be safely established that from 1947 onwards, the cities of Pakistan evolved in alienation and disconnect with respect to the rural heartlands of the country. The rural population stopped identifying with the urban and vice versa. For both, the other was an alien culture and an alien language.

In the beginning, this alienation was less antagonistic and more polite, but as the race commenced in the new state for controlling the reins of social and political power, this race became more and more a race manifested through tussles between ethnicities and ethnic perceptions of a political rival, rather than a race between economic classes per se or a simple intellectual battle between rival schools of politico-economic policies.

The first victim of this ethnicity-based competition in the new state became the Bengali Muslim. The 1950s was the decade of sidelining the

Bengali leadership of the Pakistan movement and the new state of Pakistan.

But before we elaborate on that and reflect on the ethnic-based prejudices and politics in Pakistan thereafter, we take a pause and interrogate the general essence and nature of the 'Migrant' way of thinking.

The essential components in the mindset of the 'Migrant' once he[33] is uprooted or has uprooted himself from the comfort and 'fit' of his age-long homeland, are 'risk' and 'uncertainty'. The element of 'risk' imbues him with a dynamism, an agility, and alertness to surpass the hurdles for survival and progress, without the luxury in his hand of the networking and economic support that would be there if he was historically rooted in the society he has migrated to. The 'Migrant', therefore, has historically been found to be generally more efficient, educated and self-reliant than the laid back 'Native' or 'Local' who first receive the 'Migrant', examples stretching from world Jewry including in the land of Palestine, the Chinese in Southeast Asia, the white settlers in America and South Africa, expatriate workers and professionals in the Middle East and elsewhere and ... the 'Muhajirs'[34] in Pakistan. The element of 'uncertainty' results in the emergence of feelings of 'insecurity' constantly lit in the back of the mind of the 'Migrant' to a degree bordering on a semblance of paranoia. The same fact that he does not see a social safety net to cushion his fall if ever he was to fail, a net which would be available to him had he been a 'son of the soil', constantly keeps this question alive in his mind that what would happen to him and his family if he was to fail, not only in surviving but in providing a comfortable and even prosperous life for them.

The close to paranoid feeling of insecurity and the element of risk inherently built into the life coaching of the 'Migrant', in turn, produce

---

[33] The gender 'he' or 'him' will be used here for ease of discourse, just as the word 'Man' is used often to represent 'human being'.

[34] In Pakistan, the term 'Muhajir' (literal meaning 'migrant') is reserved for the migrants and their descendants who migrated at the time of partition, and after, from the non-Punjabi and non-Bengali areas of post British India like the Upper Provinces (Uttar Pradesh), the Central Provinces (Madhya Pradesh), Bihar, the Nizamate of Hyderabad and the Indian state of Gujrat. Since they do not speak any of the local languages of the territory comprising Pakistan as their mother tongue and therefore communicate with their compatriots in Urdu, they are also called 'Urdu Speaking'.

two default traits generally present in the thought process and discourse of most migrants.

The first is a sarcastic, bordering on hostile, and belittling attitude towards the majority native population of the land in which the 'Migrant' has arrived. It has been common among 'Migrants' to term the indigenous natives as lazy, or dirty, or primitive, or backward, or illiterate and uneducated, as somehow it is these traits present in them due to which it is the 'Migrants' who are thriving and leading the way and not them. And if an indigenous native person does come up, it is due to the fact that he is using the privilege he has of having a network and social support system, being an age-long local, and still not because he really deserves on merit to be up there.

This then leads to the second trait produced and present in the 'Migrant' mindset, which is 'ultra-sensitiveness' to any kind of affirmative action or legislation, or even democracy per se, which seeks to uplift the native majority of the land. This mindset idealizes executive, often arbitrary, actions taken by career officers or middle-class individuals in positions of power in the bureaucracy or military or government, as opposed to what would legally or morally be right from the point of view of the constitution or the democratically legislated law of the land. Because the mantra in the mind of the 'Migrant' is of 'being self-made', 'merit', and of 'making it on one's own'. This, in the eyes of the 'Migrant', is more important than the efforts of forward-looking leaders of society for pursuing means of uplifting everyone in the country and evolving and implementing a policy of 'no one left behind'.

The above mindset is typically observed for 'Migrants' who came and became socially ahead of the indigenous native population. But the same elements of risk and insecurity are manifested in a different way among migrants who come to a society where the local population is already more advanced than them and positions of power and influence are already occupied by the 'Local'. Examples include migrants from the third world and the Middle East moving into Europe and the United States, including illegal migrants pouring into the United States from Latin America.

The feelings of sarcasm towards the local population and ultra-sensitiveness to any attempt by the receiving state to deport the illegal migrants and assimilate the legal ones into the socio-cultural construct of the receiving society are present in these migrants too, but their expression manifests in a different way.

These migrants expostulate and portray the local population as privileged people of advanced capitalist societies who have thrived by colonizing and exploiting third-world countries and continue to do so. Therefore, it is a right and entitlement of the migrants from these third-world countries to make their way into these advanced countries and make a life for themselves by whatever means possible. Meanwhile, they are not obliged to assimilate into the culture of the receiving society. Here enters Identity Politics and the politics of labeling any politician of the receiving country a 'racist' if the politician requires the migrants to abide by the democratically legislated laws of the country or to assimilate into the social and cultural, including lingual, values of the country. Added to this is the factor of Muslim migration, the discourse of the Muslim migrant also including the narrative of the West having become morally corrupt, decadent, and hedonistic and therefore, on a lower rung of the moral ladder, to be uplifted by the Muslim and not the Muslim to be uplifted intellectually or culturally by the receiving society.

In recent years, it has become more and more clearer and stated as such by parties and intellectuals[35] opposed to lop sided migration on the global scale specially illegal migration, that it is preferable to have economic advancement and peace in third world countries which are the source of mass migration, so that people should not feel that they have to migrate in order to obtain a better life for themselves and their children.

However, this emerging view is grossly challenged and sabotaged by vested interests served by human trafficking, cheap labor from illegal immigrants without legal protection and rights guaranteed for labor for those who are already citizens of that country and the wanton exploitation of the raw materials and resources of third world countries which would not continue as profitably for these interests if the source countries became industrialized and technologically advanced. Of course, the advanced countries of the world, where population growth diminishes, would always

---

[35] *The Case Against Immigration: The Moral, Economic, Social, and Environmental Reasons for Reducing U.S. Immigration Back to Traditional Levels (Roy Beck)*

need new immigrants, but that can be managed in a planned and legal way whereby the assimilation of the immigrants with the local population is also ensured sophisticatedly.

After the brief interrogation above of the 'Migrant' mindset, we return to the case of the 'Migrant' in the newly created Pakistani state, which was going to prove to be the determining factor in the social and political divide that then ensued.

The case of the 'Migrant' in Pakistan was the case of 'Migrants' who came and became socially ahead of the indigenous native population.

At the time of the formation of Pakistan in 1947, as mentioned earlier, the main cities of the country specially in the then West Pakistan, emptied of their dominant Hindu and Sikh demographic and were replaced by migrant Muslims coming in from northern India.

At the same time, the civil bureaucracy and military of United British India were being split up between the two new countries of Pakistan and independent India. The civil bureaucracy left behind in the new state of Pakistan, specially in West Pakistan, also emptied of Hindu and Sikh occupants in the same manner as the cities.

The military left to the new state of Pakistan was already predominantly Punjabi by ethnicity, with Pathan and Bengali ethnicities next in numbers. Due to the fact that the dominant economic and social structure of the territories comprising the western wing of the new state of Pakistan were at the historical stage of tribal and feudal modes of social organization, there was a lack of an urban Muslim middle class coming from the native indigenous populations of these territories which could have filled the gaping vacancies created in the civil bureaucracy due to the exodus of Hindus and Sikhs from the urban centers of West Pakistan.

Instead, these vacancies were filled by the incoming migrants from northern India who historically, due to their proximity to the center of power of United British India and even before that having the heritage of being descendants of the courtiers and the support system network of kings ruling India, had the advantage of being already educated and qualified to take on the running of a bureaucracy in charge of the civil administration of the state. In fact, most educated migrants pouring in from northern India were alumni of the Aligarh Muslim University, founded by Sir Syed

Ahmed Khan, and active participants of the All-India Muslim League's movement for Pakistan.

Similarly, private jobs and trade in the urban centers were taken over by these same migrants. Properties left behind by the departing Hindus and Sikhs were claimed and taken over by these same migrants, and the die was cast for the nature of future urban life in Pakistan.

In Punjab, it was slightly different, as the vacancies and properties left behind by the Hindus and Sikhs were taken over majorly by Muslim migrants coming in from East Punjab territories that had become part of the new independent Indian state. In Bengal too, urban centers were mostly filled by Bengali populations.

But when the dust settled and the new state of Pakistan moved forward into the decade of the 1950s, the civil bureaucracy was firmly dominated by migrants and not the native indigenous population of the pre-Partition territories of Pakistan.

Meanwhile, the political leadership of the country, that is the leadership of the Muslim League, was also dominated by migrants from North India and from the now eastern wing of the country called East Pakistan. The Prime Minister, Liaqat Ali Khan, was a migrant from Karnal, located at the time in East Punjab, but in fact effectively the easternmost city of Haryana, a territory bordering the state of Uttar Pradesh of India.

The Quaid e Azam, Muhammad Ali Jinnah, the Governor General and the head of the state of Pakistan, although having been born in Karachi, which was in the new state of Pakistan, was in fact a descendant of pre-Partition migrants from the state of Gujarat in India and had resided all his life in the city of Bombay and had no similarity with the natives of the province of Sindh to which the city of Karachi belongs. In fact, being the completely westernized gentleman that he was, his inability to speak Urdu, the new national language of the new state of Pakistan, is well known, and his proficiency in his own mother tongue, Gujarati, is also suspect.

The leaders next in line at the helm of the Muslim League were A. K. Fazlul Haq, Khawaja Nazimuddin, Husain Suhrawardy, and Mohammad Ali Bogra, all four Bengali Muslims, having roots in Bengali society and popular political leaders of the Muslim League with the ability to get themselves democratically elected by the people of the society from which they came. After the death of the Quaid e Azam, Khawaja Nazimuddin became the head of the state as Governor General. The first Defense Secretary of the new state of Pakistan, controlling its armed forces, was also a Bengali Muslim, Iskander Mirza.

This was the mantle of the leadership heading the new state of Pakistan as the decade of the 1940s ended.

An observation is made at this juncture regarding the migrant Punjabi from East Punjab in India coming in and settling in West Punjab in West Pakistan in the new state. While it is true that ethnically, the migrant Punjabi did not face as much difficulty in assimilating with the local indigenous population of West Punjab as did migrants of northern India in the new state, there were two factors that influenced the mindset of these Punjabi migrants too with the same migrant mindset as discussed earlier.

The first factor was that these Punjabi migrants had been the direct victims as well as perpetrators of the holocaust that had followed the announcement of the partition of India on the eve of independence in 1947. Due to this fact, these migrants carried a much deeper hatred of the Hindu and Sikh and a more frenzied zeal for an exclusively Muslim supremacist state in Pakistan than did the native indigenous Punjabis who already belonged to and resided in West Punjab.

The other factor was that the class composition of these migrant Punjabis was the middle class while the area of West Punjab into which they were migrating was dominated by a West Punjabi Muslim landed feudal aristocracy and peasantry with which they could not identify themselves. These two factors contributed into the mindset of the Punjabi migrant a sense of sarcasm and demonization towards the landed aristocracy of West Punjab, and they considered them as less genuine supporters of the Pakistan cause, specially in view that this landed aristocratic class had represented themselves for most of the period of colonial rule through the Unionist Party and had joined the bandwagon of the Pakistan movement very late in the mid 1940s.

The narrative against them was that they had only joined the Pakistan movement because the Indian National Congress had the abolition of feudalism as an inherent component of their manifesto for post-British India.

Towards the other classes of native West Punjab too, the migrant Punjabis had a cynicism that the former had not experienced the miseries which the latter had suffered during migration, so they did not really know the worth of the new state in the context of the sacrifices made for its formation.

These Punjabi migrants too replaced many positions in the civil bureaucracy, trade, and properties in the urban centers of Punjab left vacant by the departing Hindus and Sikhs, and in the first decades of the new state found themselves more in alignment with the social and political perspectives of the other non-Punjabi migrant settlers in Pakistan's urban centers than with the perspectives of those from rural Pakistan.

So, what were those social and political perspectives that emerged differently in the urban centers of the new state of Pakistan and its rural heartland?

The basic point of departure between the two perspectives emanated from the fact and realization of the electability and non-electability in a democratic polity proposed for the state. It became very clear very soon to those running the state how the configuration would work if straightforward, unremitted, full-fledged democracy via adult franchise was allowed constitutionally in the new state. It was clear, in view of the demographic of the population, as to who would be mostly elected to lead the country in a democracy.

The fact was that the Bengali Muslim had been the spearhead of a majoritarian democratic case for the Pakistan movement. The All-India Muslim League had been formed in 1906 in Dhaka, and since then Bengal had been the only state where the Muslim League, or the Krishak Praja Party which was an allied party headed by A. K. Fazlul Haq, had won in each legislative election (1937 and 1946).

In the new state of Pakistan, the majority population was Bengali. Of the approximately 70 million population of the new state, roughly 40 million, that is, about 57%, were Bengalis. Then in West Pakistan, the majority population was ethnically Punjabi, Sindhi, and Pashtun, and any democratic elections would have majority constituencies from the rural heartland of these denominations.

On the other hand, the civil bureaucracy and political leadership effectively running the country just after independence were dominated by migrants ethnically not enrooted culturally or socially in the territories now comprising Pakistan. It was clear that in the event of a general democratic election, it would be the Bengalis and politicians from the rural heartland of Pakistan who would head Pakistan.

It was an existential dilemma for the insecure and zealous 'Migrant' who had come over to run the state and considered himself intellectually and culturally superior to the local, not worthy of assimilating with, but now realized clearly that in a democratic polity, he would have to accept the dominance of the Bengali and the local West Pakistani.

However, he found a sympathetic ally even in the local West Pakistani, for whom too an existential dilemma had occurred in view of the fact that, though ethnically dominant in West Pakistan, in the overall state of Pakistan it would be the Bengali who would mostly lead the state by default of coming from the majority province of the country.

Added to that insecurity was the fact that land reforms were carried out in East Pakistan in the 1950s with resolve and political will of the Bengali leadership[36]. This too posed an existential dilemma for the landed aristocracy in West Pakistan. A tactical tacit alliance thus emerged de facto between the 'Migrant' from North India and the 'non-North Indian' West Pakistani mostly dominated by the Punjabi (native as well as migrant from East Punjab). It is pertinent to mention at this stage that this alliance did not come about through some explicit conscious expression of the need for such an alliance, but it emerged via a materialistic convergence of interests as was psychologically felt in the corridors of power of the new state of Pakistan. It is here that we see how psychology automatically leads individuals to concur, gravitate towards each other, and act together as a consequence of this concurrence. This concurrence manifested at the time through prejudices voiced as concerns of national security and survival.

---

[36] East Bengal State Acquisition and Tenancy Act of 1950

In the case of Pakistan, when this tactical alliance started emerging spontaneously, the backdrop of the Cold War was thick in the region. With the question looming of aligning with either the Soviet bloc or the Western bloc led by the United States, it became easy for this alliance to put off the formation of a democratic constitution for the country.

The civil bureaucracy, at that time the establishment of the country, went into action. After relegating Khawaja Nazimuddin from governor general to the post of Prime Minister following the assassination of Prime Minister Liaqat Ali Khan, the post of governor general was occupied by Malik Ghulam Mohammad, a Punjabi career bureaucrat and also an alumnus of Aligarh Muslim University, knighted by the British Crown. From there on, the post of governor general was used constantly in the decade of the '50s to keep dismissing political governments and leaderships and not letting a stable political government take root[37], including dismissing the Constituent Assembly, and in the meanwhile fend off the passing of any democratic constitution as a bedrock for running the state in a civilized manner.

A political party, the Republican Party, was created in 1955 by the powerful civil military bureaucracy led by Ghulam Mohammad and Iskander Mirza, in collaboration with the landed aristocracy of West Pakistan[38], to be present amidst the Constituent Assembly and throw "the

---

[37] Prime Ministers of Pakistan after the assassination of Liaqat Ali Khan in 1951 up to the martial law of 1958: Khawaja Nazimuddin (17 October 1951 to 17 April 1953) Muslim League government dissolved by Governor General Ghulam Muhammad, Mohammad Ali Bogra (17 April 1953 to 12 August 1955) Muslim League government dismissed by Governor General Ghulam Muhammad, Chaudhry Mohammad Ali (12 August 1955 to 12 September 1956) leading the coalition government of Muslim League / Awami League / Republican Party was removed by no confidence vote from within his own party the Muslim League, Husain Suhrawardy (12 September 1956 to 17 October 1957) resigned after lost support from within his own party the Awami League and compelled by pressure from President Iskander Mirza, Ibrahim Ismail (I.I.) Chundrigar (17 October 1957 to 11 December 1957) of the Muslim League removed by no confidence vote led by the Republican Party and the Awami League, and Feroze Khan Noon (16 December 1957 to 7 October 1958) removed by martial law imposed by his fellow Republican Party member, President Iskander Mirza

[38] https://www.britannica.com/topic/Republican-Party-political-party-Pakistan, https://www.britannica.com/place/Pakistan/Political-decline-and-bureaucratic-ascendancy [written by Lawrence Ziring & Shahid Javed Burki]

spanner in the works" when required. This party is generally viewed as the first of the various "King's parties" formed in Pakistan (the Convention Muslim League, formed in 1962 to support General Ayub Khan, is viewed as the second one).

Such a strategy of the unelected ruling clique of Pakistan suited and played right into the hands of the British and US establishment, who were concerned about the alignment of the new state of Pakistan in the Cold War. These international as well as Pakistani establishments succeeded in having the state of Pakistan sign into the strategic military defense treaties of SEATO[39] and CENTO[40] in 1954 and 1955 respectively, before the Constituent Assembly of Pakistan was reconstituted in 1955 and the first constitution of Pakistan was passed in 1956, proclaiming the state as the Islamic Republic of Pakistan. This constitution heavily favored the head of the state rather than the political post of the prime minister, granting the president power to declare a state of emergency in case of concern about national security and giving under-representation to East Pakistan despite it having the majority population.

In this game of sidelining a popular democratic leadership in the country and not letting a true democratic system be implemented, we see that even Liaqat Ali Khan, a politician, and Iskander Mirza, a Bengali, became unwitting players with limited foresight, signing their own death knell. Liaqat Ali Khan supported the Objectives Resolution of 1949, mixing Islam with the matters of the state[41], which was in contravention to the vision expressed in the famous 11th August 1947 speech of the Quaid e Azam, and Iskander Mirza siding with Ghulam Mohammad and General Ayub Khan against the political governments. Iskander Mirza eventually staged the coup d'état of 7th October 1958 with General Ayub Khan, only to be deposed himself by General Ayub twenty days later in the coup d'état

---

[39] SEATO (Southeast Asia Treaty Organization) signed in September 1954 in Manila
[40] CENTO (Central Treaty Organization) also known as the Baghdad Pact, signed in February 1955 in Baghdad. [41] The religion of Islam was used politically as a bulwark against 'godless' communism by the intelligentsia and strategists of Western Capitalism throughout the period of the Cold War of the 20th century.
[41] The religion of Islam was used politically as a bulwark against 'godless' communism by the intelligentsia and strategists of Western Capitalism throughout the period of the Cold War of the 20th century.

of 27th October 1958. These two players, Liaqat Ali Khan and Iskander Mirza, became the unwitting tools of an anti-democratic drama unfolding in the new state of Pakistan for the reason that both were unelectable as leaders of the country if the way was paved for full democratic rule. Liaqat Ali Khan, a migrant, would not be able to hold the mandate of the majority constituencies of Pakistan in a general democratic election, and it was inevitable that one of the Bengali politicians would become the democratically elected leader of Pakistan. Similarly, it was not possible that Iskander Mirza, though a Bengali but an unelected official of the state, could remain the head of a democratically run state.

In fact, in retrospect, even the Bengali politicians, in their goodwill towards the state of Pakistan, can be seen to be unwitting participants in this political drama of the '50s, failing to see the larger game being played in the backdrop of the Cold War. We see them cooperating with the civil-military bureaucracy and their representative political party, the Republican Party, in this 'game of thrones' and over policy issues like the 'One Unit'[42] and siding with the United States in the name of anti-communism.

This intellectual susceptibility and limitation of the Bengali politicians, falling into the trap of the civil-military bureaucracy, can be attributed to their 'original sin' of misplacing the notion of nationalism with 'Muslim Nationalism', as discussed in the preceding chapter, and working towards the partition of British India on that premise and being wary of the Hindu majority of post-British India in their mindset. In that vein, they may have considered the concerns and dissensions against the concept of 'One Unit' expressed by the indigenous classes of the three smaller provinces of West Pakistan, i.e. Sind, NWFP (North West Frontier Province), and Balochistan in the rural heartland of West Pakistan, as well

---

[42] The 'One Unit' was an administrative scheme passed in 1955 which merged the four provinces of West Pakistan, i.e. Punjab / Sind / North-West Frontier Province (NWFP) & Balochistan, into a single unit to create parity with the province of East Pakistan. It is generally viewed as an attempt by the Pakistani establishment in West Pakistan to create population parity with East Pakistan to counter the majority population of the latter. Ironically, this scheme was led, owned and carried by Mohammad Ali Bogra, a Bengali politician, and resisted by the indigenous classes of the rural heartland of the three smaller provinces of West Pakistan, i.e. Sind, NWFP and Balochistan

as from within East Pakistan, as anti-national because the selling point of the 'One Unit' scheme for Mohammad Ali Bogra, a Bengali politician, was that by having only two administrative units for Pakistan, the issue of financial disparity of East Pakistan would be resolved[43]. Similarly, it was the government of Khawaja Nazimuddin on 21st February 1952 when police opened fire on people in Dhaka, East Pakistan, who were rallying for recognition of their mother tongue 'Bangla' as one of the national official languages of Pakistan (21st February is now celebrated internationally as the 'International Mother Tongue Day').

With the signing of the international defense treaties in the name of security of the state against communism and against socialistic tendencies sympathetic to land reforms as a start, the unelected establishment of Pakistan, cheered by the feudal lords of West Pakistan, succeeded in sidelining popular politicians coming from the majority ethnic population of the state, and suppressing this population with the help of a strong military. Once the military had been brought into this equation of signing defense treaties with the West against communism and suppressing popular politicians, it was only a matter of time before the military would come out of the shadows and, with a nod and assenting silence from the hypocritical democratic Western establishment, its General would see no reason why he should not seize power and rule the country as dictator[44].

All along this timeline, historically we will find the urban middle classes of West Pakistan siding with the machinations of the civil-military bureaucracy and not the foremost Bengali leaders of Pakistan, and eventually celebrating the military takeover of the government in 1958 by General Ayub Khan[45]. The then Chief Justice of Pakistan, Justice Muhammad Munir, an 'East Punjabi', invoked the 'doctrine of necessity' a second time[46], to justify Ayub Khan's martial law.

---

[43] https://historypak.com/one-unit/

[44] https://time.com/archive/6871116/pakistan-and-then-there-was-one/, https://time.com/archive/6827839/pakistan-the-benign-year/

[45] https://www.dawn.com/news/664894/flashback-the-martial-law-of-1958

[46] The first time Justice Munir invoked the 'doctrine of necessity' was in 1954 when Governor General Ghulam Muhammad had dissolved the constituent assembly and this dissolution was challenged in court by Maulvi Tamizuddin, a Bengali, who was the speaker and thus the president of the dissolved constituent assembly

To this day, a vast section of Pakistan's urban middle classes refer fondly to the era of General Ayub Khan's tenure in power, choosing to overlook the illegality and anti-democratic nature of the martial law that lay at the root of this tenure, and the fact that it was the first step towards changing the direction of the country from evolving into a functional constitutional state to a path of turning the state into a 'banana republic' where law was to become open to arbitrary violation by anyone who possessed the might to do it and get away with it, and where 'anything goes'.

So, the decade of the '50s was the decade of sidelining the Bengali leadership of the Pakistan movement and the new state of Pakistan, and this sidelining culminated in the eventual success of this strategy with the ascent to political power in Pakistan of General Ayub Khan. However, even after this sidelining, the tirade of negative propaganda against the Bengali leadership and the Bengali per se did not cease but in fact increased in intensity under the regime of General Ayub Khan, and the West Pakistani urban middle classes bought into this tirade until it met its eventual nemesis in the civil war of 1971 and the creation of Bangladesh.

The two decades of the 1950s and 1960s in Pakistan can therefore be considered as the full duration of the first spat that occurred in the state between the electable and the unelectable forces vying for political power. This spat had heavy ethnic overtones in the fore, which were picked up and championed by the urban middle classes of West Pakistan entrenched in the seats of civil bureaucracy as well as the urban economy in that wing of the country. They were all in it together against the Bengali, i.e., the non-Punjabi migrant, the Punjabi urban middle class, and the Punjabi and Pathan politicized officers leading the armed forces of the country, who were, because of the martial law, effectively running the country. Analyzing retrospectively, in fact, there are many reasons to even theorize that it seems as if those in the echelons of power in West Pakistan wanted to get rid of the Bengalis, their majority, and all that would follow because of that majority.

In this propaganda narrative built during General Ayub Khan's regime[47], the Bengali was increasingly portrayed as being less of a Muslim, with the script of their language, their dressing, particularly that of their women, their dark skin, and lesser heights used as 'evidence' of them being more Hindu than Muslim. The racist angle came into full play, because Islam had initially and majorly been embraced by Arabs, Central Asians, including Turks, who also had been warriors and conquerors defeating non-Muslims. So, who looked more similar to them among Pakistanis with respect to the color of their skin, their heights, their perceived ancestries, and the script of their languages, West Pakistanis or East Pakistani Bengalis? Seemingly, West Pakistani. So, the East Pakistani Bengali had to be less of a Muslim than the West Pakistani.

Lost in this propaganda and racist frenzy were the facts that the Muslim League had been founded in Dhaka in 1906, Bengal had been the only province in British India where the Muslim League or its allied parties had always won through majority vote, that the majority of independence stalwarts in the Muslim League were from Bengal, and that Bengalis would be found to be more staunch practicing Muslims than the West Pakistanis if a thorough statistical evaluation was conducted from that aspect.

It can be stated with considered reflection that it was during the era of General Ayub Khan in power that the perception of being a better Muslim adopted a racist angle for the first time in the country. Whereby any personal sign resembling the race and culture found to the east of West Pakistan, in Hindu India, and in East Pakistan started being considered as less Muslim. And racial and cultural signs resembling the Muslim world to the west of the western wing of the country were considered as somehow more Muslim, and hence more 'Pakistani'.

However, during General Ayub Khan's regime, while the dominant spat for political dominance continued to be with the Bengali, some

---

[47] 'The Caricatured Bengali & the Pakistan Army' by Hafsa Khawaja (https://www.jamhoor.org/read/the-caricatured-bengali-amp-the-pakistan-army), 'What they never tell us about Ayub Khan's regime' by Murtaza Haider (https://www.dawn.com/news/1293604)

societal cracks along ethnic lines also started appearing in the edifice of the West Pakistani wing of the country.

Two phenomena occurred and gained momentum during the decade of General Ayub Khan's rule. First, as the decade of the 1960s set in, educated middle classes had started emerging in greater numbers from the indigenous population of the territory comprising West Pakistan. These classes, as they started occupying more and more positions in the bureaucracy, were less enthusiastic about Muslim communalism and supremacism than was the migrant population in urban West Pakistan. The intellectual tilt of the former was enhanced by the liberalism of the British-trained generals, which came to the fore during military rule and was also promoted by General Ayub Khan at the official level[48]. As mentioned before, this less than genuinely enthusiastic, and more pragmatic, sentiment for communalism and Muslim supremacism was also reciprocated among the upper-class landed aristocracy aligned with the Ayub Khan regime in all provinces. The second phenomenon was that there was growing resentment among the next to the topmost strata, i.e. upper middle, rural classes of the three smaller provinces of Sind / NWFP & Balochistan against the 'One Unit' arrangement of administration within West Pakistan. Both these phenomena resulted in a chipping of certain political forces away from the bandwagon of General Ayub Khan's propaganda narrative against the Bengali and crossing over and allying with the Bengali political parties and leaders.

With the first phenomenon we see the manifestation of this realignment in the form of Fatima Jinnah, the sister of the Quaid e Azam, and the constituencies in urban Sind and Punjab, comprising mostly of migrants, allying politically with the Bengali population and their leaders specially in Fatima Jinnah's presidential campaign against Ayub Khan in

---

[48] 'Forced Modernization and Public Policy: A Case Study of Ayub Khan Era (1958-69)' by Sarfraz Husain Ansari (Journal of Political Studies, June 30, 2011, Publisher: Knowledge Bylanes, Gale Academic Onefile), https://military-history.fandom.com/wiki/Ayub_Khan_(President_of_Pakistan), https://storyofpakistan.com/the-constitution-of-1962/, 'Pakistan Between Mosque and Military' by Hussain Haqqani

1964/1965[49]. Again, here we see the Ayub Khan propaganda machine turning against Fatima Jinnah herself, brandishing her as an Indian agent, playing on the fact of the similarity of her lifestyle, dressing, and language being more similar to Hindu India than to the territory comprising West Pakistan[50]. However, it is pertinent to observe that the migrant families of the civil bureaucracy and of that legacy from the pre-independence period still did not throw in their sympathy with the urban economic classes supporting Fatima Jinnah and the cause of unadulterated democracy she was advocating. They remained suspicious of it and preferred the security of standing by the civil military establishment supporting Ayub Khan and his skewed indirect system of 'Basic Democracies'.

With the second phenomenon, we see the manifestation of the resistance to the 'One Unit' arrangement in West Pakistan in the form of military resistance in Balochistan, which was countered via military action by the Ayub Khan regime in 1959, culminating in the arrest of the Baloch leader Nawab Nauroz and in the early to mid-1960s, against the insurgency led by Sher Mohammad Marri. We see in this period the emergence of nationalist parties for self-determination in three provinces, led by leaders like G. M. Syed in Sindh, Abdul Ghaffar Khan and his son Wali Khan in NWFP, and Abdul Samad Achakzai and Ghaus Bux Bizenjo in Balochistan.

In West Pakistani Punjab too, activist stalwarts and leaders like Mian Iftikharuddin, Mazhar Ali Khan, Kaswar Gardezi, and Sher Baz Khan Mazari had started questioning the unholy alliance between the landed aristocracy and the civil military bureaucracy, and eventually of both with the Western capitalist establishment in the ongoing Cold War.

---

[49] 'Fatima Jinnah's Life' by Naureen Talha
(https://pu.edu.pk/images/journal/history/PDF-FILES/Naureen-Talha.pdf), 'Fatima Jinnah Mother of the Nation' by M. Reza Pirbhai
[50] 'Fatima Jinnah's Contribution to Pakistan Movement and Democracy' by Dr. Murtaza Kamran (https://republicpolicy.com/fatima-jinnahs-contribution-to-pakistan-movement-and-democracy/), 'Crossed Swords' by Shuja Nawaz, A Brief Account Of Mohtarma Fatima Jinnah's Political Struggle And Service For Restoration Of Democracy In Pakistan by Summer Sultana
(https://www.researchgate.net/publication/342555744_A_Brief_Account_Of_Mohtarma_Fatima_Jinnah's_Political_Struggle_And_Service_For_Restoration_Of_Democracy_In_P akistan), https://time.com/archive/6627139/pakistan-trouble-with-mother/

These movements and leaders ultimately aligned and identified themselves with the Bengali challenge to the Pakistani civil military establishment and resulted in the founding of the National Awami Party (NAP), with the party in West Pakistan being led by Abdul Ghaffar Khan and Wali Khan, and in East Pakistan being led by Maulana Bhashani. This party aligned itself on the international arena with the communist bloc, with the banned Communist Party of Pakistan entering into its fold as members, along the lines of Nehruvian India, i.e. although its leadership was not communist itself, it chose to side with the left-wing bloc on the global scale with sympathy for socialistic economic policies in the domestic arena.

Later, during the mid '60s, NAP split into NAP (Wali) and NAP (Bhashani), with the former siding with the Soviet bloc and the latter siding with the Chinese bloc in the Sino-Soviet split on the international scale.

Fatima Jinnah was also helped in her presidential bid by NAP[51] and the Awami League in East Pakistan, led by Sheikh Mujib ur Rehman as one of its leaders, which was part of the Combined Opposition Parties (COP)[52] supporting her (NAP Wali in West Pakistan was also part of COP). It was Sheikh Mujib ur Rehman who later led East Pakistan towards independence and became the father of the nation of the new state of Bangladesh, formed as a result of this independence in December 1971.

Therefore, we see from the above discourse that once Pakistan had disconnected itself in 1947 from its mother country of centuries, India, like a planet on its own hurtling into space searching for and creating its own destiny, it was in the formative decades of the 1950s and 1960s that the die was cast, going forward, for the parallel existence of two basic narratives and visions for the country, with each contradicting the other politically as well as culturally.

---

[51] 'Reminiscing Moulana Bhashani, his Political Legacies and Missed Opportunities in Pakistan' by Zahid Hussain Gardezi (https://southasiajournal.net/reminiscing-moulana-bhashani-his-political-legacies-and-missed-opportunities-in-pakistan/)
[52] The Combined Opposition Parties (COP) consisted of Council Muslim League, Awami League, National Awami Party (Bhashani), National Awami Party (Wali), Jamaat-e-Islami Pakistan and the Nizam-e-Islam Party

This contradiction became antagonistic during the race for power grab and social dominance, all the more so because the social classes dominating the modern urban centers of power in the country were not organically connected with the vast majority of the indigenous historical polity of the country. There existed a deep sense of alienation from the other, among proponents of both narratives.

The first indigenous historical polity to fall victim to this antagonism were the Bengalis, because they were in the majority. But after 1971, when they had fallen out of the equation with the creation of the new state of Bangladesh, the guns of those in the urban centers of power turned towards those who were next in majority in the remaining state of Pakistan.

It is important to understand that the basic reason for this onslaught and contempt for the majority, and by extension for democracy, which is the expression of the will of the majority, emanated from the inherent 'Minority' mindset which had initially created Pakistan, suspicious of the Hindu majority of a united India. This mindset was further reinforced by the 'Migrant' mindset of those pouring into the urban centers of West Pakistan from post-British India, wary and contemptuous of the indigenous majority of the land.

These two mindsets found a further powerful ally in the dominant mindset of the cadre of the existing civil-military establishment of the country, who were not at all ready to relinquish their immense powers inherited from the British colonial past in favor of elected representatives of the people.

These three mindsets worked together tirelessly at an early stage in the existence of the new country to build a dominant narrative in the imagination of the educated classes, mostly urban at that time, which made them suspicious of politicians from the onset[53] considering them inherently as either self-serving, politically myopic, greedy or just simply corrupt and made these 'educated' classes wary and insecure with respect to unadulterated democracy arguing that in such a democracy illiterate and feudalistic people from the rural areas or 'pro India' 'hinduized' Bengalis

---

[53] A quote of the Quaid e Azam was popularized in which he had stated that 'all coins in my pocket are fake' implicitly questioning the integrity of those who had been the comrades of the Quaid e Azam during the independence movement

would come to the fore thus painting a scenario of incompetence, corruption, anarchy, and treason attributed to politicians and democracy.

This dominant narrative set in the urban centers of the country became the pivotal narrative on which the Pakistani zeitgeist was subsequently built. From textbooks[54] to the press media (specially the Urdu press media) to movies to television plays to literature to what was considered politically correct in public speeches and to internal policy debates in the corridors of power that resulted in legislation and foreign policy decisions.

This dominant narrative became the criterion for determining who was 'educated' and who was 'jaahil' (uneducated or illiterate) when it came to politics. The 'educated' were expected to exhibit and voice all the suspicions and badmouthing of politicians and unadulterated democracy; otherwise, they were considered politically 'jaahil' or intellectually stilted.

That is why as the decades proceeded, it was "educated" to support Ayub Khan and not Fatima Jinnah or the COP (Combined Opposition Parties) or the Bengalis. It was "educated" to support General Zia ul Haq and military rule and not the MRD (Movement for the Restoration of Democracy) in the 1980s. It was "educated" to support Nawaz Sharif and not Benazir Bhutto during the 1990s. It was "educated" to support General Pervez Musharraf and not the ARD (Alliance for the Restoration of Democracy) or the ousted elected ex-prime ministers Benazir Bhutto and Nawaz Sharif or their CoD (Charter of Democracy) during the 2000s. And during the 2010s and 2020s, it was "educated" to support Imran Khan and the coterie of generals and judges conniving to destabilize, sabotage, and oust elected governments and replace the federal parliamentary system with an authoritarian presidential system, and not those who had given the country the 18th Amendment to the Constitution restoring in full the federal and parliamentary spirit of the 1973 democratic constitution of the country.

At this juncture, it may be argued, against the proposition being put forth in this chapter, that this dominant anti-politician and anti-democratic narrative was adopted not only by the "Migrant" element and their

---

[54] 'The Murder of History: A Critique of History Textbooks used in Pakistan' by K. K. Aziz

descendants in the country but even by sections of the local population and to this day is owned by people across the board coming from all backgrounds, not just "Migrant."

This is true, and this argument is correct. However, it still does not overturn the proposition that the origin of this mindset is in the insecurity and contempt for the majority, which is felt not just by the Migrant but also by the unelectable Middle Class individual, as explained earlier in the book. And if the collusion of the two has in its roots also a "Minority" majority-fearing mindset, on the basis of which the country was created, then all unelectable individuals are susceptible to falling to it and being seduced by this narrative.

Moreover, the effect of years of social conditioning, done through education and the media, which started from the early years of the existence of this country and where the other narrative could never really acquire a firm foothold in the social consciousness due to unrelenting efforts to destabilize it from the moment whenever it acquired power or started gaining acceptance, cannot be understated even for individuals of the urban middle class inherently "non-migrant" in nature but overwhelmed and conditioned by the dominant narrative in urban areas.

There is a decade which was skipped in the above listing of the decades in which who were considered "educated" and who not. That was the decade of the 1970s.

The decade of the 1970s was the decade emerging after the death of the original Pakistan of two wings, West Pakistan and East Pakistan, and the birth of the "new" "only" Pakistan. The decade of 1970s was the decade of Zulfiqar Ali Bhutto.

We have to understand who was considered "educated" and who not in that decade, as per this proposition. A proposition to understand the essence of a social consciousness cannot be a correct proposition if it cannot withstand interrogation from all angles with respect to the complexities of all situations for which it is presented to be applicable.

Zulfiqar Ali Bhutto, henceforth referred to as only Bhutto, belonged to the uppermost landed aristocracy of West Pakistan who sided with General Ayub Khan in the aforementioned alignment and polarization of forces in the struggle for political power in the new state of Pakistan. That

136

is, inherently and automatically, he gravitated towards the anti-Bengali lobby and the movement to sideline the Bengali leadership of Pakistan. He was no different socially from, say, the Nawab of Kalabagh, who was Ayub Khan's governor of West Pakistan, or the family of the Nawab of Bahawalpur or the other princely states which acceded to Pakistan.

However, individually and intellectually, Bhutto leaned towards socialist ideas. In the backdrop of the demise of colonialism and the rise of heroic anti-colonial struggles after the Second World War, he had more sympathy for non-capitalistic ideas, capitalism being exclusively the foremost system of Western colonialism. It can also be proposed that for a forward-looking individual coming from a feudal background, who knew that if the capitalist stage of development, which threatened his class, was to be jumped and the power of his class to be maintained over society while at the same time bringing advancement to his country, the only viable option would be to root for state ownership of industry and agriculture and therefore, socialism.

It is here that we see how the mental makeup and intellectual self-cultivation[55] of an individual enables him to rise historically above the intellectual trappings of his class and instinctively recognize the wind of change in the air and rally to the voices coming from below as the edifice of an obsolete archaic social structure is falling apart.

As resistance was increasing against the "One Unit" arrangement in Pakistan and the Ayub Khan regime, both in West Pakistan as well as East Pakistan, Bhutto judged that this dispensation would not last long and decided to part ways with General Ayub Khan. He decided to side with the anti-India Muslim Nationalist stance on Kashmir, popular in the urban centers of Punjab and Sindh, and reached out to socialist intelligentsia in urban West Pakistan and from Bengali East Pakistan to establish a mass political party, the Pakistan People's Party (PPP), in 1967.

It is pertinent to point out here that when Bhutto seized the moment at the opportune time to capture the imagination of urban Sindh and Punjab, the anti–"One Unit" NAP had still not been able to build inroads in these

---

[55] Zufiqar Ali Bhutto is widely considered to have been the most well read and intellectually astute ruler of Pakistan, followed closely only by his own daughter, Benazir Bhutto

areas due to their indigenous nationalistic manifestos, of which the predominantly "Migrant" urban economic classes of Sindh and Punjab were wary. They were still reeling from and licking their wounds after the defeat (1965 presidential election) and demise (in 1967) of Fatima Jinnah and nurturing resentment against the Ayub Khan regime, which was also allied internationally with the capitalist West.

Here we take a further pause and look into an accentuated aspect of the popular support which Bhutto received from Punjabis all over the country, and which also factors into the Punjabi support provided to the "Migrant" classes in West Pakistan against the Bengalis, as well as against the indigenous local populations in the three smaller provinces of West Pakistan. This aspect is the mindset and role of the "Settler" in the new country of Pakistan, which manifested in thought and action in the same manner as the "Migrant" or "Muhajir" from post-British India.

The "Settler" in the Pakistani context is normally the Punjabi, and to a lesser extent, Pakhtun settler in the provinces other than their own in what was formerly West Pakistan. These are Punjabis who went into the provinces of Sindh and Balochistan either for work, business, or were ex-servicemen or civilians who were allotted agricultural lands in these provinces and then settled there for good. These "Settlers" had the same sense of insecurity and alienation from the local indigenous population and the same suspicions of the latter's aspirations for the right to self-determination lingually and economically, and the same mistrust of the majority Bengalis, as did the "Migrants" or "Muhajirs" from post-British India. Therefore, they politically sided with the civil-military establishment narrative against the Bengali and the politics of NAP.

Of course, the one difference which the "Settlers" had from the non-Punjabi "Migrants" of India was that these "Settlers" had organic family links back in their own provinces, while the non-Punjabi "Migrants" of India had no such links in the rural heartland of Pakistan.

This was the political vacuum in 1967 in urban Sindh and Punjab, which was filled by the mass movement launched by Bhutto, clamoring for "people's power" and a socialist economy. This movement overwhelmingly swept the political constituencies of Sind and Punjab, targeting the capitalist business and industrial community in these provinces including the famous '22 families'[56] of the Ayub Khan era, and even in NWFP against the traditional feudal aristocracies, with the Hindko[57]-speaking communities of NWFP, who are lingually closer to Punjabis rather than the Pashto speaking Pathans, jumping on the bandwagon of the PPP instead of the NAP.

Post December 1971, when East Pakistan had seceded, it was Bhutto who commanded the majority in what remained in Pakistan. On top of that, the military and its political generals who had manipulated and ruled Pakistan since the 1950s stood totally humiliated and discredited. They were in no position to assert themselves even if they wanted to.

Bhutto became a civilian CMLA (Chief Martial Law Administrator) as he took over control of the martial law imposed on the country from the military CMLA General Yahya Khan. The narrative which had belittled majority rule and democracy since the inception of the state stood crushed after the secession of East Pakistan, the defeat at the hands of India, and the surge of Bhutto's popular majority movement in former West Pakistan.

It was the first time, the first window of opportunity for narrative change, when it became politically correct in the Pakistani zeitgeist to enamour and work for democracy, majority rule, and a constitutional set-up like a civilized country and not a 'banana republic'. The leaders of NAP from the three smaller provinces were roped in, as were the political parties, including religious parties, from urban Sind and Punjab, and the first democratic constitution was framed, passed, and given to the country in 1973.

At that time, for the first time, it became considered 'educated' to talk of democracy and the constitution and not of dictatorship and martial law, getting rid of all the politicians. The Left-wing intelligentsia and art scene took dominance over the social imagination and the zeitgeist for the first time, and progressivism and federalism became signs of intellectual sophistication and political correctness.

---

[56] 'Who's the richest of them all?' by Dilawar Hussain (https://www.dawn.com/news/1463164), 'Family business in Pakistan-The ghost of Mahbub-ul-Haq' by Ikram Sehgal (https://pakobserver.net/family-business-in-pakistan-the-ghost-of-mahbub-ul-haq-by-ikram-sehgal/)
[57] https://en.wikipedia.org/wiki/Hindko, https://hindkopoint.wordpress.com/hindko-history/

It was also the first time, specially with the first lady belonging to urban Sind and technically from a 'Migrant' background, that a window of opportunity arose for a crossover between the 'Migrant' and the 'Local' and for social integration, with Bhutto being the bridge between the 'Migrant' and the 'Local', between the 'Settler' and the 'Local'.

And with India having conducted its first nuclear test in 1974, and Pakistan being far from having a similar counter deterrent, it was Bhutto's ingenious skill at diplomacy which succeeded in mobilizing leaders of the Islamic world to Lahore for the OIC (Organization of Islamic Countries) conference, which not only kept any risk of cowing down to India at bay but also won the hearts of religious-leaning political people in the country.

It was also the same year in which the 2nd amendment to the 1973 constitution was passed by parliament, and although it can be termed, ad nauseam, as controversial from the point of view of secularism and contrary to the views of even the founder of the country as explained before, it showed the maniacal religious fundamentalist minds a more civilized and constitutional way of asserting themselves in the Islamic Republic of Pakistan, while not stripping the Ahmadis of any other right as constitutionally due towards the religious minorities in the country.

However, five factors rekindled the flames of reaction and caused a reversal of the dominant narrative back to the anti-democratic and anti-politician one and kept the rural-urban alienation and divide alive.

Firstly, due to the overkill of Pakistan's business and capitalistic industrial community in the urban centers by Bhutto's socialist policies of nationalization, anti-Bhutto sentiments simmered among these classes, and it was considered 'educated' among them at least not to support the socialism and nationalization of Bhutto, in which they were right.

Secondly, the anti-India sentiments were simmering in the rank and file of the humiliated military who had been defeated and had surrendered shamefully in East Pakistan, and they could not tolerate the existence of the two 'India-friendly' 'Nehruvian' NAP provincial governments in Balochistan and NWFP. This led Bhutto to succumb to this sentiment by dismissing the two governments on the pretext of the 'Hyderabad

Conspiracy' case[58], imprisoning the NAP leadership, and starting another military operation in Balochistan.

Thirdly, as it happens when state bureaucracy is strengthened in an attempt to create a socialist state, the leader becomes less and less tolerant of pluralism and criticism, and starts relying more on state agencies than the democratic set-up. And so it happened with Bhutto, who became less tolerant of dissent and criticism from comrades and political adversaries alike, started relying more heavily on his security forces, and indulged in high-handedness against perceived opponents, even physically at times.

Fourthly, as was inevitable, what had started during the Ayub era continued, that is, the education and advent of more and more middle classes from the indigenous population occupying positions in the state bureaucracy helped more by the quota system[59] and the receding of the non-Punjabi 'Migrant' or 'Muhajir' numbers in these jobs, which caused a simmering of resentment among the 'Urdu-speaking' 'Muhajir' middle classes against Bhutto. Although it was not he, but the natural course of history responsible for this phenomenon, which they could have avoided had they organically and socially integrated and naturalized with the indigenous population through intermarriages and learning and owning their languages, rather than keeping distant and aloof from them.

Fifth, and lastly, there was growing resentment among the religious parties and fundamentalist forces in the country, who were mostly concentrated in the urban areas (predominantly of Migrant or Settler backgrounds), against the liberal progressive wing of Bhutto's movement which dominated the education and cultural establishment and landscape during Bhutto's rule. Therefore, these reactionary fundamentalist forces considered the Bhutto regime as being anti-Islam.

What Bhutto could have done differently to have made this correction of perspectives with respect to democracy, constitution and federalism a permanent repair and keep it from rotating back to the old anti-democracy,

---

[58] The Hyderabad Conspiracy case was a case made by the government of Pakistan against the leaders of NAP (National Awami Party) in 1975, alleging that they were conspiring to break away the provinces of NWFP (Northwest Frontier Province) and Balochistan from the state Pakistan to create 'Pakhtunistan' and Independent Balochistan respectively
[59] 'Quota system in Pakistan' by Abdul Wajid Rana
(https://tribune.com.pk/story/1553353/quota-system-pakistan)

anti-majority perspectives, has been the subject of extensive discussion and research in writings by many prominent intellectuals and writers.

However, an argument could be made that such was the force of the historically entrenched strength of the country's military and the international machinations and geopolitical strategies for the region that it was inevitable what happened to Bhutto, and he could not have avoided it.

But it is my opinion that a current political situation is pregnant with many possibilities, not just one, and it depends to a great degree on the acumen of the protagonist in the situation to go forth with the proper balancing act and realize the best of those possibilities into becoming the reality of the next political situation. That is the eternal dialect between the subjective and the objective.

The analysis of Bhutto's tenure and politics is not the subject of this chapter, or even this book, but before we continue on our journey of interrogating the Pakistani zeitgeist, I would like to record my opinion on what I think were Bhutto's prime mistakes which he could have avoided that would have paved the way for a different possibility to become the next reality, notwithstanding the fact that these mistakes still do not justify or excuse the capital crime against the constitution and the country that was committed by the perpetrators of the military coup of 1977.

Bhutto made four prime mistakes which he, as a subjective player in the objective backdrop, could easily have avoided and his downfall would not have been as final as it eventually became.

Firstly, in his drive for nationalization, he could have limited the drive to big industry, which was out of reach of the then-existing entrepreneurial classes of the country, and not taken over their businesses as well. In that, he could have done well to follow the Nehruvian model of state capitalism for heavy industry, infrastructure, and transport, while not touching and allowing the budding capitalist classes of the country.

Secondly, he should not have succumbed to dismissing the NAP governments in Balochistan and the Frontier Province, imprisoning their leaders who had been his allies in creating the 1973 democratic constitution of the country, and sanctioning military action in Balochistan. He should have relied on fighting political battles with political opponents instead of resorting to state executive action against them, and thus not losing the opportunity at any time to make allies with them again against any conspiracy and sabotage initiated by political generals.

Thirdly, and this is linked to the second mistake, he should not have been seduced by the allure of power to rely more on his Federal Security Force (FSF) than on his political comrades and allies. The seduction was inadvertently leading him towards the path of creating a one-party state along the lines of Saddam Hussein, Hafez al-Assad and Colonel Qaddafi. This is also what led to the 1977 elections being perceived as rigged. He had won the elections even without the high-handedness demonstrated by his political goons and forces in certain constituencies eager to give him a two-thirds majority.

Stanley Wolpert writes in his book 'Zulfi Bhutto of Pakistan'[60], quoting Henry Byroade the US ambassador to Pakistan at the time who had been invited by Bhutto to his house on the night of the elections, that initially elated at the results coming in of those elections, when Bhutto realized what his people had done, he became increasingly sullen as the night progressed. *"...on the whole in the three provinces, he was in by about 70 percent, which was a fair, honest, correct vote. Then the returns of the Punjab, which was politically the most important province, started to come in, and Bhutto was winning by 98-99 percent, and everyone knew that this was phony." I said, "I saw him the next morning and he wasn't himself; he had been on the telephone all night calling Lahore. He was asking his lieutenants there, 'What the hell have you done?'"*[61].

Fourth and finally, he should not have given in unilaterally to the Islamic Dogmatic Fundamentalist forces[62]. He should not have appointed the Islamic Dogmatic Fundamentalist General Zia ul Haq as the Army chief. He should have correctly assessed that at that time, in the backdrop of the Cold War, the forces most prone to being infiltrated and manipulated by the American CIA were the Islamic Dogmatic Fundamentalist forces the world over, specially of the Wahabi "Ikhwani" variety, of which

---

[60] 'Zulfi Bhutto of Pakistan' by Stanley Wolpert (Chapter 15 'Elections and Their Aftermath (early 1977)')

[61] https://www.trumanlibrary.gov/library/oral-histories/byroade

[62] For the first time, Friday was declared as the weekly holiday instead of Sunday and alcohol was legally banned in Pakistan by Bhutto in 1977. The weekly holiday was returned back to be on Sunday by the Nawaz Sharif government in 1997.

General Zia ul Haq, a "Maudoodiite," was the perfect example who should have been most avoided.

He should have known that any attempts by him to reconcile with Afghanistan's president Sardar Daud and lean more towards the Chinese bloc were sure to be sabotaged by these same forces. He miscalculated the dividends of appeasement, and made the same mistakes as the early Bengali leaders of Pakistan since he too had been a proponent of "Islamic Socialism," had he not? And he too, like them, had the original idea of Pakistan emanating from Muslim insecurity from a Hindu majority and could not divorce the religious from the political.

Indeed, it is often said in Pakistan that the weaker their rulers will be or feel themselves to be, the more they will rely on Islamic jargon and perceived Islamic actions and words as representative of their prime political standing. They prefer to go this route rather than proceeding with the idea of autonomous federalism as the raison d'être for the continued existence of Pakistan, which this book advocates.

Had Bhutto not made these prime four mistakes, it can be theorized, going out on a limb of "what-if" hypothetically intellectualized scenarios of political science, that he may have lost power, may have needed to build coalitions and alliances, but he may have lived to come back another day, as did Indira Gandhi in India in the 1980s.

But so much for the digression towards Bhutto and the brief window of opportunity that came with him to stand truth back on its legs in Pakistan, and we return to concluding our chapter on the "Migrant" and "Settler" factor in the urban-rural divide in Pakistan. There are ethnic and economic angles to this divide, also, but these we will raise and deal with a bit later in the book.

Recapping the crux of this chapter, we find that it is the troika mindset of "the three Ms" of "Minority," "Migrant," and "Middle Class" which stoked and continues to stoke the fire, rather than extinguish it, of the divide between the minority urban population and the majority population of the country's heartlands.

There is hope for redemption only if two of these "three Ms" fall away in a Pakistani's mindset. If a Pakistani can cultivate himself or herself to get rid of two or all of these "three Ms," he or she can enable oneself to see the larger picture, analyze the needs and correct way forward for the country in an objective and impersonal manner, rid oneself of personally nurtured petty prejudices and choices based on personal likes and dislikes, transcend their own social class, and think beyond their noses.

However, one of the two "Ms" to be rid of must be the "Minority" mindset because it is the most powerful of the three, which paralyzes the mind from accepting majoritarianism[63] or the verdict of democratic exercises and is most prone to being seduced by connivances of tiny coteries against unadulterated democracy. It is important to point out that what is being criticized here is the mindset and not the existential background of an individual being as such. A person can be from a minority, migrant, and middle-class background, but what is required is to rid oneself of the prejudiced subjective mindsets that come subconsciously from being born in that background. It is only after the cultivation of social consciousness that humanity is able to rise above the realities of a particular stage of its social being and change those realities in a progressive manner to create a new social being. So, it has been in history that a slave owner was an abolitionist, an industrialist a Marxist, a feudal lord a socialist and a democrat granting adult franchise to the people of his country, clergymen who gave humanity modern genetics and the big bang theory, and monarchs originating from feudal history who championed capitalist industrialization, democracy and constitutionalism in their countries.

However, with the increasing flux of the rural population towards the big urban centers of Pakistan and the high birth rate in the cities, there is a likelihood that the demography may tip in the not-too-distant future to make the urbanites the majority in their respective provinces of the

---

[63] Majoritarianism is a fourth 'M' which can boomerang like a parabola and become dangerous when taken overboard, by the 'M' of an assertive identity based 'middle class', at the expense of the 'Minority' and also becomes susceptible to fascist programs as happened in Nazi Germany or shows these leanings in the Hindutva project in India. Rejection of pluralism and diversity can turn majoritarianism too into fascism. In the context of Pakistan this phenomenon is manifested in the chauvinism of the majority religious grouping in the country and its attitude towards religious minorities.

country[64]. With a reactionary anti-democracy, anti-federal, and anti-'Hindu India' narrative dominating the urban centers, one very likely possibility is that there could first be a 'Red-Indianization' of the indigenous populations of the provinces, and then Pakistani society would function like the urban ganglands of present-day India, minus the industrialization, plus the service industry and consumer goods society as a cover for an undocumented black market and money laundering, with jingoism and religious fanaticism ruling the roost.

This is not a rosy scenario, as the masses would lie impoverished, the risk of belligerence with neighboring states could increase, and society could again be ruled as a police state.

The only positive answer to such a scenario is the development of Pakistani rural areas, its infrastructure, strengthening and modernizing of agriculture, building industry on an agrarian-based economy, and bringing the entire economy under documentation and taxation reversing the situation of the public and the upper classes being wealthy privately while the state remains poor. It also involves exploring the mineral resources in the provinces and giving the prime share of the profits and its benefits to the locals of each area, thus preventing any resentment among locals and the mass exodus of population into the cities.

This can either be achieved by state socialism (the days of which are, and hence its feasibility, bygone) or by supporting the progressive ruling classes of the rural areas, who still control the majority demographics of the country and the means of production, in other words the material productive assets (land, industry) in their areas, easing their journey of conversion into being capitalists (as historically happened in the UK, without an anti-feudal revolution per se).

That, therefore, seems to be the only way out. Only that can ensure the victory of democracy, the liberation of national cultures, tolerance and the rule of law in Pakistan, and a new pro-democratic, liberal, and pacifist narrative overcoming the reactionary one.

---

[64] In fact, as a side observation, with Pakistanis from all backgrounds having members of family in the West as expatriates, thus being migrants ('muhajirs') in those western countries, churns around the migrant mindset to set in as a mental perspective in those families back in Pakistan too.

This book hopes to unpack these ideas contained in the last few paragraphs of this chapter a bit further in the remaining ones.

Skepticism of the Majority and Diversity, Puritan Cleansing and Infinite Regression

It is well known that the word 'Pakistan' came into being as an acronym combining the first letters of the words 'Punjab', 'Afghania' (denoting the Pathan), 'Kashmir', 'Sind', and throwing in the 'stan' of 'Balochistan' at the back of the word. Peculiarly, no one, least of all the Bengalis, had an issue with adopting this word as the name for their country, considering that the 'B' of 'Bengal' was missing, ironically indicating as if the parting of ways with the Bengalis was a foregone conclusion from the beginning. Some versions would tend to say that the 'I' in the word was from 'Islam' and it would correspond to the concept of 'Bangistan', which the coiner of the word 'Pakistan', Chaudhry Rehmat Ali, had reserved for Bengal.

However, very soon the name also started to be conveniently read as meaning 'the land of the pure' since the Urdu word for 'pure' is 'pak'. The name suddenly had a meaning, too.

To be pure means not to have any impurities, to be clean from any impurities, to be 'absolutely' clean, because impurity is the negation of purity, the death of being pure.

Normally, all countries of the world ending with the word 'stan' (land) have the forename indicating the national ethnicity or religion of the people living in that land. Therefore, Balochistan is the land of the Baloch, Afghanistan is the land of the Afghans, Uzbekistan is the land of the Uzbeks, Tajikistan is the land of the Tajiks, etc., and 'Hindustan' (India) is the land of the Hindus. In that sense, if at all, the logical name of the new country being created in the subcontinent could easily have been 'Muslimistan', that is, the land of the Muslims. It would be logical because everyone understood that calling India 'Hindustan' did not mean that only Hindus lived there, but that the majority population of that land was Hindu. Similarly, the new country for the Muslims in the northwest of the Indian subcontinent could be called 'Muslimistan', that is, understanding that not only Muslims lived there but that the majority population of this country was Muslim.

However, this name could not be chosen for another logical reason. 'Hindustan' was accepted as a name for India because it was the only country in the world where the Hindus were in a majority. But choosing 'Muslimistan' as a name for the new country for the Muslims in the subcontinent would not work because it would not be the only country in the world with a Muslim majority.

So, what worked for a new name was the word 'Pakistan', based on the original vision of the poet Iqbal and the creator of this name, Chaudhry Rehmat Ali, of having a federation of independent Muslim states in the northwest of India, coming into being as mentioned, as an acronym of the federating states of northwestern India, with the mystery continuing why the Bengalis of East Pakistan accepted that name.

It should be admitted by all who still criticize the adoption of an acronym as a name for Pakistan that the name can still mean 'the land of Punjabis, Afghanias (Pathans), Kashmiris, Sindhis and Balochistanis' and make sense as a name based on the principles of political science. A land where these nationalities are a majority in each of their federating provinces. And so, it should be taken forward, this name for the country, that is how it should be interpreted.

Because 'the land of the pure' means nothing. What does it mean? Is it a land of the pure people? Pure in what respect? Is it pure, as in pious? Or is it pure, as a Muslim, that is, free from any sects? Or is it pure racially, but then what race? Or pure as being absolutely honest, and not corrupt financially?

And if it is any of that or all of that, then do not people who have those traits live in other countries? If they do, and more in every respect, then again, this meaning, this interpretation of the name 'Pakistan' falls flat on the ground. It is a nonsensical interpretation of the name and an unrealistic representation of the people living in the country.

But this meaning of the name, this concept of purity and puritanism, has seeped into the mindset of Pakistanis, specially in those with a religious tilt and those of the middle classes who are resentful of those upper economic classes who prosper through wheeling and dealing, technically not breaking laws but going around them unscrupulously through loopholes. It strikes a chord with people who continue to see the raison d'être of Pakistan through the communal Muslim supremacist lens or with those who resent the dominance of the wheeling and dealing classes even in the corridors of political power and would like to see a clampdown on them by a person or persons of similar backgrounds as their own.

It is these two categories of people who also remain wary of majority rule and unadulterated democracy, which seem dirty (impure, impious), religiously wayward (Islam being in danger, the indigenous cultures and languages of the land being considered as paganistic), anarchic (giving the illiterate the right and power to vote, whom they think can be fooled by politicians from the upper classes), and corrupt (driven by greed and material benefits) to them.

This concept of puritanism leads those infected with it straight into the hands and agenda of religious fundamentalists or of military adventurers seeking to stage a coup or to sabotage democratically elected governments.

And so it has been, since the inception of the state, this figment of an imagined puritanism driving the 'self-made', self-righteous, unelectable, middle class individual, suddenly thrust in the seat of political power due to the weakness, and even absence, of an organically evolved national democratic class and of democratic institutions in the frail new state, finding himself wielding immense political power, to push back on majority rule over this country.

After the Muslim minority in united British India had pushed back against a Hindu majority united India, this mindset was fertile to collude with those in the stronger civil-military bureaucracy of the new state, to push back against the next majority around the corner, which were the Bengali citizenry of the country. All with this mindset cooperated in this push back, as we saw, including even individual Bengali bureaucrats and politicians. Leaders who would represent the majority Bengalis were sidelined, and intentionally or unintentionally, this push back culminated in the creation of Bangladesh as a separate state.

It was clear that a policy of push back against the majority was self-destructive for the state, but this mindset persevered obstinately and with

149

petty, myopic prejudice. Once the Bengalis were gone, what this mindset did not like was the existence of pluralism and NAP majority governments in two provinces of the country, who had earlier been sympathetic to the Bengalis and had a friendly perception of Hindu majority India.

In that push back, the Bhutto government colluded with this mindset against the NAP governments. Once these governments were gone, the next in line was the majority of Bhutto that had to go. This mindset, eventually leading to the military coup of General Zia ul Haq, found allies in the smaller parties of the country, and once again the majority of the country was suppressed.

When this mindset went on the back foot because of the death of General Zia ul Haq, a collusion was formed to push back against the majority will and elected government in the post-Zia ul Haq period. Once this majority had been sidelined through presidential dismissals and subversive events in collusion with an alliance of opposing political parties[65], the push back had to happen against the next majority which coincidentally was enrooted in the majority province of post 1971 Pakistan, that is, the province of Punjab. This push back against the majority will of the majority province of Punjab continued for two decades, consuming the decades of 2000s and 2010s[66] as had the push back before against the majority Bengalis consumed the decades of the 1950s and 1960s[67]. In this push back of the 2000s and 2010s against the will of the majority, the urban middle classes and those politicians who had fallen

---

[65] With reference to the 'Islami Jamhoori Ittehad' (IJI), an alliance of parties cobbled together by active intervention of key individuals from Pakistan's military establishment, opposed to the government of prime minister Benazir Bhutto in the early 1990s and all their illegal political machinations, conspiracies, briberies and subversions of that time.

[66] With reference to the regime of General Musharraf, which came in power in 1999 after toppling the federal government of Punjabi prime minister Nawaz Sharif in a military coup, and continued till 2008 and the post Musharraf machinations by Pakistan's establishment to undermine the governments of political parties, that were signatories of the 'Charter of Democracy' (CoD) signed in London in 2006 and had passed the 18th amendment to the constitution in 2010 restoring the federal democratic essence of the 1973 constitution, up to the dismissal of Nawaz Sharif as prime minister in 2017 and bringing to power in 2018 of the establishment's then favoured party, the Pakistan Tehreek e Insaf (PTI).

[67] It was this same Minority mindset which for a long period after the 1971 debacle, till the rise of Nawaz Sharif, promoted the politically accepted 'wisdom' that the prime minister of the country should not be from Punjab, which was now the majority province of the country, as if that would be bad for successfully retaining the federation.

out or not teamed up with the majority leader of the country, colluded with full force with this mindset. Finally, when this majority leader had also been ousted conclusively, this mindset found itself suddenly popular among large swathes of the masses. Decades of social conditioning and narrative building by the state establishment had borne fruit and had seeped deep into the rank and file of this very establishment. Moreover, it was backed by powerful monied interest groups and lobbies supporting it, domestically as well as internationally, to the extent that it was ready and had become powerful enough to take over the state itself, eliminate all political opposition as well as opposition within the civil military bureaucracy, and establish a one-party fascistic state.

The 'praetorian' state then had to save itself from this eventuality by colluding with the political parties representing the remaining two thirds of the electorate at the time, who were providing resistance to this mindset and vision for the country. More about this last leg referred to, of the self-defense of the 'praetorian' state, will be written later in this book.

We see three strong threads running through the fabric of this story which, if we unravel, will provide us with the basic understanding of why the battle for the supremacy of democracy and the constitution has been a battle of survival for this goal rather than a battle for victory, and why this battle is filled with bitterness and hatred of one side for the other.

The three threads are: one, **Collusion** of the relatively smaller political forces with the minority dictatorial power (mostly having been generals in the country's history) against the majority political force of that time, and in the end themselves coming at the receiving end of the dictatorial power; two, **No Outrage** on the part of the educated middle class about the illegality and unconstitutionality of the generals' intervention in politics, glorifying them and identifying itself with them, considering them as beacons of the 'self-made', 'self-righteous' and 'self-proclaimed' morally superior middle class; and three, **Intolerance**, i.e., the political battle in the country not being a tolerant one towards the opposite camp as compatriots having differences of opinion and different political manifestos for the country which could be debated as ideas, but a battle to eliminate that opposite camp entirely, if not physically then at least brandishing them as mortal enemies of the state with the hatred and abuse that would then naturally come with such a perception.

The psychological source of all three of these threads again exists in the **Minority** mindset residing in the basis of the state's formation, which this book has identified, i.e., the fear of the majority, contempt for the choice of the indigenous people of the land comprising the majority at a certain time, and identifying the acceptance of that choice with conceding to chaos and perceived corruption in political rather than administrative decisions, and an insecurity about their own short-term petty vested interests.

It is because of these three main threads of **Collusion**, **No Outrage** about military intervention, and **Intolerance** in the fabric of the country's socio-political story that political rivalry in Pakistan between compatriots never became a normal, sane, and tolerant rivalry, but rather an enmity full of hatred, debasement, and abuse the other[68]. Thus, in each epoch of the country's history, the struggle for political domination became an exercise in 'infinite regression', always trying to defeat the majority, always trying to seek to purify the body politic from the dirtiness and curse of chaos, corruption and treason that was perceived to happen if majority rule and the results of unadulterated democracy were to be accepted. This 'infinite regression' resembled the splitting of an element into its molecules, its molecule into its atoms and then the atom to be split again to achieve the purest, the most 'pak', form of Pakistani existence, forgetting that this 'infinite regression', this splitting of the atom, would logically only end in a nuclear explosion destroying everything, the society as well as the state itself.

So continued the search for the 'purest' Pakistani who abandons one's own indigenous culture and language in favour of only one type of culture and language, the search for the 'purest' Muslim who adheres to only one approved sect and interpretation of the religion, thus converting it from being a personal matter into a matter of concern for the state, and the

---

[68] In fact, the hanging of Bhutto can be taken with considered reflection as the turning point in post 1971 Pakistan when the concept of political rivalry was taken to the next level to mean not coexistence with the political adversary but the target to physically eliminate the adversary.

search for the 'purest' political being who rejects all possibilities for pluralism and a multi-party democracy in favour of being a straitjacketed individual hailing and saluting only one party and one leader as being the most patriotic and all others either less patriotic or even worse, traitors and betrayers of the country.

Such a search was bound to 'split the atom', and this 'infinite regression' was bound to reach a stage where society and state would be full of people calling those who were different from themselves as 'kaafir' (infidel) or 'ghadaar' (traitor). Reaching such a stage could be a moment of self-destruction for the state itself, and all those who pursued and colluded in this policy of 'puritanism' would be guilty of this self-destruction.

This yearning for 'puritanism' in the imagination of the urban middle classes dominating the press and intellectual landscape of West Pakistan before the creation of Bangladesh and of Pakistan, per se, after the secession of East Pakistan, became specially acute after the end of the Zia ul Haq era in 1988 and has not relented since then, extremely resentful of all political governments that were formed as a result of general elections held in the country after Zia ul Haq, regarding them as representatives of the country's upper classes and not of themselves, and therefore these representatives had to be corrupt, immoral, selfish and unpatriotic and treasonous.

Thus, collusion had to be continued with the invisible hands of military intervention in politics, the generals of course being perceived as being from the stock of the 'self-made', self-righteous and 'self-proclaimed' morally superior middle class. It is for this reason of considering 'puritanically' the political adversary and rival as an enemy to be eliminated, and not to be coexisted with, that political expression by the middle classes in Pakistan is found to be almost always full of hatred, personal abuse and name-calling.

As we have seen sufficiently by now, the chapter of 'infinite regression' against the Bengali ended in 1971 with the splitting of the state and the creation of Bangladesh.

The army and bureaucracy of the middle class stood absolutely defeated, humiliated and discredited and was left with no power at that stage to reassert its fascism on the state.

The shattered state was picked up by the historically organic economic upper classes of West Pakistan, next in line after the departure of the Bengali as representative of the true essence of the majority of West Pakistan. These historically organic economic classes were mostly from the rural heartland of West Pakistan and tribal or feudal in nature.

The foremost leader of these classes was Bhutto, who we have seen was a progressive individual who was forward-looking and a modernist rather than an orthodox reactionary clinging to old economic structures. As explained earlier, since he himself did not derive his economic strength from urban industrial capitalism, his modernism wanted to jump the capitalist stage of development and therefore rooted for the socialist mode of economy and state ownership of large-scale industry and the macro economy. But we have also seen that in his desire to jump capitalism, he went into an overkill and hurt small urban businesses and budding industrialists.

The period of the Bhutto regime was therefore tolerated and digested by the urban middle class of Pakistan unwillingly and resentfully, as they did not possess the strength to assert themselves immediately after the debacle of 1971.

But with time, partially because of Bhutto's mistakes identified earlier in this book and partially because of the geopolitical considerations and machinations of international powers in the region and the resonance of the same found among certain political and ideological forces favoured by them in the country, a narrative against the modernism, socialism and heavy-handedness of the Bhutto regime was built and gained strength.

And when General Zia ul Haq, of a middle class 'Punjabi migrant' background[69], came along with his coup, given supra legal protection by another individual of a middle class 'Punjabi migrant' background. Chief

---

[69]General Zia ul Haq belonged to a Punjabi family which migrated from Indian East Punjab to West Punjab in Pakistan as India was partitioned.

Justice of the Supreme Court Anwar ul Haq[70], the 'minority' urban middle classes were back in business of controlling the reins of power in the state and among them the removal of the Bhutto regime was cheered, condoned and justified. Not for a moment did they stop at the time to reflect or consider or voice that the coup was illegal, unconstitutional and treasonous and that those who had carried it out were criminals who should be summarily condemned and punished. In not doing so, they too, in effect, became criminals and accomplices in the crime. This was the third time history gave them a chance, but they lost it like they had done before. First, when Justice Munir invoked the 'law of necessity' to justify the dissolution of the country's Constituent Assembly in 1954, and second, when General Ayub Khan imposed the first martial law in the country in 1958.

After the secession of East Pakistan, as one qualitative chapter in the history of Pakistan ended, and as the new country of 'only' Pakistan emerged from the ashes after the passing and implementation of the 1973 democratic constitution, the educated urban middle classes could have atoned for their previous collusion in the connivances against the Bengali by understanding what had happened in East Pakistan, rising above their class prejudices, and leaving behind the cancerous and fascistic 'Minority' mindset. But they chose not to change and once again became accomplices in the crime against the constitution and democracy.

Once a person becomes an accomplice in a crime, his[71] future and his stakes become eternally entangled with that crime and all that would follow as a result for the criminals who committed that crime. If he sees that the legal reprimand for that crime is not forthcoming and room has been given to indulge in mental gymnastics to justify the crime, his entire life thereafter would be spent in doing so, and eventually, he will attempt to portray the crime as an act of justice.

So, it has happened with the urban middle class of Pakistan after the Zia ul Haq period. They have spent their lifetimes since then spitting venom against political parties coming into power after each election and

---

[70] Justice Anwar ul Haq belonged to a Punjabi family from Jullundur in Indian East Punjab who opted for Pakistan after partition.

[71] The gender 'he' or 'him' is used here for ease of discourse, just as the word 'Man' is used often to represent 'human being'.

portraying ensuing events in a way as if subversive and conspiratorial acts of connivance and sabotage carried out by political generals against these elected governments were, in fact, attempts to impose the 'rule of law' against political decisions and perceived corruption of those governments.

Truth was made to stand on its head, and those generals who were violating the constitution by interfering in politics were portrayed as defenders of the 'rule of law,' and elected governments possessing the constitutional mandate to rule the country were perceived and labeled as criminals.

How this narrative of the country's anti-democracy middle-class intelligentsia seeped deeply into every nook and corner of social consciousness, and how it manifested itself in socio-psychological discourse over the years after Zia ul Haq, becoming ever acuter in its displeasure and frustration as it saw that this middle-class fascism was not coming back through the constitutional dispensation in the country, will be seen in the next chapters.

But this chapter is concluded with the statement that: a vision for the country based on a concept of 'puritanism' or being a 'land of the pure,' summarily cleansing the country from all forms of 'impurities,' including the 'dirtiness' of diversity, indigenousness, pluralism, family dynasties in business or politics, and so-called 'corruption' not evidenced in a court of law, will only serve to be a recipe for the death, in fact suicide, of the country.

Middle Class Clichés

"We are not political" or "We are not interested in politics."

Anyone who has grown up in Pakistan, specially in the urban areas, is certain to have repeatedly heard these two sentences being used *ad nauseam* throughout one's life, in one's household, social circle, or the media.

And immediately on the utterance of any one of these two sentences, this expression of the default position of the person uttering it regarding all matters is taken in by the listeners with an enhancement of the stature in their eyes for that person. It is as if, by stating that "I am not political" or "I am not interested in politics," the prestige of the person saying so has increased, and he or she is considered as possessing a superior intellectual level or moral compass than the rest who "are political" or who "are interested in politics."

There are a few socio-psychological nuances built into these sentences which will be unpacked in this chapter. But before we do that, it would be worthwhile to state upfront two truths which were found to be validated in almost all cases of those who uttered these sentences, while acknowledging that a few really mean it when they say "We are not political," to which there should then be genuinely no objection.

One, is that subscribing to the view that being not political was somehow a sign of possessing intellectual superiority and a higher moral compass turned out to be the very opposite, with those doing so found to be completely lacking in any deep understanding of their country's history or how statecraft for their particular country would work, and instead just found looking for or waiting for a "messianic leader" who would arrive and fix all problems singlehandedly and unscrupulously, and illegally, trampling on the democratic and human rights of compatriots in doing so.

The second truth is that those who stated "We are not political" or "We are not interested in politics" turned out to be the ones with the 'most political' pent-up views and an immense hatred of democracy and democratically elected politicians running their country, and were normally the first to hail and actively side with martial laws or any attempt to stifle democracy and pluralism in the country. The second truth complemented the first when these "we are not political" people considered, every time, the general imposing the martial law or a fascistic leader locking up all politicians as the "quick fix" *Messiah* they were all waiting for. In fact, they are so invested in this political perspective, hiding behind the façade of "We are not political," that when they come out in the open their expression and behavior is not that of normal sane political people and borders on the maniacal, seeking the elimination or silencing of all differing political perspectives.

The inherent socio-psychological nuances packed in these two sentences were as follows: that politics was a negative thing, a dirty thing, something that we in our lives and the country could very well do without and still go on, in fact, do much better. And then, who is the most apolitical potent entity in the country who could be relied on to take over the reins of power, get rid of the politicians "doing politics," this dirty negative thing? Of course, the military, who else!

And therefore, better to build your confidence and sense of security, to the extent of being complacent, by considering that whatever the generals are doing, in power or out of power, must be right for the country. And if any politician is criticizing the generals for interfering in politics, damn that "dirty" "f$%@!**" politician.

In countries where democracy is the historically evolved mode of government, with the three pillars of the democratic state functional and the rule of law effective, e.g. the foremost democratic states of the world like USA, UK, Canada and France etc., citizens of the middle class[72], derive their confidence and sense of security, from their belief that the constitution of their country is supreme and no individual, least of all from the military which is a department subordinate to the ministry of defence, is greater than the constitution. And if any individual adventurer attempts to take over their state as a dictator, the democratic institutions, including the three pillars of the state and the media, are so strong and conscientious that this individual is bound to fail. In fact, the largest democracy in the world, India, too, can be considered as falling in the category of these countries where, despite the political victories of a non-secular party, this party has still not succeeded in superseding the constitution of India, which still reigns supreme. And this party faces pushback across the federating Indian states and in general elections, with no chance of any military adventurer or fascist individual imposing a dictatorship there.

However, in Pakistan, the 'educated' middle class sought its comfort not in the constitution of their country, which they considered to have been formulated and passed by classes with whom they did not identify themselves. They preferred to seek that comfort from a hope of eventual

---

[72] Though it must be admitted that the middle classes in these countries are devoid of two of the three 'Ms' identified in this book, i.e. the 'minority' and the 'migrant' mindset, historically having become organically connected to the majority composition of the country and technically no longer being of 'migrant' stock but having become the locals themselves with the urban and the rural being of the same stock.

intervention, no problem if illegal, by the military, with whose officers they identified themselves more, coming from middle-class backgrounds.

This is a clear case of moral and intellectual bankruptcy because, logically, it would be expected of any educated people to identify and align themselves more with the constitution of their country, which is an exercise of intellect and places the 'rule of law', i.e. the pen, as superior to the sword, the gun of the military in this case.

But due to their historic and organic disconnect and alienation from the political class that had passed the constitution of the country, in Pakistan, it was considered as being 'more educated' to side with the sword than the pen. The base instincts of the Pakistani middle class called for the blood of all those who called for democracy, because, in the considered subconscious and even sometimes consciously expressed opinion of the Pakistani middle class, democracy would mean their being subservient to the political class of the country, which traditionally belonged to the upper economic classes.

This contempt for the democratically legislated law and constitution of the country also manifested in identifying more with unelected but politicized or compromised judges, who, instead of merely interpreting the law and the constitution passed by an elected parliament, sabotaged elected governments and condoned military takeovers through verdicts based on supra-legal, supra-constitutional judgements[73].

There is no objection to, or harm, if someone is genuinely 'not political', for that is their right. But then, they should not come out from the shadows later to badmouth politics and politicians, per se, both of which are protected and encouraged by the constitution of the country as the legitimate mode of running the country. But the overwhelming fact about Pakistan is that nobody is not political. One just needs to scratch

---

[73] From the 'Doctrine of Necessity' invoked to justify the dissolution of the constituent assembly in 1954 to justifying the martial laws of General Ayub and General Zia to the judgement after the military coup of October 1999 giving the power to even amend the constitution single handedly to General Musharraf to dismissing elected prime ministers of the Pakistan People's Party and Pakistan Muslim League (N) in the 2010s by supra constitutional requirement to act against a constitutionally immune sitting president and invoking the supra legal 'Black Law Dictionary' respectively, to few other vital such decisions which will be referred to in this book.

away just one layer of a Pakistani's personal makeup, and the politics will burst forth like a fountain bearing the real political self. 'We are not political' is almost always a façade that the fascist minded wear over themselves to defeat the pluralism of democratic politics and the sway of 'one man one vote' democracy in the country.

A cliché following close on the heels of the "We are not political" cliché is "We are with the one who wins" (expressed in popular Punjabi vernacular as "Jehrra Jittay Ouhday Naal" or JJON, literally having the same meaning). This cliché is expressed in jest, highlighting it as a point of humor to again show a perceived intellectual superiority of the one uttering it, as if "this dirty politics is beneath us," but in its depth too reside a couple of socio-psychological nuances.

The first is, as already explained, a deep-rooted contempt for democratic and pluralistic politics. But there is a second, which is saying that what is important is winning, and it is not about any principle. However so that winning is achieved, — even by hook or by crook, or even by bypassing or violating the law and constitution of the country — it is acceptable. This mindset makes fun of and looks down cynically at those who raise issues of principle based on law and constitution, condones military coups, and expresses glee at tricks and treachery adopted by dishonest political players, considering them as very smart instead of characterless and crooked.

"Nation needs danda" ("danda" is the Urdu word for "stick" or "rod" in English) or "Nation only understands danda." These are another two clichés much popular among Pakistani middle classes. They are meant to say, as is obvious, that the nation needs dictatorship and that force should be used on it regardless of any human or democratic rights to make the people do what the ruling dictator wants them to do, and that the people of this country are like animals who are not developed enough intellectually to abide by laws unless they are beaten with the rod like animals and made to do so by use of physical force on them.

This again betrays the anti-democracy and fascist mindset of the Pakistani middle class, but there is another socio-psychological nuance hidden inherently in these two clichés. These clichés of the middle class which are saying that the nation needs the rod, or that the nation only understands the rod, are telling something about themselves also. They are saying that "WE need the rod" and "WE only understand the rod," meaning that unless the rod (force) is applied on us, we do not recognize any other authority — democratic or constitutional — and we will do as we please, and we will do everything in our power to fail democracy and the constitution. We will only stay or become quiet if we are made to do so by applying force on us.

Thus, a gauntlet is thrown in the face of those who want democracy and constitution to reign supreme in the country, whereby the democratic and human rights provided for by the constitution are misused and abused by this middle class to subvert a democratically elected and constituted government to such a degree that eventually the democratic government is forced by circumstances thus created to use physical force and incarcerations, although sanctioned by the constitution, to control this subversion.

In this way, the reactionary middle classes say to those advocating for the supremacy of democracy and the constitution that *"see, in the end there is no such thing as civility even in your democracy and constitution, and it is only physical force and the principle of might is right which is the real law in this world."*

Of course, the use of executive force and incarceration in the face of mischief, abuse of law and order, and subversive activities is sanctioned by the democratic constitution. But the optics of police charge on a demonstration breaking the law or incarcerating political opposition because they broke the law would seem to validate this point of view being put forth by a seemingly educated middle class.

It is truly a malicious and contemptuous attempt by a reactionary middle class to weaken and fail democratic and constitutional rule in the country, instead of playing a positive role expected of sane, educated people to bring civility and respect for democratically legislated law and order into politics.

Another cliché often finding assenting expression among the Pakistani middle classes has been that "how can illiterates be given the right to vote?" or that "how can you equate an illiterate person with a person holding a degree or a PhD?"

As the Italian Marxist Antonio Gramsci was quoted earlier in this book, such a view is an attempt by a fascist outlook to disenfranchise the common man in society from even the one power he has through the vote — to affect public policy and the course of his future. Repeating what Gramsci writes in 'Modern Prince': *"everyone tends to confound his own 'private interest,' it may be, with that of the nation, and hence find it 'dreadful,' etc. that it should be the 'law of numbers' which decides; it is better of course to become an elite by decree. Thus, it is not a question of the people who 'have the brains' feeling that they are being reduced to the level of the lowest illiterate, but rather one of people who think they are the ones with the brains wanting to take away from the 'man in the street' even that tiniest fraction of power of decision over the course of national life which he possesses.."* [74] This concept of universal franchise has also been debated historically in Western democracies, which are the pioneers in providing it and voting rights to their people. For instance, during the passing of the Ballot Act in the UK as early as in 1872, voting secrecy was ensured to avoid the sway of influence by the rich, and in Ireland this worked for the peasants to vote against the landlords. And then this Ballot Act was re-debated again in 1892 on the topic of providing voting rights to the illiterate.

Those who oppose voting rights for the illiterate consider the illiterate to be less human than the literate and educated citizens of the country. The fact is that all human beings are capable of knowing what is best for themselves with respect to the material considerations of their economic existence, be they farmers or workers or of any other vocation in the economy of the country. Every human being has the capacity of intellectual rationalizing by instinct. The only difference which literacy or education makes in this is that the person becomes capable of structuring his or her thoughts and giving expression to it in so many words through education.

Verily, this proposition is validated if by nothing else than by the fact that the very first humans in human history who philosophized and built the foundations of human knowledge were not literate in the meaning of

---

[74] Antonio Gramsci (Modern Prince, Chapter 13 'Number and Quality in Representative Systems of Government')

the word as we have today. And in this day and age, with the presence and dividends of modern technology abound, it would be intellectually dishonest to state that an illiterate person today would not be capable of knowing what is best for him.

On top of this, when we see that highly educated individuals conscript in terrorist organizations like Al Qaeda, while on the other hand an almost illiterate person like Abdul Sattar Edhi knew what needed to be done to rescue and serve his compatriots in the most efficient and organized way, this theory, of illiterate people not deserving the right to vote or not being equal to educated ones in all faculties as a full human, falls flat on its face there and then.

And to shut up once and for all all those specially in Pakistan who still subscribe to this cliché, need we remind them of the fact that the one considered by us as the greatest person of mankind, i.e. our Prophet (pbuh), too was an illiterate by worldly standards, but a respected arbiter among the families of his city and a successful merchant before prophethood was bestowed upon him?

We finally address the most deeply entrenched cliché of the 'moralist' middle class in Pakistan, which is also a basic misconception in thought carried and nurtured by this class in its mindset. Its origin emanates from the much larger intellectual problem affecting not just Pakistani Muslims but Muslims globally, of the dogmatic and literalist way of Asharite thinking dominating their thought process since centuries, pointed out earlier in the book.

We will see that this cliché in fact is so deeply problematic that it turns out to be the fountainhead of various maladies in the thought process not just on the political level, virtually incapacitating even highly educated middle class individuals from submitting themselves to the rule of law and constitution of the land, but even on the social level, succumbing to intellectual retardation with diminishing ability to understand, and the agility to interact with, the dynamics of a progressively advancing modern contemporary world.

For pre-partition Indian Muslims, the 'renaissance' initiated by the educational work of Sir Syed Ahmed Khan, carried forward by the intellectual work and poetry of the Allama Iqbal, and the practice and speeches of Jinnah, briefly pulled them out of this intellectual morass. But as the dogmatic fundamentalist thought process, which had initially opposed the creation of Pakistan, replaced this 'renaissance' and gradually gripped the new state in its shackles, from the passing of the Objectives Resolution in 1949 to the 'Islamization' of the Zia ul Haq era, all along favored and egged on by domestic as well as international forces opposed to Communism during the Cold War, the window of this brief period of enlightenment was shut close and the mind of the Pakistani Muslim fell straight back into the intellectual morass of pre Sir Syed times.

This cliché presents itself in the following forms: "Take Deen (religion) and Dunia (the world or worldly matters) hand in hand together" or "Excel in both, Deen and Dunia" or "We have to take Deen along with Dunia" (meaning that we should not forget religion while excelling ourselves in worldly matters).

On the face of it, if looked at superficially, it would look like a secular premise. As if someone is separating religion from worldly matters because one is looking at religion and worldly matters as separate entities, which should be a good thing, as it would lead to a separation of religion from politics or state affairs in the mind of that person.

However, in fact, when interrogated deeply, this cliché is found to be the manifestation of intellectual groundwork making the case for bringing the domination of organized religion into politics and establishing theocratic rule.

Because the nuance which is contained in this cliché is that this world is satanic, and it is only the ritualistic practices of religion and its overt symbolism which are Godly and the means for the salvation of the soul.

This thinking negates the proposition that the means of salvation pass through what you do entirely, holistically, in your life in this world. That 'Dunia' is in fact 'Deen'. That is why this cliché downplays the practice of daily practical life, the interaction between human beings, the quest for worldly and scientific knowledge, and the achievements resulting from this knowledge, and glorifies religious ritualism and religious discourses devoid of 'this worldly' knowledge and the telling of tales of the hereafter.

It views salvation in terms of bean counting in quantitative terms and God as some kind of a bean counter whereby good deeds and bad deeds are put on two scales of a balance and whichever weighs more will decide the fate of an individual on the day of judgment, not recognizing that one qualitatively overwhelming evil deed or one qualitatively overwhelming good deed could be the determining factor for the individual's fate.

It does not see science as a Godly work, as a quest for knowing the divine, but proposes that the divine cannot be known. It rejects the Sufi proposition that by knowing yourself, you will get to know the divine because we and our universe are part of the divine (in the image of God) and not entities exterior to the divine[75]. Such a proposition would complement the scientific bent more as we now know that we are all made up of elements found in star dust. This cliché scornfully views science as failed and pathetic attempts by Man to know the truth, initially declares all new scientific inventions, innovations and discoveries as satanic, yet at the first opportunity when these scientific breakthroughs translate in everyday life into means of moving ahead in the world, it pragmatically justifies the adoption of these means for itself to reign supreme over the rest of the world. And while it is belittling science, it continues to glorify clerics and leaders of religious ritual as being the ones foremost on the right path and works for worldly domination by them and not by those who understand the advancements of science and scientific thinking and those who intellectually philosophize and try to build systems and societies based on newer and newer scientific findings.

When Protestantism emerged in the West and challenged the political rule of the clergy, it laid the foundation stone for secularism in society by proposing a direct link between man and God with no need for any intercessory. What it did in fact, and the princes in Europe who backed it, was not the elimination of religion from society but to break the hold of the clergy over political power and push back their influence and reduce it within the boundaries of the church to be dealt with there theologically. Thus, the field was cleared for kings and princes, who were not devoid of religion but imbued with Protestantism, to steer the ship of state, free from the paralyzing and retrogressive edicts of the clergy, as they saw fit

---

[75] The debate between 'Waḥdat al-wujūd' (Unity of Existence, as objective) and 'Wahdat Al shuhūd' (Unity of Vision, i.e. whatever we see, as subjective) in Islamic philosophy.

according to their own conscience and rationale for practical sociopolitical requirements of the contemporary present.

This also opened up the opportunity for the work of intellectuals of that time to come into play, who were rationalizing based on the faculties of logic and considerations of contemporary scientific advancements to discover what was the best way forward for human society. They were not godless people, but they had just rejected and broken free from the shackles of a reactionary monopolistic clergy for whom the world was satanic, for whom 'Deen' and 'Dunia' were separate, even opposed to each other.

Since the emergence of Islam up to the present day, it is commonly stated among the Muslims that there is no priesthood ('rahbaaniyat' in Urdu) in Islam. The fundamental point on which the original theological proposition of Islam rested and still rests is that there is no need for any intercessory between man and God. Any attempt in thought or practice to deviate from this fundamental proposition risks such a deviant to enter the realm of 'shirk' (the Arabic word for belief in more than one God, that is, associating divine powers also with anyone other than God). According to fundamental Islamic belief, a person can directly ask God's help or direction through 'dua' (supplication). Supplicating to anyone but God pushes the person doing so into the realm of 'shirk'. According to Islam, God has sent His direct word through the Quran, and all humans are free to read from it directly. In all these ways, Islam was already like the later emerging phenomenon of Protestantism in the Christian West (minus recognizing any divinity for even Jesus Christ, of course).

That is why initially, imbued with this theological concept, the early Muslims did not have any clergy as a separate entity within themselves. No one had a monopoly on religion. And yet here we are, many centuries later, where we find the Muslim society hostage to a clergy which proclaims monopoly over all things and concepts religious, which propounds that ordinary Muslims do not qualify to be able to read the Quran and understand it or interpret from it, more so those who do not even know Arabic, and we see millions of Muslims subordinating themselves to 'Pirs' (holy men), whom they ask to pray on their behalf to God and to, a hierarchical and eventually elitist, clergy.

As was mentioned earlier in the book, as dynastic rule overpowered the Islamic world and the upper classes of society adopted Islam as their official religion, similar to what happened when the Romans adopted Christianity, the official interpretation of religion was sanctioned to a set group of people and a monopoly over the interpretation was acquired by the state. Thus, was established, as happened in Roman Christendom, a clergy or a kind of 'papacy' holding monopoly over the interpretation of the religious doctrine given by God.

We have already talked about the tussle between the Mutazalites and the Asharites concluding in victory for the Asharites, thus ending the Golden Age of Islam, with the Asharites rejecting the 'cause and effect' nature of the material world identified by science and considering scientific laws susceptible to the will of God and miracles if so be the wish of God to suspend this nature, while in the real material world it never manifested or manifests that way.

Since then, the monopoly over Islam and the Quran has been held by a clergy existing as a separate entity within the Muslim society, and the thread of epistemology connecting the Muslim world to the past, present, and future human journey of knowledge was broken.

So, while in the West humanity freed itself through Protestantism from the monopoly of the papacy, in the Islamic world, theology lost its freedom to an anti-science reactionary clergy similar to a Christian papacy of the famous Dark Ages.

While it is not to be denied that any extensive work in theology which would enable Muslims in the modern world to do 'ijtihad' (collective intellectual effort) or come up with updated 'fiqh' (jurisprudence) suitable for modern times would require deep scholastic study of the Quran and Islamic philosophy, it is unfair and belittling to the citizens of the Muslim world not to consider them worthy of making their own democratic decisions and running their state as they deem correct.

It is also intellectually dishonest to state that any Muslim, by reading the Quran, will not know what is explicitly written in that divine book about what is right and what is wrong, and the dos and the don'ts.

Once a Muslim has read the Quran and has picked up the broken thread of epistemology by educating and enlightening oneself with the latest modern scientific body of knowledge, he (or she) is fully qualified to function as an independent citizen in a modern democratic state, voting according to one's conscience and consciousness, without being intimidated or subordinated by an exclusive group of people known as the clergy or 'Pirs' (holy men).

This would be no different from those Protestants who are known as the founding fathers of the United States of America. Acting as per their conscience and knowledge, and not controlled by any clergy in the practical world and the running of their state, and for improvement in their religious conscience, voluntarily referring to the latest theological work being done by scholars and experts dedicated to that work.

In that sense, the 1973 Constitution of Pakistan is already there, whereby it proclaims that although the sovereignty of the state belongs to the Almighty, this sovereignty is exercised by the elected representatives of the people, and the judgment to make laws not repugnant to Quran and Sunnah also rests with them (although this prerogative was later distorted and defaced by overemphasizing the role of the unelected Council of Islamic Ideology (CII) and the unelected Federal Shariat Court in the periods of Islamization by the Zia ul Haq regime, as well as similar leaning governments).

However, as discussed earlier, in Pakistan, a state in the Islamic world founded on the principles of democracy and by the force of the ballot, bridging this gap between the citizen and independent, enlightened, self-cultivated theological conscience has always remained an uphill task since the passing of the Objectives Resolution of 1949 and the strengthening of religious parties and the clergy during the Cold War.

It is due to this overbearing atmosphere of the domination of the clergy in matters of religion and the lack of understanding of the thread of knowledge which was broken in the Islamic world with the victory of the Asharites in history, that a vast majority of the educated middle class in Pakistan remained confused about the matters of the world and matters of religion, thinking them to be at odds with each other.

They failed to read and understand the Quran themselves (a vast majority of Pakistanis do not know firsthand what is written in the Quran) and did not understand that the advanced successful system of the West stood on intellectual work of Western people who had not rejected religion per se but only freed themselves from the domination of their clergy, and had in fact built their societies on the continuity of concepts taken from Muslim intellectuals of yore, like Averroes (Ibn e Rushd) and Ibn e Khuldun, who in turn had built their philosophical work on the legacy of ancient Greek philosophers infused with the ontological implications of the new faith.

Due to this failure of insight, what happened with most middle-class individuals of Pakistan was that either they initially became too westernized, looking down on their own cultural heritage, and in later life, after rebounding from things they were unable to understand about the West, became 'born again' Muslims, falling into the pits of the religious interpretations of the clergy, or they always remained subscribed to the reactionary religious interpretation of their clergy, considering all modern scientific knowledge and Western societal or political norms as satanic and adopting or adjusting to those only as a matter of pragmatism or 'taqiyyah' (concealment).

This lack of independent self-cultivation based on one's own theological legacy using one's own faculties of logic and rationality, and this lack of understanding of the combined collective epistemological legacy of humankind, results in the mindset of considering 'Deen' and 'Dunia' as contraposed to each other.

This becomes more problematic when, due to this mindset, the Muslim mind rejects the laws of the land in which it lives as being man-made and not divine (disregarding the fact that these laws of the land have been made by the will of religiously conscientious, or just conscientious, people who are created by God), and therefore not to be obeyed, thus becoming susceptible to theocratic movements and sympathetic to Islamic dogmatic fundamentalist forces like the Taliban, etc.

Individuals lacking this self-cultivation and understanding are prone to indulging in mob violence or 'sleeper' terrorism as a means of catharsis for themselves, to compensate for these deficiencies through acts of violence against non-believers and perceived blasphemers, while in their practical lives they behave with sheer pragmatism. The citizen of the hereafter, acting or speaking out against citizens of this 'satanic' world, in search of salvation, atonement, acclaim, and glory.

Solipsistic Personal Prejudices

An initial cultural chasm was instilled in the new state at the time of its birth in 1947 between the rural and the urban, as explained in an earlier chapter of this book, and there was a lack of effort on the part of the drivers of the new state to bridge this chasm. Instead, in fact, growing resentments on each side of the chasm were fanned, time and again, by the downplaying or suppression of the indigenous cultural manifestations, including the languages of the constituting provinces of the federation, by a centralist view for the state.

This lack of bridging chasms resulted in various ethnicities, sects, and social groups becoming defensive and inward-looking, causing 'Compartmentalization' in society.

Instead of the new state becoming a seminal pool for Pakistanis interacting, and even procreating, dynamically with each other, considering all kinds of backgrounds to be equal and to be equally respected, and producing a synthesis between the citizens of the new state in a progressive atmosphere and manner, this defensive compartmentalization resulted in the various groups contained in the new state to become socially stationary and closed, and reluctant to synthesize with a different group.

As a side observation, this attitude was and is compounded, making this phenomenon of compartmentalization more problematic, by the practice of intra-family marriages which has permission in the religion of Islam.

This kind of compartmentalization has not been that intensive in the case of India after Partition. The primary reason being that the initial Indian leaders at the helm after independence promoted the viewing of each other by Indians as equals, with no ethnicity, language, religion, or sect considered as superior to the other and none suppressed officially per se, although in recent years this mindset has deteriorated there too. But it happened so contrarily in Pakistan, as has been discussed earlier.

Such compartmentalization has resulted in the introduction of a kind of solipsism in the psyche of the average Pakistani, whereby he[76] views events and personalities from a personally subjective lens. In other words, he is not able to think 'beyond his nose'.

So, it is that the migrants ('muhajirs') pouring in from post British India looked down on local cultures, the locals started resenting and eventually hating the 'muhajirs' who in turn became resentful and hateful too against the locals when faced with prejudice and exclusion from the latter's side, the West Pakistanis started looking down on and resenting the majority East Pakistanis, the East Pakistanis eventually started hating the West Pakistanis, the Punjabis who were the majority in a centralist One Unit West Pakistan started considering the Pakistanis of the three smaller provinces of West Pakistan who wanted their self-expression and self-determination as less patriotic Pakistanis (all the more so because Punjabis had abandoned their own mother tongue and could not understand why the other ethnic groups stood for their mother tongues), the Pakistanis of the three smaller provinces of West Pakistan started hating Punjabis as Punjabis comprised the majority of the Pakistan Army which was the face of state action in the event of a martial law or a military action; and with the advent of the Sunni Wahabi martial law of General Zia ul Haq the resentment of Shias and Sunnis towards each other advanced into hatred of each other and the final nail in the coffin came with the non-Party based elections of 1985, after which the subjective solipsism of ethnicity, sect and caste became the mental norm. These solipsistic tendencies, specially in the context of the internal tussle of the middle classes among themselves based on ethnic, linguistic and sectarian leanings are nascently fascist in their essence. They possess high risk of fascism. So do such individuals with that kind of bias.

In Pakistan, it is very normal to ask a person in the very first meeting where he is from or what is his family name. This seemingly innocent question is, in fact, the in-built screening mechanism in the psyche of the person asking that question through which he gauges how close or how far the other person is from him. Based on that evaluation, he will determine

---

[76] The gender 'he' or 'him' is used here for ease of discourse, just as the word 'Man' is used often to represent 'human being'.

in what way he is going to interact with this person because, for him, that person is a non-entity on his own and has to contain and represent all styles, characteristics, and viewpoints that the questioner perceives about that person's cultural background. The closer he finds the other person to his own cultural background, the more comfortable he will feel himself to be with him and the more he will open up on an intimate level with him. What the other person is as just a person, by himself, does not count, and neither is the questioner interested in it. For how can anyone be different from their respective cultural background, because in Pakistan, we stick by and are stuck in stationary, non-interacting cocoons of our respective social existences, are we not?

Though, among progressive and open-minded Pakistanis, this solipsism is disappearing through conscious decision and initiative by such individuals and still not spontaneously, generally this solipsism continues in the mindset of the majority.

It is for this reason that in the post Zia ul Haq era, as pluralism returned in the political process, parties of a federal nature having strong presence in all provinces gradually diminished, and the major political parties of the country became reduced to one province or the other. The fault for this lay not as much with the leaders of these major political parties as with the electorate who are gripped by this solipsism.

For one reason or the other, the majority electorate of one province thought of a political party as closest and most responsive to their own cocooned perceptions and interests, so they voted in that political party to power in their province and to the national assembly seats from their province. Here, it is very important to note that the consideration for that electorate was not who would be most beneficial to them in material terms and performance-wise, but who is the closest to their solipsistic perspectives.

That is why, when pluralism returned after the Zia ul Haq era, initially sub nationalist parties succeeded in the western provinces of the country. The feudal agrarian Pakistan People's Party succeeded in feudal Sind and the agrarian areas of Punjab, the Muhajir Qaumi Movement (MQM) succeeded in the major urban centres of Sindh where the migrants ('muhajirs') of India and their descendants were in majority and the pre dominantly capitalistic Muslim League led by a Punjabi succeeded in urban Punjab and the areas in Punjab where feudalism was weak.

In subsequent years, as the hold of Islamic militias strengthened in the Northwest of Pakistan with the success of the Mujahideen in Afghanistan in the 1990s and later with the ascent to power of the Taliban, the religious parties in the Pakhtun areas of Pakistan gained ground and came to power in the northwestern province through elections in 2002. Although it must be pointed out that due to the sensitivity of the province and areas of the Pakhtuns being nearest to Afghanistan, the role of the country's security establishment in determining, through their influence, who will come to power there cannot be understated. Because when the military dictator General Musharraf, who was often perceived as 'running with the hare and hunting with the hounds'[77] in the 'War on Terror', was cornered into becoming a lame duck president subsequent to a mass movement against his regime in 2007, the party to win in the Northwest Frontier Province was again the sub nationalist Awami National Party (ANP). Subsequently, as the United States lost foothold in Afghanistan and the Tehreek-e-Taliban Pakistan (TTP) gained ground within Pakistan, stalwarts of the ANP were gunned down and their candidates intimidated, and the pro-Taliban Pakistan Tehreek-e-Insaaf (PTI) was voted into power in the province thrice, in the 2013, 2018, and 2024 elections. To what extent intimidation plays a role in bringing a pro-Taliban party to power in the Northwest Frontier Province, now renamed Khyber Pakhtunkhwa, can be a subject of debate, but it can be safely stated that if the intimidation is taken away, there is more chance that a sub-nationalist rather than a federal party will come to power in that province, which is a validation of the observation that solipsistic considerations are the prime criteria for the electorate in the way they vote.

---

[77] 'How Musharraf Survives' by Pervez Hoodbhoy (https://www.project-syndicate.org/commentary/how-musharraf-survives), 'MMA, Musharraf and Pakistan's enduring political enigma' by A. Masroor (https://www.khaleejtimes.com/opinion/mma-musharraf-and-pakistans-enduring-political-enigma), 'Pakistan spy chief seen as tough on militants' (https://www.nbcnews.com/id/wbna26952834), 'No pardon for Musharraf' by Liaquat Ali Khan (https://www.thedailystar.net/news-detail-28488), 'Does the West need Musharraf?' by Ahmed Rashid (http://news.bbc.co.uk/2/hi/south_asia/6710597.stm), 'Bush And Pakistan' by C. Raja Mohan (https://www.forbes.com/2008/09/22/bush-pakistan-afghanistan-oped-cx_crm_0922mohan.html)

It will be to the credit of the leaders of federal parties if they succeed in breaking this mindset and are able to build a narrative of objective and not solipsistic nature which captures the imagination of the electorate and gains popularity as a voting point for them, but so far this solipsism persists.

Even voting for parties of a federal nature with a federal agenda revolves around voting for the personalities leading those parties rather than their political programs. It is more a case of personality worship than of genuine evaluation of and identification with the economic and political program of that party, hence here too solipsism is at work. And each individual of the electorate has a solipsistic reason for identifying oneself with the leader of that federal party.

In the case of the Pakistan People's Party (PPP), it has been the personality worship of Bhutto and his charisma, which continued to be the reason for its electorate to vote for his daughter Benazir, although a big portion of the PPP electorate loved and admired Benazir in her own right. In later years, this electorate was reduced to the province of feudal Sind and the context and considerations which that characteristic brings, most adeptly taken forward by Benazir's widower Asif Ali Zardari. This kind of politics also found resonance in the feudal areas of Punjab and areas where agrarian politics still dominates on a local level and where the traditional big wigs have been wary and resentful of the growing power in the province of an urban capitalist leading the dominant Pakistan Muslim League in Punjab. However, on a federal level, it is still this importance more of the person leading the federal party rather than the program of the party that the family of Bhutto and Benazir, represented by Benazir's son Bilawal and daughter Asifa, commands the respect of PPP's electorate. Coincidentally, considering the sacrifice and struggle of the Bhutto family for democracy in Pakistan and the chance that the family leadership of PPP shows advanced levels of political maturity, this is not necessarily a negative, but the point of concern is that the criteria for the electorate on a federal level are personalities rather than programs and performance.

The case of Pakistan Muslim League-Nawaz (PML-N) led by Nawaz Sharif and his family is again clear and a reaffirmation of the observation that the criterion of the electorate for a federal party is personalities. The core support for Nawaz Sharif is derived from his 'Punjabiness' and the fact that he has been the most successful and most popular Punjabi leader in the history of Pakistan. He is loved by his core support in Punjab, specially among the Punjabi middle class with a sub-nationalist bent of mind in their own turn, in whom these reasons combine with a weariness among them of always being blamed by sub-nationalist parties of other provinces for their woes. Here is a Punjabi majority population of the country who has found their popular leader who can win a majority in national elections just by sweeping Punjab and winning only a few constituencies in other provinces, form a government on the federal level and even deliver for the country through performance, which will be for the good of all of Pakistan. However, again it has to be Nawaz Sharif or one of his family, his daughter or his brother who should lead and if the party was to be handed over to another individual out of that family, the party may succumb to infighting and internal groupings for no one else would be considered of the stature attributed to the Sharif family and all will look at each other pettily as competitors.

It is the compartmentalization in Pakistani society and the solipsism which results from this compartmentalization that elevates the stature of family in the Pakistani mindset as an entity where only loyalty can reside and survive, and not outside of it. This importance of family loyalty acquires even more meaning and significance in facing and resisting the suppression of military dictatorships and arm-twisting which has been a norm in Pakistan. These are the foremost reasons why families dominate political parties, federal or sub-nationalist, in Pakistan. This mindset is also inherently built on the age-old trend in the subcontinent in particular but which can still be seen even in advanced western societies, of the son adopting the same profession or trade as of the father, which is a phenomenon that lingers from that stage in societies when they had not fully evolved out of tribal or feudal modes of life into becoming a modern democratic capitalist nation-state.

The case of the third party to emerge as a major federal party in Pakistan with genuine electoral support, the Pakistan Tehreek e Insaaf (PTI), is also the same, personality worship rather than program. In fact, whereas the former two major federal parties, the PPP and the PML-N, generally represented the upper classes of the rural areas and the capitalist interests of the country respectively, in PTI and its leader the growing urban middle class of Pakistan found for the first time a political party of a federal nature with which they could identify themselves on a personal level. On the first sound of it, this may seem to be a positive progressive occurrence in the body politic of the country. But on closer examination, it is found that this phenomenon too, in fact more than for the other two major federal parties, is heavily beset with acute solipsism. This solipsism diverted the party onto the same lines as those of the politics of the most famous of the middle-class parties in history, the parties of Mussolini and Hitler[78]. Because the urban middle classes, which backed the PTI, were, as we already observed earlier in the book, the same classes that historically had grown up and lived with the cliché of 'We are not political,' rejecting and ticking off politics and their contemporary political parties as dirty and corrupt. These were the same urban middle classes for whose contempt for the 'din of democracy' and the seemingly slow pace of the country's progress, the solution was an oversimplistic and 'quick fix' one, that is, the elimination of pluralism and uniting under one autocratic and unscrupulously ruthless 'Messiah.' In other words, fascism.

Before, this 'Messiah' used to always be the Chief of Army Staff (COAS), who would be seen as the epitome of pureness and honesty and the real driver behind all things good, even if that good was being delivered by political governments. However, the catch to the idealization of the person of the COAS was that if ever this 'Messiah' was to take charge openly, it would be through a military coup and martial law, which had every time eventually been defeated by the democratic and multiethnic federal nature of Pakistan's body politic. And it was more the position of the COAS than the persona per se of the person occupying that post which carried that messianic aura, with the person once having retired from that post losing all so-called popularity and influence.

---

[78] "*Hitler hated the Weimar Republic* because *it was weak and he admired the industrial and military leaders because they had power. He never fought against established strong power but always against groups which he thought to be essentially powerless. Hitler's- and for that matter, Mussolini's-"revolution" happened under protection of existing power and their favorite objects were those who could not defend themselves.*" (Eric Fromm in his book 'Escape of Freedom' chapter 5 'Mechanisms of Escape')

This fact was recognized even by the political generals in the military, who were bent on keeping political parties as far from real power as possible. And with the defeat, fourth time around, of their fourth stint of direct power in the form of the ouster of General Musharraf, the realization had set in that repeated martial laws were becoming an impossibility in face of the growing assertion by the major political parties commanding the sway of the electorate of a multiethnic, diverse, federal country with the sixth largest population in the world at the time.

Even during the last two stints of direct power by the military during the regimes of General Zia ul Haq and General Musharraf, the military rule had to rely heavily on launching and ensuring victory of their "King's party" in elections, which they could not put off due to the force of history and objective circumstance[79], and less on directly placing military officers as direct rulers ('Martial Law Administrators' or military rulers) of districts, provinces and the country. On the other hand, it was also clear to the political generals that with the exponentially growing population of the country, the population and the concentration in cities of the urban middle class had also increased in proportion, sufficient to have enough nuisance value and paralyzing effect for any political government in power. They knew that this urban middle class had traditionally been anti-constitution and pro-martial laws and extensively occupied influential positions in the civil bureaucracy, military, judiciary, and the print and electronic media. Therefore, whereas it was a fact that it had become increasingly difficult to impose further martial laws in the country, it was also a fact that the urban middle class with all their prejudices and contempt for pluralistic politics had grown too in population and influence and for the intelligent political generals the time was ripe to shift the image of the 'Messiah' from

---

[79] In the author's view the force of history and objective circumstance being: the increasing reluctance on part of governments of western democratic countries towards the end of the Cold War to be associated with and support military dictators in the third world, the exponential growth in population of Pakistan, which as a multi ethnic federated state could not continue to be ruled by direct martial laws and it was imperative for any driver of the state to engage with and govern the majority civilian population through politics, the Charter of Democracy (CoD) signed in London in 2006 majorly between the PPP and the PML-N and the passing of the 18th amendment to the constitution in 2010 restoring the federal democratic essence of the 1973 constitution and building into the constitution the impossibility for the judiciary to validate the imposition of a martial law.

themselves to a political leader from the urban middle class. This leader was to hold enough sway over the solipsistic imaginations of the urban middle class to fire them into abusing the liberties provided by the constitution through the electorate to checkmate those political parties whose leaders were no longer in the generals' control. But who could that ideal candidate be, that perceived nonmilitary 'Messiah'? Knowing the solipsistic nature of the Pakistani body politic which made the criteria for voting to revolve more around personalities and personality worship, with solipsistic personal identifications projected onto the person of the leader one would vote for, that ideal candidate had to be someone who possessed the stature of a national hero but at the same time who had the same mindset of contempt for pluralistic politics and the federalist essence of the country as did the political generals and the urban middle class.

This ideal candidate, as we all know very well now, was found in the person of Imran Khan, the ex-captain of the country's cricket team, which had won the World Cup in 1992.

Here, we will have to take a pause in the chapter and reflect and dwell for a while just on the uniqueness of the persona of Imran Khan and how it is that this persona found popular resonance among the Pakistani urban middle class in the most electrifying manner, even more than was expected or liked by the political generals who had catapulted him into the seat of power in 2018.

The case of Imran Khan is not the case of just another puppet propped up by the military whereby the pro-military or pro-martial law sections of the population go along with this puppet just because the military propped it up. That kind of trend holds good for individuals like Mohammad Khan Junejo when he was propped up as prime minister by General Zia ul Haq, Nawaz Sharif in the 1990s when he was backed fully by the political generals against Benazir Bhutto, and successively for Zafarullah Khan Jamali and Shaukat Aziz when they were propped up as prime ministers by General Musharraf. In all these cases, the urban middle class played along till each of these listed individuals either fell out of military favor or no longer held power. Once these individuals were out of favor and out of power, they were done and dusted with and forgotten by the urban middle class.

The examples of Zulfiqar Ali Bhutto and Nawaz Sharif are two cases where we see the popularity of these individuals continuing even after these two leaders had fallen out of favor or were out of power. However, for these two leaders, the popularity was not as pervasive among the urban middle class as has been for Imran Khan for one main pertinent reason: the reason of self-identification.

In the cases of both Bhutto and Nawaz Sharif, these two individuals belonged to the upper classes of Pakistan. Therefore, the extent to which a solipsist individual of the urban middle class identifies himself on a personal level with them becomes limited after a certain degree. With Imran Khan, it is not just easiest for an individual of the urban middle class to identify with because Imran Khan himself belongs to the same class, but also because each individual of the urban middle class identifying oneself with Imran Khan is projecting his own self onto the persona of Imran Khan and perceiving him to be what he perceives himself to be, whereas in fact Imran Khan himself may not be at all what he is being perceived to be.

Thus, a middle-class individual with a liberal outlook on life views Imran Khan as a liberal. A democratic-minded middle-class individual considers Imran Khan as a democrat. A middle-class individual with a religious bent of mind considers Imran Khan as an Islamic leader. And intellectually sophisticated middle-class Pakistanis think that Imran Khan is as sophisticated as themselves. All these perceptions exist side by side among his supporters, with each perception thinking that Imran Khan is tactfully dealing with the other perception but actually he is really "what I perceive him to be."

This unity of opposites is also reflected in the colors of the PTI flag which contains both green (traditionally the color of Islamism in Pakistan) and red (perceived as the color of the Left or socialism in Pakistan). This solipsism projected onto the persona of Imran Khan continues regardless of the facts about Imran Khan's life and the actual behavior of Imran Khan himself, which at various times will contradict the self-made and self-projected perception about him by his supporter from the urban middle class.

But even if contradicting facts from Imran Khan's life and behavior are presented to his supporters from the urban middle class, they will either go into denialist mode, terming that presentation as a falsehood, or try to justify these facts and behavior through endless mental gymnastics, which would not withstand an interrogation based on pure logic or rationalization.

Before we attempt to find out who the real Imran Khan is, we have to understand why his personality gripped the minds of the urban middle class in such an overarching and irrational way.

Till the early years after the downfall of General Musharraf and before he was launched as a front-runner leader of the country by the political generals of the country, Imran Khan was an unwinnable candidate politically, but he was immensely popular and respected as a national sports hero in Pakistan. Since the early 1970s, the young and old generation of that time and generations coming after them had lived, breathed, and grown with the rise of Imran Khan as a star of cricket in their lifetimes. So that by 2011, which can be pinned down as the year when the aspirations of the urban middle class converged with the new strategy of political generals to formally launch Imran Khan as a frontrunner in politics[80], in a period of 40 years, Imran Khan had become a virtual household member of almost all Pakistanis, as if he was a cousin or uncle or son, or love interest (in case of females) for each of them. As if he was them and as if, each male thought that 'he is me' and each female thought that 'he is mine' or 'I am his'. All generals, judges and media persons who worked to bring him to power, keep him there and stuck with him when he was thrown out of power and provided him with insider facilitation, grew up with him with his presence always in the background of their households as a source of pride for them. He became a culminating personification of the Pakistani middle class, all aspects and tendencies, even if contradictory to one another, rolled into one embodiment. This has been a unique socio-psychological collective experience of Pakistanis, starting in the same year as East Pakistan was seceding from them and the new post-1971 Pakistan emerging out of it.

---

[80] 'Explaining the rise of Imran Khan' by Huma Yusuf
(https://foreignpolicy.com/2011/10/31/explaining-the-rise-of-imran-khan/)

We have to understand why it happened. Why did it not happen with any other sports hero and why with Imran Khan? There have been other sports heroes for Pakistan, much greater than Imran Khan, like the squash champions Jahangir Khan and Jansher Khan, whose performance and achievements belong only to them as individuals, while in the case of Imran Khan, achievements in his sport, cricket, rely more on the efforts of the whole team. Or for that matter, Pakistan's great hockey players who won the world championships multiple times for the country.

So why did Jahangir Khan and Jansher Khan or the hockey greats not become those kinds of virtual household members as did Imran Khan? What psychological factors are in play here?

Cutting to the chase and shunting aside all beating about the bush which may come with overthinking, the answer is really very simple, staring directly at our face, but it is threefold. And it is that threefold pack which needs to be unpacked and got rid of, 'thrown into the Arabian Sea,' putting it rhetorically, if Pakistanis are to move forward as a mature nation state, free of personality cult, fascism, and fascist psychology, and worthy of constitutional institutionalizing and the stability and progress that comes with it.

The threefold answer is: (i) the looks of Imran Khan, (ii) his proficiency in the English language as an alumnus of the Oxford university in Britain, and (iii) his conquest of white women.

The first reaction to this answer can be one of jest or dismissiveness. How can a complex political phenomenon be reduced to this kind of seemingly superficial oversimplification?

But it is the author's considered, reflected opinion, which I will attempt to defend with logical interrogation and explanation, that the causes of the overwhelming socio psychological sway that the personality of Imran Khan holds over the imagination of Pakistanis, the middle class in particular, can be found in this threefold answer and the psychological nuances on which this answer rests.

Not only in Pakistan, but in the whole of the Indian subcontinent, particularly in the northern half of it, there is a fascination and awe with the fair color of skin and beauty features of the face more aligned and identifiable with beauty features belonging to the human species residing towards the west of the subcontinent. This definition of beauty further gets promoted to be the epitome of beauty when the beauty features under scrutiny seem more European, more of the Greco-Roman Caucasian kind.

This fascination and awe are not without reason. The Indian subcontinent has been attacked and invaded almost always from the West all through its history and was eventually subjugated under colonialism by a foreign power belonging to Western Europe, the British. Therefore, it is only natural that in the collective subconscious mind, the conquerors from the West loom large as the winners and of superior strength and wit, in possession of and master of that superior wisdom, technological or societal, which outwitted and knocked out the indigenous people and rulers of the subcontinent.

This is the curse of colonialism. The curse of being conquered and subjugated and the curse of being so effectively demoralized by the conquerors that even if unwillingly, unwittingly, or unknowingly, this awe seeps deep into the collective conscious of a subjugated and colonized people. The task of liberation is really never complete just by the end of the physical colonization, but also only when the mind breaks itself completely free of this awe.

And so it has happened in the case of Pakistan, that even though the British left, there had been no socio psychological movement, no social reformers, who had done any work to break this awe in the minds. In fact, not only was this awe of the western white-skinned man not broken, but independence for the territories constituting Pakistan had been attained looking down on the rest of the non-Muslim Indian subcontinent as a land and people who had been previously conquered by the ancestors of those who were making Pakistan before the British arrived. This has already been discussed in more detail in the previous chapters of the book.

So the struggle was to free ourselves from those who had conquered us, but keep intact and reinstate ourselves as part of the heritage of the conquerors from the West and rid ourselves of any possibility ever of being governed by those whom we had always conquered and ruled.

That is why, to this day, even in the streets, villages, and hovels of Pakistan, even among the poorest sections of the population, this awe pervades so deep that white skin and western features are considered as some kind of virtue, and dark skin and less Aryan and more Dravidian features are looked down on not just as some kind of disability but even as if it were a vice to look like that.

In the case of the rest of India, this slavish mindset was broken to a certain degree by various Indian reformers, but above all by the completely rejectionist figure of Gandhi, who by living example rejected and inspired rejection of any awe for visible symbolism of western superiority and, through the symbolism of the 'charkha' (the spinning wheel), imbued in his followers, including the future leaders of India, a passion for self-reliance.

It is in this context of socio psychological mindset that for Pakistanis, whenever a figure appeared who seemed to surpass and look better, sound better than the westerners on the criteria of their own western culture, language, and mannerism, then it was this figure who had to be their hero. And on top of that, if they saw western ladies dropping dead and being bowled over by the beauty, vocabulary, and style of that hero, this was their man, their blue-eyed boy to be proud of. Because what more satisfying can it be for the ego of a conquered people when their hero goes out and conquers the bodies and souls of their conquerors' women?

It speaks for the deeply ingrained male chauvinism of a primitive oriental society where a woman's body is seen as the carrier of honor, whereas the body of a man is seen as the weapon through which any honor can be deflowered. If the genders were reversed and Imran Khan was a female conquering white men, he or so to say, she, would be labeled as a hussy whose very life would be under threat of honor killing in her (his) own country.

But since he was a man, so all promiscuity was forgiven, as long as it was white women who were being conquered. He was our pride. And we opened the doors of our homes to include him as one of our family. There was no one else around like him.

This perfection in beauty features, particularly of the Greco Roman kind with a fair skin, this proficiency in speaking English sounding even better than the British, and this long line of white women fallen in love or infatuation for him, all this belonged to no other sportsman of Pakistan, for that matter to no one else in Pakistan, but to Imran Khan.

So, it was he who was the best, he was the one who had to be right in everything, he was the one who had to be the purest of them all (notwithstanding any promiscuous liaisons he may have indulged in), and he was the one who had to be the most non-corrupt of them all. Any facts or proof of his factual behavior that indicated anything otherwise were either met with outright denial or mental gymnastics to explain why that in fact was the best thing that could be done by anyone.

And when he entered politics, he was the one who had to rule and all others were just corrupt, petty pygmies who either had to now go away or subordinate themselves to him, because he said so. The one to be supported was supposed to be better than us, on these criteria. How could people who looked like us or even lesser in looks and style than us be our leaders? Those were the ones who had to be ridiculed and humiliated if ever they were placed in the seat of power over our heads. Unless of course, it was a general who sat on us by force of a military coup, so back to basics, the original thread line of the middle-class story.

In his attempt to show himself higher than the British, when Imran Khan used the term 'brown sahib' to degrade the political system and the civil military bureaucracy left by the British which had been continued to be used post-independence as the foundational basis to run the country, it was not as if he was some kind of a revolutionary who would replace all those systems with a more progressive system he had in mind. But it actually meant that he was asking the 'brown sahibs' to replace their awe of the British and western systems with an awe for him, in that he was better than the westerners on the same criteria which were the basis of that awe.

And then, when the awe shifted towards him, and it was expected of him to give something more progressive, he came up with asking the people to subscribe to either his personal dictatorship or to primitive retrograde fundamentalist views held by the likes of the Taliban[81], which

---

[81] It is a matter of record validated over the course of years in various electronic and print media that Imran Khan vocally sided with the Taliban in their war with the United States, he was proposed by the Taliban themselves to be their spokesman in negotiations with the government of Pakistan, his government provided financial assistance in the millions to seminaries which were the source of training for the recruits of the Taliban, during his

was a step back into a dark past rather than a step forward into a bright future.

The fact was that the fascination and awe of the white man had never gone away, and he himself and his followers were the quintessential 'brown sahibs' who believed in bettering the British on their own superficial criteria of looks, mannerism, and behavior, and believed in conquest rather than understanding the real reasons for the progressiveness of western democratic societies without abandoning one's own indigenous heritage. The usage of the term 'brown sahib' for others while being one himself was as big a self-deception as was the later slogan of 'Absolutely Not' attributed to him, answering a hypothetical proposition of providing air bases to the USA, whereas in fact, by his actions he had made Pakistan capitulate to the IMF (International Monetary Fund)[82] and to US / British interests by de facto closing down the CPEC (China Pakistan Economic Corridor) project during his tenure in government. Externally, while he adopted a religious Islamist image and overtones, he preferred to campaign for his ex-brother-in-law Zac Goldsmith against the Pakistani-origin Sadiq Khan in the elections for the mayorship of London, and when incarcerated

---

government in the name of mainstreaming the Taliban instead of scientific approach being tutored in Islamic seminaries the reactionary fundamentalist outlook was entered into the textbooks of mainstream schools in Pakistan, under the watch of his government many Taliban prisoners escaped under dubious circumstances, his political competitors were gunned down by the Taliban during elections in the northwestern province of Khyber Pakhtunkhwa, he declared Osama bin Laden as a 'martyr' in a speech in parliament, during the August 2021 takeover of Afghanistan by the Taliban he stated that 'the Taliban have broken the shackles of slavery' while women across Afghanistan were being brought to a condition of literal enslavement and his intelligence chief was found in Kabul liaising for the successful formation of the Taliban government, he advocated the Taliban move to close down education for Afghan girls by stating that the Pashtuns culturally did not want their girls to go to school and during his tenure in government the Taliban were rehabilitated in the Khyber Pakhtunkhwa province who later destroyed the writ of the state in the territories where they had been rehabilitated and entered into armed combat with the Pakistan army.

[82] The government of Nawaz Sharif had succeeded in exiting Pakistan from the IMF program in 2016, but Imran Khan's government went back to IMF although it had been Imran Khan's slogan that he would prefer 'to commit suicide rather than go to the IMF'. In fact, in January 2022 Imran Khan's government got a bill passed in parliament which abided to an IMF dictation to free the state bank of Pakistan from government control for the first time in the history of the country and stopped the government borrowing from the bank. This effectively, under the stance for giving autonomy to the state bank, made it easier for the IMF to have the state bank act according to its conditions and made it difficult for the government of Pakistan to control the monetary policy.

ended up groveling to US lobbyists to ask the US government to interfere in Pakistan's internal affairs and get him released. It is only a 'brown sahib', intellectually unaware of the historical thread of epistemology which joins, not pits against each other, the West with the Orient, and who is unaware of the real indigenous culture to which he belongs, who substitutes superficial symbols of perceived racial superiority with chauvinism of primitive and contemporarily bankrupt reactionary orthodoxy, prisoner to the same kind of supremacist counter-racism, whose character is most likely to be compromised to come full circle and fall subservient to the very colonialist domination he claims to remove. In other words, empty vessels make the most noise.

Returning to the main topic of this chapter, we have already talked about the solipsism which drove the migrant dominant culture at the time of the inception of the country which looked down on the indigenous culture of the territories comprising Pakistan, and the solipsistic hatred in return which it received from the indigenous cultures. We have talked about the solipsistic middle class envy and resentment which drives it to belittle and work against the upper classes of society and which glorifies military coups carried out by military officers of middle class backgrounds, and we have just now talked about the solipsism at the root of the personality worship of Imran Khan.

But, in the post Zia ul Haq period, eventually the compartmentalization in Pakistan became so acutely solipsistic in political manifestations that the reason for political support or opposition for an individual became myopically internalized based on very personalized basis for like or dislike of political figures. So, the majority electorate of the three smaller provinces could not bring themselves to vote for a national political figure emerging for the first time from the biggest province of Punjab, that is Nawaz Sharif, more so in consideration of the fact that General Zia ul Haq was ethnically a Punjabi who always backed Nawaz Sharif as his foremost political protégé, and the Pakistan Army imposing his military rule across the country was also predominantly Punjabi by numbers.

The Punjabi majority electorate in turn voted mostly for Nawaz Sharif just because of him being a Punjabi. However, most of those who had historically been with the Pakistan People's Party (PPP) could just not bring themselves to vote for Nawaz Sharif because he had initially been a protégé of General Zia ul Haq, who had hanged Bhutto, the founding leader of the PPP. These PPP supporters were so invested in their personal dislike of Nawaz Sharif that in his fallout with General Musharraf and the eventual military coup carried out by General Musharraf, they could not stand by the principle of siding with the elected prime minister of the country being illegally removed by a general, and many of them in fact supported General Musharraf during his tenure[83].

Later, when the Pakistan Tehreek e Insaf (PTI) was brought up by machinations of the country's military intelligence forces, these same PPP supporters chose to join PTI just out of spite for Nawaz Sharif, abandoning the democratic principle of not siding with the machinations and subversions of political generals.

Similarly, the majority of the Urdu speaking community (descendants of migrants from the non-Punjabi territories of post British India) chose to support General Musharraf just because General Musharraf also belonged to this Urdu speaking community, and in a tussle between an Urdu speaking and a Punjabi it was a no brainer for them where they would stand, all the more so because it also satisfied a secret resentful wish to get back at the Punjabis who had been the prime ethnic group, being in the majority with organic cultural connection with the biggest province of the country, which had gradually and naturally overtaken them in the state's power brokering. Later, post Musharraf, most of them chose to side with the PTI just because of this spite for Nawaz Sharif.

Opposition to Nawaz Sharif, a figure from central Punjab, is also seen among 'Seraikis' (speakers of the Seraiki language) who also find more resonance with Imran Khan, him being in turn the son of a 'Seraiki' father[84].

---

[83] Pakistan People's Party 'Patriots' formed after the elections of 2002 was the prime example of this phenomenon

[84] Imran Khan's father Ikramullah Khan Niazi was an ethnic Pathan belonging to Mianwali, a city in the Seraiki speaking belt of Punjab while his mother Shaukat Khanum belonged to a migrated East Punjabi family of Burki Pathans. Both sides of the family were distant descendants of Pashtun tribes now speaking the Seraiki and Punjabi languages respectively.

Most of the country's Shias traditionally supported the PPP because Bhutto's wife, Nusrat Bhutto, was a Shia and this became even more personal because the man who removed Bhutto, General Zia ul Haq, was a Sunni Wahabi with even an agenda to impose this version of Islamism on the country. Their spite for Nawaz Sharif continued for the same reason of him initially having been a favorite of General Zia ul Haq, and they too mostly supported General Musharraf and later the PTI for this reason.

Wahabi elements in Pakistan were mostly found to be siding with Nawaz Sharif and considering the PPP an anti-Islam party, some even considering it as a Shia party.

Agrarian classes mostly also sided with the PPP or PTI, wary of increased power for an urban capitalist.

Wannabe revolutionaries for whom rebellion against a state and a capitalist dispensation, which tilted towards Western capitalism and did not rail against the USA, was more important and the preferred mode of existence than the stability and prosperity of the economy with the status quo intact, they too joined every move in the country which could lead to a confrontation between government and people, between state and people, and the toppling of an election-based system where only the monied people had more chances to win. The state was looked at as if it was still a colonial state and the property, assets, and installations of the state were open game for destruction and carnage, even if this caused loss in the millions or billions to the state exchequer. For a 'revolutionary' too it is easy to, if not support a military coup, to coexist with it as he would with a constitutionally elected dispensation, because for a 'revolutionary' all law is the law of a decadent system which he has already declared as illegitimate, and it does not matter if that law is trampled by martial law. For a 'revolutionary' too, the accepted worldview is that 'might is right', and whosoever can overpower the other, even through force, gains the right to rule.

The result of this internalized solipsism was that an individual affected by it could not externally provide or voice a rational reasoning for his or her political support or opposition, nor could he stand the test of objective facts, which would clearly show that his choice was not correct. So, instead of rational reasoning, the reasoning was externally oversimplified into resorting to blanket labeling or branding of political adversaries, an attempt to dehumanize them, as 'corrupt' or 'looters' or 'chor/daaku' (Urdu for thieves and dacoits), and those being favored as the 'honest' ones.

And of course, the 'honest' ones were those favored by the military because how could 'self-made' officers coming from middle-class backgrounds running the most efficient organization in the country not be honest? This dominant narrative was adopted while ignoring in a stride that facts would show that the reason why the military was left as the only efficient organization in the country was because all other institutions and departments had been destroyed and neglected due to long periods of military rule, with military officers even entering as heads into nonmilitary departments and institutions, which was the most dishonest and corrupt thing that could be done to a country, not to speak of the heavy involvement of military officers in corruption and smuggling.

The point is not whether the allegations of corruption against democratically elected and popular politicians were correct or not, but the fact that these allegations were hurled with prejudice, without any substantiating evidence and without any stomach for due legal process, considering these allegations as enough reason to conspire against, subvert, and bring down elected governments by any means possible. And all the while choosing to ignore, again with prejudice, that the protagonists who were being supported to replace these political leaders were, maybe in fact, and in many instances, visibly proven, the really corrupt or more corrupt than the legitimate elected governments being brought down[85]. 'Corruption' was never the real issue with those clamoring that corruption was the biggest ill of the country. The real issue was their hatred and

---

[85] The trend for the Corruption Perception Index (CPI) reported by Transparency International shows that Pakistan reached an all-time high in corruption perception of 144 out of 180 countries in the ranking for 'least corrupt countries' in the year 2005, which was the period when Pakistan was under the rule of General Musharraf. It was as low as 116 in the year 2016 under the regime of Nawaz Sharif (meaning that it was the 116th least corrupt country) and during the regime of Imran Khan in the years 2021 and 2022 it returned to a high of 140. (https://tradingeconomics.com/pakistan/corruption-rank). The serious cases of corruption against Imran Khan and of the PTI regime are further examples of this socio psychological contradiction and self-deception.

189

prejudice against those they had already made up their minds, for personal solipsistic reasons, to dislike and oppose.

We see, therefore, that it is solipsism and solipsistic personal reasons, and not reasons of the political manifesto or performance in government of a party, which compel an electorate to vote the way it votes if it is not motivated by economic class interests through any organized class movement or if it has not educated itself consciously to mature and vote with the larger interest of the country in mind. If this solipsism is not overpowered and eliminated and persists, a political party or government can display the best performance and service to the people, but when elections come again those driven by this solipsism who had opposed them before will still vote against them, and those they had supported before due to this solipsism will again receive their votes.

Solipsism is thus not only a major nuisance in the body politic of the country but becomes harmful for the country's interests when it affects and overwhelms the educated middle class of the country like a psychological disease or contagion.

This solipsism became all the more harmful when this contagion gripped the Pakistani middle class residing outside the country.

There have been two kinds of Pakistanis who left the country to earn a living or even settle down abroad.

One was the category of people who mostly belonged to the working class or the lower middle class who went outside due to poor economic conditions inside the country for the sake of survival of their families back home and eventually raising the standards of their living as they continued to stay longer outside.

The second category has been of people for whom survival was not the issue, who belonged to the middle or upper middle class of the country. This category of people left the country in search of prosperity much more than they perceived they could achieve by staying back in the country. The search was for receiving the maximum dividend possible by the maximization of their potential in societies which they perceived could maximize their potential, and Pakistan was not that society.

This second category of expatriate Pakistanis has proven to be the most adversarial and misrepresentative of Pakistan's interests when gripped by the solipsism which this book speaks about. The first category also joins the second category in being affected by this solipsism, as survival becomes less of a concern for its continued residence outside Pakistan, and it becomes more affluent.

It needs to be understood that what was the vocal rationale for leaving the country that the second category of expatriates voiced when leaving Pakistan? The rationale has not been limited to just the fact that we are leaving to maximize our potential to receive maximum dividends for ourselves, in other words, for purely selfish reasons.

Since the issue was not just survival, because if it is for survival the person is blameless, an element of guilt entered the equation in the conscience of the departing individual. This guilt needed to be addressed because if the issue was not survival, then the individual could stay in the country and everything that he or she would then do would be a direct part of the country's nation building and a direct life's work of contribution to that end. But the departing individual was abandoning that role, so this feeling of guilt needed to be addressed.

This feeling of guilt was addressed in two ways. First, the guilt was transferred from the individual onto the country which was being left behind. The country's system was bad, there was nothing for the individual in that country because the system was rotten, the people running it were corrupt, and nothing was fixable in the country. All the time forgetting that it was the same country which had produced this accomplished and educated individual badmouthing it now. Secondly, it was voiced that this departing individual will do and could do more for the country once outside the country. He[86] will send back money as remittance, as if this will be the real force driving the country without which the country will collapse, and he will make the country proud by his achievements abroad and his representation as a Pakistani to the outside world with his conduct. He will become the sole spokesman of Pakistan and not the ones living inside Pakistan. He will be the representation of the good Pakistani and not those living inside Pakistan. He is the better Pakistani and not those

---

[86] The gender 'he' or 'him' will be used here for ease of discourse, just as the word 'Man' is used often to represent 'human being'

living inside Pakistan. He loved his country Pakistan so much that for its sake he was going to take the oath of loyalty to another country.

The result of this twofold solipsistic rationale has in turn manifested itself among expatriates of Pakistani origin in two ways:

Firstly, although Pakistani expatriates may spend their whole lives outside Pakistan, they remain constantly passionate about politics inside Pakistan more than about the politics and contemporary issues of the country they chose as the country of their new citizenship.

Secondly, they have historically and majorly always backed military coups which were brought about in Pakistan, blaming the politicians for its occurrence because this narrative aligns with their voiced rationale of leaving the country that the country's system and those running it were bad. Therefore, whenever a general, trampling over the constitution of the country, that is its system, took arbitrary and dictatorial power, here was a like-minded individual who had stepped out of the box like "us," and he was going to fix the system from outside. We were the physical expatriates; this military dictator is the mental expatriate.

Enter Imran Khan, who not only, like the military adventurer, badmouthed the home country's system, but also glowed as the Greco-Roman Godlike figure, looking and sounding better than the white man in whose country we now live, so let us tell the white man, this is our leader, better than you, so we are no less than you, in fact better than you.

What a military dictator or Imran Khan did inside the country was immaterial. How any of their actions may have been illegal or unconstitutional, how they may have destroyed any institutions, imprisoned people with no legal or evidentiary basis, how they may have compromised the security or economic interests of the country, and how they destroyed the social fabric of society through their divisive politics, was not a matter of study or serious logical discussion for them. What mattered was the outer face, the optics of false strength and swagger. The imagery of glamour. It was this which satisfied their egos, and ego is nothing but solipsism refined.

To be an expatriate is not a crime. To change passports is not a crime, not only legally but even morally. But what is a crime legally is to side with the violation of the home country's constitution. What is a crime morally is to badmouth the home country and those running it under its constitutional mandate when you yourself have chosen to leave the country. And even worse, it is a crime, legally as well as morally, to actively take part in any effort that would threaten, sabotage, or badmouth the democratically formulated and evolved constitutional dispensation of your home country or in any way throw a spanner in the works for its economy.

Before we conclude this chapter on the solipsism which pervades the Pakistani zeitgeist, a final observation is made with respect to a 'chicken first or egg first' like question.

It has normally been perceived and said in Pakistan that it is the military which is the real boss and whatever stance or direction the military will adopt at a certain time will be towed blindly by the media and the political forces, specially by those middle classes which we have spoken about who always supported martial laws or military interferences in the politics of the country.

While this proposition has been challenged all along the country's history and shown to be not always true, thanks to the democratic and constitutional struggle of the organic economic classes of the country and their intellectuals and activists (about which we will discuss more in the next chapter), it is also true that on closer observation this proposition also falls flat when interrogated in context of the urban middle classes who seem to always have been glorifying the military and the generals, eager to follow them in whichever direction they took them.

This book proposes that it is not the political generals per se who are the prime drivers of military takeover and military interference, in other words, the real bosses who steer the country and its people through direct or indirect military interference. But it is the three "Ms" mindset identified in this book, which is the real boss of such subversion, the real disease that repeatedly resulted in military takeovers and interference.

If ever an army chief chose not to impose martial law or interfere in politics to subdue the politicians and the constitutional process in the country, or in fact actively sided with it, that army chief was considered a weakling and a figure of ridicule and joke by the constitution-hating middle classes.

It is they who cannot digest the continuation of a constitutional dispensation in which they see the upper classes of the country dominating the political scene. They expect the army chief to bring down such a system, although they know that if he does that it would be illegal and unconstitutional. But if he does not do that, then he is a traitor, because he is a traitor to their class[87].

So, if there is an army of the enemies of constitution and pluralist democracy in Pakistan, then the boss of that army is not the chief of Pakistan's military which has had a history of imposing martial laws in the country. The boss of any such army is that part of the Pakistani middle class which is fascist leaning because of being beset with the three 'Ms' mindset, identified in this book, as its originating subconscious.

---

[87] *"There is one feature of the authoritarian character which has misled many observers: a tendency to defy authority and to resent any kind of influence from "above." Sometimes this defiance overshadows the whole picture and the submissive tendencies are in the background. This type of person will constantly rebel against any kind of authority, even one that actually furthers his interests and has no elements of suppression. Sometimes the attitude toward authority is divided. Such persons might fight against one set -of authorities, specially if they are disappointed by its lack of power, and at the same time or later on submit to another set of authorities which through greater power or greater promises seems to fulfill their masochistic longings. Finally, there is a type in which the rebellious tendencies are completely repressed and come to the surface only when conscious control is weakened; or they can be recognized ex posteriori, in the hatred that arises against an authority when its power is weakened and when it begins to totter. In persons of the first type in whom the rebellious attitude is in the center of the picture, one is easily led to believe that their character structure is just the opposite to that of the submissive masochistic type. It appears as if they are persons who oppose every authority on the basis of an extreme degree of independence. They look like persons who, on the basis of their inner strength and integrity, fight those forces that block their freedom and independence. However, the authoritarian character's fight against authority is essentially defiance. It is an attempt to assert himself and to overcome his own feeling of powerlessness by fighting authority, although the longing for submission remains present, whether consciously or unconsciously. The authoritarian character is never a "revolutionary"; I should like to call him a 'rebel.' There are many individuals and political movements that are puzzling to the superficial observer because of what seems to be an inexplicable change from 'radicalism' to extreme authoritarianism. Psychologically, these people are the typical 'rebels.' "* (Eric Fromm in his book 'Escape of Freedom' chapter 5 'Mechanisms of Escape')

Statecraft, Upper Classes

As discussed earlier, in August 1947 when the state of Pakistan came into being, the territories comprising the western wing of the country, West Pakistan, were predominantly in the feudal or tribal stage of social and economic development. Urban industrialization was nominal, as was urbanization, and heavy industry was nonexistent. The genuine indigenous upper classes of West Pakistan consisted of feudal landlords and tribal chieftains.

And as discussed earlier too, the bulk of urban demographics after the formation of Pakistan was filled by the migrant populations from the territories of post-British India, who majorly contributed by occupying positions in the civil bureaucracy running the new state. Any business families that preexisted in the urban areas of West Pakistan were involved in trading, banking, or an infant textile industry, but there were no Pakistani capitalists owning and running heavy industry like machines' manufacturing, which has historically been the spine of the industrial revolution in the West. Possession of technological knowledge or wherewithal was absent.

Many scholarly studies and well-researched books with exhaustive statistics have already been written to analyze the growth of industry and business in Pakistan over the years and the agriculture-based economy of the country through which the country exported food commodities and raw materials to the world.

The objective of this book and this chapter is not to delve into any such statistical analyses, but to see how whatever modes of economic production existed when the state came into being were important as a launching pad for effective statecraft and nation building, and how these should be allowed to advance to the next modern stages in a way which is beneficial for the people as well as for social cohesiveness and the stability of the state.

In the course of mankind's history, as is very well known, human society has moved from primitive stages of development to advanced stages of development through wars, conquest, revolutions, mass upheavals, all underpinned by physical violence. This physical violence happened every time those who had power and control over the means of production, and the state manifestations of that power and control, resisted and did not cooperate with the change that was required to move into the advanced stage of development.

We have seen this in Europe in the form of wars as states were formed under monarchies and feudalism from the previous stage of scattered tribalism and primitive slave societies, as the continent gave birth to bourgeois capitalism from the womb of dying feudalism, primarily in the form of the French Revolution of 1789, and as communist revolution attempted to overtake capitalism with socialism after the success of the Russian Revolution in 1917.

This story of monumental tussle between the opposers of proposed change and the advocates of it has not just been violent but also filled with bitterness and hatred against the other among the contesting parties. Such hatred also gave way, as a side effect, to the rise of fascism and fascist states in the 20th century AD, which were overpowered by the forces of democracy through great effort, and human society was brought back to the main track of economic evolution and a sane and civilized dialogue and interaction between the state and the citizen in democracies.

However, as the 20th century AD approached its end and as communism and communist states failed and collapsed on the anvil of history, humankind suddenly took pause, took a deep breath, and got the opportunity to think whether the trendline of progressive change was really the one that had been accepted for so long as political correctness based on the readings proposed by Marxism. That is, from primitive man to tribalism to slave societies to feudalism to capitalism to socialism to communism. Was this trendline, which was considered as progressively correct, really correct? Could it be that the proposers and ideologues of revolutionary change had been wrong in some respects? Maybe the conservatives, who always resisted change until it became inevitable, had a point in questioning every proposed change on very strict logical criteria, and maybe some things were better to be maintained or brought back, although improved in many humanist ways.

We see England restoring the monarchy after the era of Cromwell. We see the bloody and ruthless French Revolution, in which many learned intellectuals and people of science were also executed, followed by Napoleon's dictatorship and then his eventual dismissal and the restoration of the French monarchy. We see the de-Stalinization of Soviet Russia where the supposedly 'Leftist' force had politically become a force of 'the Right', that is, anti-people, and so too in its satellite communist states. We see the end of hippieism of the 1970s and the toning down of the sexual revolution in the West that had exploded in the 1960s. We see Zimbabwe destroy itself and its economy through reverse racism after gaining independence, and we see the boom of economic growth of China only after it freed itself from the left-wing infantilism of the Cultural Revolution and communist 'command economy'.

As it objectively stands, on a macro level, the accepted political correctness still arrives at the conclusion that feudalism is better than tribalism once man enters the agricultural mode of production. That capitalism is more modern, advanced, and people-friendly once economy is based on industrial technology, discoveries of science, and forces of free market. And that decentralization, deregulation, employee participation and opportunities for ownership, and government oversight through legislation to ensure the rights of workers and consumers is better and more efficient for the economy than unbridled raw capitalism with concentrated capital in the hands of the few and negligible rights for the many.

However, with the advantage of retrospect at hand, and democracy as currently the foremost accepted concept of political correctness, specially after the defeat of fascism in World War II and the fall and/or discredit of communism and third world military or fascist dictatorships towards the end of the 20th century and the beginning of the 21st century respectively, mankind also sees now that there are nonviolent ways to implement the change which is required, and it is now possible that all parties with a stake with respect to that change can be made to see that. This is a sociopolitical phenomenon which has created the possibility for civilization to become 'more civilized' in matters of social change within societies.

The epitome and first example of such nonviolent but epoch-making revolutionary change in the third world, coming out of the clutches of western colonialism, was demonstrated in India as feudalism was abolished there.

For many, maybe most, it is very easy to say that feudalism was ended in India after independence. They do not take a pause to appreciate the magnitude of what they are talking about. Let anyone try to abolish feudalism in Pakistan today, or in any other country where it still exists, and see how much blood is spilled, and how any such society attempting to do so will implode and the state in which it exists will collapse on itself.

That India ended feudalism after independence is no mean feat, from whichever angle we may look at it. A multiethnic, multinational country in 1947 with a population of about 350 million and about 584 princely states still not incorporated into the federation at the time, faced every risk of civil war and balkanization as the ruling Indian National Congress (INC) proceeded to implement its post-colonial sociopolitical and economic agenda.

Why did it succeed and why was the least possible amount of blood spilled in implementing this reform?

Because the Indian National Congress, led by Prime Minister Nehru, was not just a political party. It had at its back the might of the burgeoning Indian capitalist classes who had already established themselves in the economy in an integral way since decades during British rule. And it had at its base the mental social revolution that had finally been spearheaded by Gandhi in the last decades prior to independence in a way never done before anywhere, and which had fired the imagination of the vast masses of India and generated a new inspiration across the globe.

Without these years of homework, just a political party headed by Nehru or whoever, could never have been successful in implementing its agenda using state power only without any bloodshed. The extensive mass movement of Gandhi, and the different thought process he provided, and the deep roots of the pro-INC capitalistic economic classes in the economy of the emerging new state were too overwhelming for any feudal lord or princeling to put up a worthwhile stand against and succeed.

Now we look at the Pakistan movement and what do we see?

We do not see any burgeoning capitalistic classes as the core supporter of the All India Muslim League (AIML). In fact, we see the Muslim feudal classes of India as its core backer, with the educated Muslim middle classes, who were its cadre, although enlightened due to the works of Sir Syed Ahmed Khan, not challenging the feudal premise of the economy to be inherited in the new state, nor building any anti-feudal movement of thought or action in any way. In fact, as discussed earlier, at the back of even the educated Muslim mindset was the nostalgia and desire for revival and preservation of the Muslim courtiers' culture and supremacy belonging to the pre-British past of Muslim India.

Without any such homework or spadework, it was not possible for anyone, even the Quaid e Azam, to dismantle the feudal or tribal setup that formed the spinal cord of the socio-economic structure of West Pakistan.

In retrospect therefore, and it is famously said that a retrospective analysis provides 20/20 vision, an impersonal objective analysis of the new state of Pakistan that came into being in August 1947 will beget various pertinent questions which should be asked to the exclusion of the external interests favoring the creation of this new state for purposes of their own self-serving designs. That is, the questions that need to be raised in this retrospective analysis have to be related to the internal thought process of the previously colonialized people who were now to be the masters of the new state, the people who were now going to be called Pakistanis.

That a third world feudal state where the socio-economic structure was not going to be changed and where the upper classes of that state, who were feudal or tribal by nature, were in no mood to relinquish their properties, power or privileges, would be more prone to side with that superpower in the world which would keep its status quo intact, is a secondary consideration. The primary consideration should be for any patriotic Pakistani retrospectively analyzing that situation now, as it was for the leaders of the new state in 1947, that such a state with a relatively backward societal stage of development had come into being, it was a reality, and just because the archaic socio-economic structures of the new state were not going to be changed any time soon, did that mean that this state did not deserve to exist or survive? The answer to this question, as it was recognized to be so also by the founding fathers and the father of the nation, the Quaid e Azam at the time, is a resounding 'No'.

Feudal states, or states where patriarchal tribal systems dominate, have existed as sovereign states in human history. Several such sovereign states existed to the west of the West Pakistan of 1947, including Afghanistan, Iran, and Arabian states in the Middle East. Being a predominantly feudal and tribal state did not and does not discredit Pakistan from being a sovereign state in its own right. Not only was this proposition sustainable by the laws of political science, but it was picked up with the correct political acumen by the father of the nation as a matter of realpolitik to be addressed with the attention it deserved.

The Quaid e Azam actively engaged and brought on board the ship of Pakistan all feudal lords, tribal chieftains, and rulers of the princely states from all territories and provinces that were now part of the new state of Pakistan without any agenda for the reform of the socio-economic structure that propped them up as the upper classes of the new state. This was a policy diametrically opposite to the policy of Nehru and the INC in the new state of India, but it was a policy of conservatism with the intention of the survival and the sustenance of the new state in the absence of any movement worth mentioning for social change in the territories that now comprised Pakistan.

So we see the Quaid shaking hands with Nawab Akbar Bugti of Balochistan as his friend and a friend of Pakistan, who was criminally eliminated physically by an illegitimate military dictator many decades later in 2006. We see the feudal gentry of Punjab and Sind teaming up behind the Quaid, the Khans of the North West Frontier Province siding with him against representatives of the INC there, and the rulers of the princely states like Swat, Bahawalpur, Khairpur and Kalat[88] acceding to the new state.

This preservation of the feudal tribal society in Pakistan, with the subsequent dominance of the organic upper classes of such a society in representative politics and the running of the state, was and is undigestible not only for the middle-class mind but also for Marxists and self-proclaimed revolutionaries.

---

[88] The accession of the state of Kalat to Pakistan is a subject of controversy whereby the proponents of an independent state for Balochistan hold the view that the Khan of Kalat was forced to accede by the Pakistani state forces.

It was also undigestible for the leaders and cadre of the INC in undivided India, but they had the degree of maturity to recognize in time that these territories were out of bounds for their influence and their movement for social change, or the strength of the burgeoning classes supporting them was weak in these territories. Perhaps, this was also one of the reasons why, after the results of the 1946 Indian elections, the leaders of the INC eventually softened their stance and finally gave way to the acceptance of the creation of Pakistan.

However, as we will see, that degree of political maturity was and still is lacking in the middle class and the 'revolutionaries' existing in the state of Pakistan. This indigestibility and confusion with regard to the natural dominance of the feudal tribal upper classes in the state of Pakistan, found not only among the middle classes but also the 'revolutionaries' living in it, is where the situation becomes problematic.

There are two major layers of complexities shrouding this problematization, which make this problem unique with respect to Pakistan, and we will peel off these two layers one by one to reach the core substance of the matter.

The first layer of complexity relates to the lack of any noteworthy all-encompassing pre-independence movement for social change that existed in the territories that became Pakistan, mentioned earlier[89]. Due to this absence of a popular movement for social change, both the middle classes of the new state of Pakistan and its 'revolutionaries' fell into the trap of looking for short cuts to counter the dominance of the organic upper classes of the new state. The name of this shortcut was 'military coup'. Reference was made very early in this book to the failed coup of 1951 in which Marxist 'revolutionaries' were supportive and encouraging of that attempt. Indeed, the modus operandi of Soviet-backed 'revolutionary

---

[89] There was a 'red-shirt' movement in the North West Frontier Province (NWFP) led by Khan Abdul Ghaffar Khan, popularly known as 'Bacha Khan', who was influenced in turn by the methods of Gandhi, which sought to bring a change in the thought process of the people of NWFP, but it was limited in extent to its own province and even in its own province it was not owned by an overwhelming majority. Moreover, Bacha Khan's movement also lacked any reciprocity economically as there was no bourgeoning capitalist class in that province to give it legs. It was more of a 'revolution in the mind' than a revolution on ground.

change' in those times had largely been reduced to communists or pro-communist bloc 'revolutionaries' seizing power in their countries through military coups. This method of power capture was inherently anti-democratic and sought to impose a one-party dictatorship and implement social change from the top without any spadework done at the grassroots level in society.

Enough has already been said with respect to the non-Marxist middle class of the country, who were less inclined for real social change per se and more a victim of their resentments and hatred of the organic upper classes of Pakistan, and more interested in just dominating them through state power and eliminating them physically if possible, while no meaningful reforms or policies were introduced to qualitatively change the socioeconomic structure of society.

Indeed, none of the military dictators who ruled Pakistan abolished feudalism in the country and in fact acted like a feudal lord themselves as an institution, the most powerful feudal lord in the country, generating and disseminating feudal attitudes to the lowest rungs of society, all the while engaging with the feudal tribal upper classes as their subjects, coercing them to cooperate with them, without initiating any socioeconomic reforms.

We have already discussed what they did to the Bengalis and how the feudal classes of West Pakistan all ganged up against the Bengalis when the Tenancy Act of 1950 was implemented. In fact, the perpetrators of the civil bureaucracy and military coups in Pakistan proved to be the agents of neocolonialism and defenders of the status quo of the backward socioeconomic structure in the country which allowed the export of raw material to the West, and a market for Western imports, and the establishment of a mechanism for an interest-paying indebted economy.

Therefore, the pose of being an 'anti-feudal middle class' or an 'anti-feudal revolutionary' was more of a deception, even self-deception, and the emphasis was more on the capture of state power through undemocratic means without any real social or economic change on the ground. The possibility of an organic evolutionary change from archaic socioeconomic structures towards modern capitalism was not even considered and neither was a serious study conducted and put into practice to achieve that through democratic means.

The second layer of complexity relates to the political face of a feudal or tribal state. As we mentioned, sovereign states existed to the west of the West Pakistan of 1947 which were feudal or tribal in their socioeconomic structure. However, what was their political face, or what is the political face of a feudal or tribal state? What is the political manifestation in terms of form of government in a state which is predominantly feudal or tribal in nature?

Of course, it is Monarchy. And such was the case of the sovereign states existing to the west of the West Pakistan of 1947. They were monarchies. But could Pakistan be a monarchy? And if so, who would be the monarch?

Monarchs do not turn up overnight. Monarchs are the product of centuries of tribal evolution, of royal families emerging out of tribal pacts and territories acquired over the course of history which pledge allegiance to those royal families. Monarchs are the historical heritage of states from the times when modern democracy had not taken over as the more powerful political phenomenon within the state. That is why monarchies are still kept intact, although as constitutional monarchies, even by modern Western states where now it is democracy and pluralism which rule the roost. Monarchies represent the social balance and equilibrium of human nature in societies which were not foolish to have abolished them through violence and bloodshed and thrown themselves onto the rocky road of instability and then difficult recovery from that instability during the course of which millions of lives suffered and were destroyed.

Monarchies organically ingrained in a society are an asset of that society and wise societies value and preserve them and evolve gradually away from their absolutism. As mentioned earlier, we can see, as an example in Arabia, societies which preserved their monarchies eventually came out as the more stable and prosperous, rather than those in Arabia who fell victim to coups by adventurer military officers who were supposed to be loyal to and saluting their monarchs as the legitimate heads of their states.

The example of Afghanistan is also a case in point, with the society, which was stable and liberalizing and moving forward gradually, sabotaged by the coup against King Zahir Shah, and from there onwards the country only went downhill. Only those societies have succeeded when opting to become a republic where the legacy of a historical monarchy was missing or did not exist. In that case, for any new state achieving independence, it was the wiser option to choose to be a pluralistic constitutional democracy.

The eventual destination of mankind is democracy. But it is the author's considered opinion that the next best thing to democracy is monarchy if a society already has it historically.

Coming back to the complexity related to the new state of Pakistan in 1947, here lay its dilemma. It was a feudal tribal society, but it had no legacy of a locally evolved monarchy, which still existed. The closest candidate to become its monarch, with the consensus of all at that time, could have been the Quaid e Azam himself. He could have become the monarch, and Pakistan could have become a monarchy, with all feudal and tribal upper classes hailing him as their monarch.

In fact, considering that Pakistan had been a product of a movement for Muslim nationalism and renaissance, Quaid e Azam could even be proclaimed Caliph. This is all very good considered in retrospect, theoretically. Practically, neither did this happen nor could it have happened. The biggest reason for this was not just because the Quaid e Azam himself was not on board with any such idea, but because the political machinery that had thrown forth Pakistan as a new state already had a monarch, the King of the United Kingdom (UK), who was to be represented in the new state by his Governor General. This political machinery was built with the nuts and bolts of the Westminster form of democracy, which envisioned a federal state consisting of multiple subsidiary states joining the new state as provinces and with constituency-based representation in the parliament.

All feudal lords, tribal chieftains, and rulers of princely states falling under Pakistan already had their monarch in the person of King George the Sixth, who was to be represented in Pakistan by the Governor General of Pakistan. Thus, it would be a more solid argument, which can be put forth and debated credibly, that whether it would have been wiser for the new country to remain under the British Crown as its sovereign after independence, as did Australia, New Zealand, and Canada and other such countries, rather than opting to become a republic.

However, it goes to the credit of this much of anti-colonial and nationalistic awakening of the Muslim League movement and of the Quaid e Azam, an ex-INC leader himself, that they were clear when they achieved independence in the form of Pakistan that they wanted to shed away all remnants of their allegiance to the British summarily. They could not bring themselves to identify with them racially or religiously and eventually wanted to proclaim themselves as an independent sovereign republic "of their people, for their people, by their people."

So, these were the constituting parameters of the new state, or we can also say the ingredients with which the new recipe was to evolve for the new dish: a predominantly feudal and tribal socioeconomic structure, a civil-military state structure inherited from the departing British rulers, the new state having been successfully created through an exercise of the Westminster form of democracy in which the elected representatives predominantly consisted of individuals of feudal or tribal background. But the body elected thus was the only legitimate and legal entity to exercise power and rule the country. And lastly, the lack of any mass movement for social change or developed capitalist or working classes on the ground which would prove to be an essential prerequisite to rapidly take the territories comprising the western wing of the new state of Pakistan to the next stage of societal development, more in line with a functioning capitalist mode of economy.

In these circumstances, looking back retrospectively, what were the correct choices for anyone running the new state to achieve successful statecraft? And were those correct choices made?

It is the author's considered opinion that those correct choices were not made by those in power, and it is because of that reason that the task of achieving successful statecraft for the state of Pakistan has to this day remained turbulent and problematic. It is for that reason of not making the correct choices in the nascent years of its existence that despite accomplishing many great feats and producing some of the foremost persons and professionals of intellect, science, sports, arts, and business who contributed on an international level to the advancement and betterment of human society, the ship of the state of Pakistan itself has wobbled on the sea of statecraft and always seemed to be an almost failed or a failing state, barely surviving and at risk of capsizing any time.

The correct choice to be made in the foundational or earliest years of the new state of Pakistan would have been to continue the line of action that had been taken by the father of the nation, the Quaid e Azam, in positively engaging with the indigenous upper classes of the territories now constituting Pakistan. Continuing to use the elected parliament, where representatives of those classes were seated, as the mother of all bodies of the state and the source of all legislation, formation of the constitution, and the supreme power of the state exercised through the elected executive derived from that parliament.

The correct choice would have been to acknowledge that the new state was going to be a federation of various subsidiary states, in each of which their organically evolved upper classes would naturally come forth as the most in number as the elected representatives of that subsidiary state. (Here we take a pause in our retrospective analysis and look at the federal states of the United Arab Emirates, where the tribal patriarchal societies of seven emirates—each ruled by an Emir or king—chose to federate into a single federal state and all logical modes of governance entailing from such a federation became part of its constitution; and of Malaysia, where the role of the constitutional monarch is rotated among nine hereditary rulers of nine of the thirteen federating Malayan states, and the federal Malaysian state is a constitutional monarchy.)

If such a choice had been made, there would have been less risk of instability from the outset and there would be more possibility that differences over policy and the way forward could be resolved through debate and voting in the parliament, and the societal shift of the predominantly feudal and tribal socioeconomic structure into a modern capitalist one achieved gradually in due course of time. We will indulge in a discussion about this proposed gradual change in a moment.

However, this correct choice could have been made by individuals in power who were equipped with the required wisdom, political training, and political acumen. By individuals who had sufficiently thought about it before the historical moment arrived for making their choices.

Instead, as we have already discussed in the book in enough detail, those who occupied positions of state power immediately after the creation of the new state were disconnected from the organic economic classes of the territories constituting the new state. The indigenous economic classes of these territories were not stronger than the civil and military organs of the ex-colonial state, and the feeling of compartmentalization thus caused resulted in the feudal upper classes of West Pakistan ganging up with state bureaucracy against the strongest bastion of democratic power at that time—the East Pakistanis and the East Pakistani leaders, who in turn could have compensated for the weakness of the West Pakistani organic economic classes against the power of state bureaucracy if those West Pakistani organic economic classes had chosen to be their allies and not of the state civil and military bureaucracy against the East Pakistanis.

In that sense, someone could still say that if this was the case, that there was a disconnect between the state bureaucracy and the indigenous population of the country, and that the West Pakistani feudal lords were wary of East Pakistani (read Bengali) domination in elected government with all the racism and insecurity about feudalism being thus abolished flowing from that wariness, then maybe it was inevitable what happened. It had to happen that way, and it did, and it could not have been any otherwise.

The response to such a deterministic stance is that firstly, if we accept a deterministic stance on history, we underplay and neglect the value of subjective thought process becoming strong enough to override the determinism of objective circumstances, which has been the prime agent of change in human society. To take the attitude of underplaying and neglecting this value is dangerous for the future as well because those who succumb to this determinism will lose the ability in the present and the future to rise above a situation if they can and change it for the better.

Secondly, taking this deterministic stance would be bad for providing a wholesome and comprehensive scholastic study, as it would overlook the many instances of possibilities that came along the way, where if those possibilities could have been turned into realities, the results could also have been different. For instance, after the elections of 1970, when two different types of political forces had dominated in the two wings of the country respectively, if political dialogue had been allowed to be continued between the two, some mechanism for the continuity and the running of the state could have been agreed upon, including the possibility of a confederation, and the massive bloodshed and secession of East Pakistan that occurred in 1971 could have been avoided. Or, if the general in power had called for the session of the national assembly despite the objections of the political force that was dominant in West Pakistan, then too, some agreement within the national assembly could have been achieved through political dialogue.

Thirdly, to reject such a proposed deterministic stance is important because we are conducting this retrospective analysis for the purpose of learning lessons for the future and at a stage in human history at the cusp of the second quarter of the 21st century AD, when the Cold War is over, when there is more clarity among humanity about communism, military dictatorships are on the backfoot, the West's love affair with immigration is over, technology is much more advanced and has qualitatively changed the way a functional society operates, and humanity is at a much greater distance from the end of colonialism which gives the benefit of greater hindsight in assessing the mistakes made by previously colonialized societies and chalking out a course for their future.

We reject a deterministic way of looking at our history because we believe we can choose to behave differently and for the better if similar circumstances are still found in the present or arise in the future.

So, we establish that the correct choices were not made in the early years of the new state of Pakistan. In the process, approximately one half of the new state was lost. But we find that the other half still exists as Pakistan. The journey of this ship has been turbulent, but it has still not capsized. It is a ship full of hundreds of millions of living souls, and if this ship were to capsize, many millions of lives could be destroyed before the survivors of this 'Titanic' could be rescued.

There is no need for this capsizing. We still have time to apply the correct choices for the state in view of the lessons learnt for similar circumstances from the past. And if these correct choices are made and successfully applied, this ship can sail completely smoothly for the rest of its journey.

Therefore, we bring ourselves back into the present and look at the nature of the socioeconomic structure of Pakistani society as it exists now, at the end of the first quarter of the 21st century AD. We see that although capitalist upper classes have emerged over the course of previous decades, who are asserting their power in politics too, the socioeconomic structure of the state is still predominantly feudal and to a lesser extent tribal. Technological wherewithal as the basis of Pakistan's capitalist classes is still absent. There is still more lopsided concentration of population in the few big cities of Pakistan than in smaller towns and the rural or tribal areas of Pakistan. The power of the military, which has previously directly ruled the country many times, though on the backfoot, is still omnipresent. And the population of the country's middle classes, specially the urban middle class, has increased substantially compared to thirty or forty years ago and this demographic is increasingly asserting itself through politics and the media.

It is in this backdrop that we have to assess what is the best way forward for successful statecraft and which ensures stability within the state, less rocking of the boat, and smooth sailing for the ship of Pakistan.

As stated before, having the benefit of 20/20 hindsight, we will have to acknowledge that none of the classes mentioned above who are asserting their presence and power are going anywhere anytime soon. And that it cannot be accepted that only one of these classes will dominate the others or rule at the detriment of the others or eliminate all others and exist alone as the sole wielder of political power in the state.

If any of these classes represented by the political party with which it identifies itself seeks to eliminate or suppress the others, we will call such a political action as fascism and such a political force as a fascist entity.

For a federal, multi-ethnic state such as Pakistan, in which more than one stage of economic development exist, any attempt to rule by dictatorship will always fail. And the only viable way in which the ship of the state can sail smoothly, the equilibrium of society maintained, is through pluralist democracy exercised under the ambit of the supremacy of its federation-based constitution. The constitution which is the social contract between all the diverse forms of economic classes, ethnic groups, and federating territories constituting the state.

Unless this social contract, this agreement, and the rules, regulations, and roles defined by it for all are honored, respected, and implemented, the state will fall apart sooner than later. The ship will most definitely capsize.

However, the above stated prescription or remedy is still found difficult to be digested by some quarters, and they are still active to do their utmost to put a spanner in the works needed for the success and eventual victory of constitutional, pluralist, and democratic rule in the country.

Needless to repeat, which the reader may already have guessed, these quarters consist of elements in the civil military bureaucracy who are not ready to relinquish their unelected illegitimate power which they exercised and still do from behind the curtains, and those middle classes and social revolutionaries who cannot stand the continuation of political power asserted by the feudal, tribal, and capitalist upper classes of the country.

Needless to repeat also that the source of this misgiving with respect to constitutional, pluralist, and democratic rule in the country is the three 'Ms' mindset, identified in this book, as the originating subconscious of these quarters.

But these quarters do have a point which carries substantial weight as a genuine valid argument which cannot be just shrugged off as being part of the prejudiced three 'Ms' mindset.

This argument raises the concern that if constitutional rule and democratic exercise as it is conducted in the background of the current socioeconomic structure of Pakistan is accepted, then the status quo will never change. Rulers will keep coming from the feudal and some capitalist upper classes of the country, and the conditions of the common people will never change, and society will never progress to become a modern developed economy.

This is a genuine argument and needs to be addressed logically, and to see whether it would be possible to transform Pakistan into a modern developed economy through constitutional democratic rule with the predominance of the existing feudal and capitalistic upper classes, as is also being advocated by this book.

But before we do that, let us first look at the alternate which these quarters propose as the way forward for the country. Their proposed alternate so far has not consisted of a revolution in which feudal lords are eliminated and land reforms implemented, but merely a reversion to martial laws or dictatorial rule of one party or one leader, in which all other classes of society are suppressed and then potshots are taken at the whim of the dictator in charge at various times against perceived adversaries of choice without in any way changing the socioeconomic structure of the country.

That is, as stated before, a feudal lord more powerful than all other feudal lords, acting like a king. And this mentality of course has its roots in the three 'Ms' mindset and the "nostalgia and desire for revival and preservation of the Muslim courtiers' culture and supremacy belonging to the pre-British past of Muslim India" mentioned before in the book.

Therefore, if the argument of these quarters was for a genuine revolution, even if bloody, for the immediate abolition of feudalism, then these quarters could have been given the respect due for revolutionaries and their lead followed. But these quarters are no revolutionaries, and are in essence, petty and envy-stricken reactionaries who would merely establish fascist rule, and the results of their actions, if successful, would only cause the state to stagnate.

However, this book proposes that even a revolution for the immediate abolition of feudalism through executive action from the top is not necessary, and Pakistan can move towards becoming a modern developed economy with its feudalism dissipated without violence, through a continuation of its constitution and democracy as they exist now.

So, let us now proceed to see how that is possible.

The best way to do this would be to first ask the question whether feudalism, wherever in the world it has been abolished or overtaken by the more advanced capitalist mode of production, was always abolished through land reforms or a revolution?

We will find the answer to this question in the negative. In fact, in more instances than not, we see the advanced capitalist societies of today having had moved away from the feudal mode of production without overnight revolutions[90] or radical land reforms. We will come to interrogate the case of Nehru's India in a while but before that, we have to take a look at the experience of the oldest 'modern' democracy of the world, which was also the international power that carried the subcontinent into the 20th century AD, and to which we owe the legacy and modus operandi of all our foundational state institutions on which the body of our state rests, i.e., the United Kingdom (UK), or Britain.

We see in the experience of Britain the diminishment and erosion of the power of the feudal lords, and the dominance of feudalism over society retreating not overnight but spread over a period of centuries, with some flashes of uprisings[91], plague, and peasants' revolt playing the role of qualitative milestones or turning points for the liberation of the peasant and the common man in general from the stifling grip of feudalism.

However, to this day, there is no prohibition on land holdings by law, and the outwardly expressed social structure still stands on class rankings leaning on titles and associations, drawing authority in society, beckoning to a system of yore. But economically, everyone, including the descendants of feudal lords of the past, now choose to invest in and profit from modern capitalist industry and commerce. And politically, no government or a member of the upper class can suppress or exploit the common man, who is equal in rights in the eyes of the law, one-on-one to any member of the upper class, and further strengthened with the concept of 'one person one vote' to get to choose the kind of government he or she wants in the country.

The structure of British feudalism stood on the concept of all land belonging to the monarch who in turn had delegated large pieces of that land to his nobles, read feudal lords, who used the peasantry to till the soil who passed to them the produce. The first turning point in the weakening of feudalism in Britain came in the first half of the 14th century AD, with

---

[90] The French Revolution abolished feudalism through a decree of the National Constituent Assembly in August 1789
[91] Magna Carta (1215 AD)

the Black Plague in 1348[92], after which due to massive deaths, the relation between the peasant and the feudal lord became 'wage based' rather than the previously 'produce based'. Subsequently, the English parliament passed the 'Statute of Labourers' in 1351, which sought to reverse or limit the newfound power of the peasants to ask for higher wages and higher prices for their produce. This fueled outrage among the peasants leading to the peasant revolt of 1381 that was eventually defeated. However, as happens with all revolts and uprisings, which are although crushed, the reasons for their occurrence are taken into account by the authorities of the time and society does not remain the same. The other major milestone or qualitative turning point, in the weakening of the feudal system in Britain can be considered to be the Tenures Abolition Act of 1660. It was passed by the English parliament which reduced the obligations of the peasantry to the monarch, and limited it to only a system of "free and common *socage*," which involved fixed payments by the peasants at specified intervals to the feudal lords that could be either in the form of cash or in the form of the produce of their land. Thus, the relationship between the farmers and the feudal owners of the land became more transactional than being that between a master and his 'slave' or serf. With the parallel rise of the burgeoning classes of trade and industry and the breakthroughs in scientific discoveries and inventions, society at large became more and more industry-oriented and urbanized. Labor became more free to depart agricultural land and work in factories, legislation ensuring such freedoms came into effect, and it became clearer for political representatives of the capitalist classes that eventually it would be the power of the ballot and voting rights for all to choose their government which would ensure that their economic progress and advancement could be maintained.

In this way, the monarch and the nobles were pushed into the background, with them also eventually choosing to jump on the bandwagon of capitalism and electoral democracy to maintain their influence over the changing society.

---

[92] Drop Dead, Feudalism: How the Black Death Led to Peasants' Triumph Over the Feudal System' by Maren Clay (https://clas.ucdenver.edu/nhdc/sites/default/files/attached-files/entry_147.pdf)

For the purpose of this book, we look at the experience of only Britain as referred to above, but to this day there are still many countries, including Brazil, where feudalism or large agricultural land holdings continue to exist. But this does not necessarily serve as a brake to the onward march and progress of their economies.

The key discerning point to understand in undertaking an intellectually honest review of the concept of large agricultural land holdings by individuals is not the feudal mode of production per se, but to see what the efficient system of management for agricultural production and the human relations, or "production relations" as a Marxist would put it, derived thereof would look like.

Here we now turn to interrogate, as promised a while back, the experience of Nehru's India with respect to the land reforms carried out there and that of the communist systems like the ex-Soviet Union and the People's Republic of China. In the former, the land was redistributed among the farmers, while in the case of the latter example of the communist system, the land was usurped by the state and then run as collectives.

So, in the case of Nehru's India, private property was allowed to be continued, although under a specified limit, while under the communist system, private property was abolished to be replaced by state ownership.

At this juncture, we will let go of the communist example of state ownership of land, as history has already shown the utter futility of it and the massive famines and millions of deaths[93], which entailed from it in the two countries we used as prime examples where it was implemented, thus determining for us now retrospectively in no uncertain terms that it is a model never to be emulated again.

Left then with the case of Nehru's India and the agricultural land reforms carried out by the Congress government in the formative years of independent modern India, we make two pertinent observations regarding this experience.

---

[93] Read about the famines in the Soviet Union including the 'Holodomor' in Ukraine and the consequences of the 'Great Leap Forward' in the People's Republic of China

The first, as has already been stated earlier in the book, is that although it may seem that the Nehru government abolished feudalism in India overnight with the single stroke of a pen, the reality is that this was able to be achieved due to the momentum of an already burgeoning indigenous capitalist class behind the Congress Party, its on-ground roots in the emerging economy of the newly independent country, and the intellectual spadework already done and taken to capture the imagination of the masses through the final movement in the years before independence by Gandhi, which had 'self-reliance' and universal adult franchise, in other words, democracy, as its core values.

That is why we see that although Nehru chose to take under the umbrella of state ownership all those industries and infrastructure for which the local indigenous capitalist classes did not possess the magnitude of concentrated capital or technology required to create or run them, he did not implement any crackdown on privately owned capitalist industries in his country or nationalize them. The policy, therefore, was not that of 'socialism forever' or 'socialism as a dogmatic principle,' but socialism or state ownership of large-scale industry as a pragmatic or transitory policy till private capital did not grow and become capable to run it on its own. Nehru's economy for India was a hybrid one, with state ownership and private capitalism existing side by side.

That this was a transitory policy for the country to become self-reliant and advance economically is verified to be so when we see India, under the same Congress Party government of Prime Minister Narsimha Rao and Finance Minister Manmohan Singh from early to mid-1990s, steering the ship of its economy away from a socialist system and entering it head-on into a completely free-market capitalist system.

It is this concept of large-scale production, or 'economies of scale,' which could not be owned and run by the private capitalist classes of the time, which led Nehru to adopt state ownership for the same. This leads us to the second pertinent observation that we make when assessing the anti-feudal experience of India.

This second observation relates to the extent of success in achieving an efficient system of agricultural production based on a structure which stands on small-scale farming or small agricultural land holdings. While initially, under Nehru's leadership and the coordination successfully achieved under his Five-Year Plans between all facets of the economy, the agricultural production of India sustained the needs of the country, in the long run, again looking retrospectively, specially with the economy having moved towards the free market model, the Indian farmer increasingly came under the strain of debts and not being able to profit in the same proportion as investing on his own to produce on his land.

Indeed, in recent years, India gained notoriety for suicides occurring in large numbers among farmers, and there are many studies evaluating the downside of small land ownership[94].

We therefore establish two conclusions from the above two observations. First, that the prime driving factor for the advancement of any country's economy is large scale production or 'economies of scale' which also must be a concerted effort among producers of either industry or agriculture with an insightful understanding of the larger picture being determined by market forces. This order of magnitude can be served either by the state itself taking charge and control over the means of production or by big capitalists possessing the required magnitude of concentrated capital and technological know-how.

The era of 'state capitalism' or 'state socialism', whatever one would like to call such an arrangement, is for all practical purposes over, and history has now designated it to the dustbin of history. In the end, it proved to be a system devoid of the required incentives for human producers to produce and reap the profits of that produce for themselves, and eventually, this leviathan came to a grinding halt and state economies functioning under this system stagnated.

---

[94] 'Over 112,000 Suicides in India's Farming Industry in 10 Years' by Anna Fleck (https://www.statista.com/chart/32258/reported-suicides-of-farmers-farm-laborers-in-india/), 'Farm size limits agriculture's poverty reduction potential in Eastern India even with irrigation-led intensification' (https://pmc.ncbi.nlm.nih.gov/articles/PMC10114281/), '11 Major Problems Faced By Indian Farmers In Agriculture In 2024' by Deepika M (https://kisanvedika.bighaat.com/11-major-problems-faced-by-indian-farmers-in-agriculture-in-2023/), 'Agrarian Distress in Indian Agriculture: Causes, Socio-economic Consequences and Coping Strategies' (https://journalajaees.com/index.php/AJAEES/article/view/2540/5065)

It was good, as stated earlier, as a transitory system for previously colonialized countries to boost large scale industrial production under state control till their capitalist classes did not become capable to do so, and that too was possible till the Soviet Union existed as the leader of an alternate socialist system on the international scale to materially back such transitory economies. With the collapse of the Soviet Union and the international system that existed with it, it is no longer possible for any ex-colonialized state to again take even this transitory route. This transitory route is no longer there. It is a dead road which leads nowhere. The maximum a country can do in this direction, and that too again as a transitory policy, is 'public private partnership'.

What are we then left with, more specifically speaking, for Pakistan?

We can see that any route involving abolition of feudalism with a stroke of the pen by an executive authority ruling Pakistan or nationalizing all land is not going to be taken and was never taken before when 'middle class' military dictators ruled the country, because both the objective as well as subjective prerequisites are missing on the ground.

Objectively, the indigenous organically evolved economy lacks the existence of any kind of self-sustaining and technologically independent industrial base and the kind of bourgeoning classes who would be leading such an industrial base. Subjectively, there is no political movement or party with sufficient grassroots popularity and narrative with a well-thought-out resolute manifesto for the abolition of feudalism and the alternate economic structure which would replace the feudal agrarian relations and modes of production and delivery to the domestic and international markets successfully and in a profitable manner.

In the absence of such objective and subjective prerequisites, an executive action from the top will not only upset the only remaining organic balance in society resulting in unrest, violence, and implosion of society, but also the economy of the state will stagnate if not collapse, and a serious security situation, food security as well as national security, will arise.

Moreover, such a summary executive action could also be illegal and illegitimate constitutionally, without backing derived from a supporting legislation which would be needed to be passed by the parliament. Of course, advocates of such an executive action could argue that this could be achieved under a Martial Law which would give that Martial Law the status of a revolution and revolutions do not recognize or need validation from organs of the system which they have replaced.

But we have already seen in this book, as well as in our country's history, the ramifications of actions taken by military rulers who stood on lack of legal legitimacy and the on-ground situation not reciprocating their executive actions, with the forces of history thus unleashed proving much stronger than their intentions and resulting without fail in the downfall of every one of those military dictators.

It is for this very reason that after the debacle of 1971, with one half of the country having seceded, representatives of all social classes and political thoughts got together and with unequivocal unity and concurrence passed the first truly democratic constitution for the remaining country in 1973, which to date is revered and referred to as the 1973 Constitution of Pakistan.

This constitution of the country is the social contract made by representatives of all kinds of people of Pakistan through which they committed to interact with each other and proceed forward together as a country. This constitution is actually the set of the 'rules of engagement' through which immensely diverse, at times even antagonistic, political and ideological viewpoints have agreed to engage with each other and proceed forward democratically while protecting the voice and opinion of the 'political minority'.

This constitution and abidance by this constitution in action are the two things which maintain the organic balance of Pakistani society and prevent it from collapse. That is why violation and overriding of this constitution by military usurpers and compromised judges who attempt to give legal sanctity to this violation, when they do not possess the constitutional authority to do so, has been and is resisted tooth and nail by the pro-constitution political forces in the country.

Because the 1973 Constitution of Pakistan is in fact Pakistan. It is the embodiment, the persona, of all people of Pakistan. It is federal, i.e. it recognizes that the country is a federation of provinces or sub-states who are socially, economically, and culturally different from each other. It is democratic, i.e. it proclaims that political power in the country can be given only by the will of its people and their voices cannot be suppressed. And it is 'Islamic', i.e. it proclaims that no law in the country can be made which is in contravention with the principles postulated in the Quran and the 'Sunnah', which the author believes should finally be decided through democratic vote in the elected parliament after debate based on logic and rationale rather than give that final say to an unelected body other than parliament, and acknowledges the primarily Muslim ethos of the country while ensuring protection of all rights and human freedoms of the religious minorities.

Extreme hues of both variants, Islamic or Liberal, may view on their own that this constitution is not the ideal one they want, and they do not like it, but they have to accept it as it is the most democratically constructed and mandated constitution of the country so far and serves as a vessel of maintaining equilibrium in society.

If Pakistan is to continue to exist as a multiethnic, multinational, multi-sect state which ranks among the top six or seven most populous countries of the world, it can only do so if the democratically mandated constitution of the country is strictly abided by its citizens.

Returning to the discussion about abolition of archaic socio-economic structures and the value of organically evolved indigenous upper classes in a country, we see that the leader in the formulation of the 1973 constitution was Zulfikar Ali Bhutto. We have already seen that Bhutto as an individual was a progressive and modern thinking person, but he belonged to the feudal upper classes of the country. We have already discussed that since Bhutto had no chance of overnight turning himself into a member of a commercial or industrial capitalist class, he opted to go the route of the non-capitalist way of development by propounding state socialism and nationalization and trying to skip the capitalist stage of development in society. At that time, this attempt was not all that unfeasible since the socialist international bloc still existed.

However, what is important to remember at this juncture, and what this book is attempting to drive home, is that there were and there are individuals, including the example of Bhutto, who although born in the feudal class, recognized then and even recognize now that a modern state to which they belong, which needs a modern economy synchronized with modern world economy, cannot advance solely on the basis of maintaining archaic feudal modes of production and feudal nature of relations between peoples. This is to say, that not all members of the feudal class are reactionary, cruel, and conservative, and there can be people belonging to the feudal class who are progressive thinking, humanists, and thinking about how to move forward their country as a modern economy.

With the option of a state-run economy out of the picture after the collapse of communism in human history, the only viable option for any country to move forward and advance in modern international economy is through the strengthening of its upper classes, where capital is concentrated, who own and run the productive sectors of the economy.

Here we take a pause and reflect on what was just stated, i.e., the 'productive sectors of the economy'. Because what is being said here is not that the strengthening of the rich classes per se is good, but that it is necessary to strengthen those classes who own and run those sectors of the economy which actually produce commodities, industrial products, and services goods, including information technology in the present era.

People can get rich or become very rich, even the richest in society, through 'mercenary economy' or 'casino economy', i.e. through real estate, speculation, receiving commissions for services, retail services, banking, trade etc. This book is not advocating for their glory, although it recognizes that there is no harm in the existence of such classes as a sidekick of an economy primarily producing palpable agricultural, mineral, or industrial products. This book roots for those classes who are the direct owners of the means of production in the country.

It is the author's opinion that economically speaking, the military rule era of General Zia ul Haq in Pakistan was better than the military rule era of General Pervez Musharraf, in the sense that under General Zia ul Haq, with the country having just exited the 'socialist' era of Bhutto and his nationalization, the windfall of dollars received by the regime during the Afghan jihad was funneled in financing the emergence, rise, or return of many locally owned industries and capitalist classes owning those industries. Whereas during the era of General Musharraf, whose regime was on a vendetta against the biggest and single most powerful industrial capitalist Pakistan had ever seen, the windfall of dollars received by his regime during the period of the 'War on Terror' in the first decade of the 2000s was funneled and dissipated in sectors like real estate, cars' financing, banking, and the speculative economy without contributing to or advancing in any way a modern capitalist economy standing on palpable production of industrial, agricultural, or mineral products[95].

Any country's real human economic assets in the present era are those who own and run the prime economic means of production in that country. In the modern world, they are all called 'capitalists'. This book takes the view that in Pakistan, the 'progressive' feudal classes also want to become 'capitalists', just like their counterparts did over a period of centuries in their ex-colonizer country, Britain.

Therefore, we see, at the end of the 1980s as the international communist bloc had collapsed, Benazir Bhutto, the daughter of Bhutto, coming into power in Pakistan without any agenda for the continuation of agricultural land reforms or a return to nationalization, but with a modern economic outlook whereby the market economy and FDI ('foreign direct investment') was encouraged. Her regime considered engagement with incoming foreign capital as a counter-strategy against the urban capitalist leadership of her political rivals, as well as a conduit for the feudal class backing her to become capitalists themselves, and work was initiated for privatization of publicly owned economic enterprises.

The feudal classes supporting the Pakistan Peoples Party, the party of Bhutto and Benazir, can safely be considered as the economically, and we

---

[95] It was an irony that during General Zia's era, the intellectual superstructure rested on conservative and reactionary thought specially as during that era ideas of socialism in the context of the previous Bhutto regime as well as the fight against the Afghan communist revolution were the intellectual foe of the regime, while during General Musharraf's era the intellectual superstructure rested on the general's formulation of 'enlightened moderation' specially as it had just unseated a political entity which had risen in power during General Zia's era and Musharraf's regime was now serving a master and receiving money for this service against the Al Qaeda and the Taliban in Afghanistan. However, this irony was more superficial than with genuine substance and once Pakistan had moved out from the legacies of both military regimes, it were the political democratically elected regimes after General Musharraf which genuinely cracked down on domestic and international terror networks and rid the country from the dominating intellectual influence of the Islamic Dogmatic Fundamentalist racket including the Taliban, in their own interest and the interest of the survival of Pakistan as a modern state.

see invariably in terms of democratic legislation as well as in social matters, progressive elements of rural Pakistan. However, these classes will not forego their social and economic privileges completely till their economic insecurities have not been addressed, and their continuing profits ensured, through their successful transition into becoming full-fledged capitalists themselves. But we will always see them advocating the modernization of the system of agricultural production and delivery and the setting up and the consolidation of a modern economic infrastructure in the country.

The existence of such a feudal upper class is not a bane for the country, and neither, on the other hand, should its rival upper class in urban Pakistan be too smug about its own moral superiority over the former, because the latter also is not entirely a fully developed, self-reliant, technologically independent and advanced capitalist class. It is important that conditions in the country are created to enable both these classes to invest locally, even if initially through 'public private partnership' or through partnering with foreign direct investors, unlock the full potential of the country in terms of agricultural, mineral and industrial production, profit from this endeavor and invest further, thus also enhancing jobs and ancillary business creation and the prosperity in general for the rest of the population of the country.

The patriotic duty of individuals from the middle classes is not to succumb to their envy of these classes but to understand why the existence of these classes is necessary for the development of the country. Of course, the patriotic duty of any individual from the middle classes would be to actively work politically to ensure that the democratic and human rights of the people are not trampled, either in the rural areas or through brutal economic exploitation in any industry. The patriotic duty, and the real revolutionary and progressive activism, would be to speak out and write vociferously against the exploitation or suppression of anyone in the country.

And in this modern world of international human rights bodies, media outreach, and even within the country the sheer assertion of the democratic legal and constitutional setup by courageous and freedom-loving individuals, it is much easier now to do that than centuries or even a few decades ago when the feudal system was less transactional and less fluid.

But if the middle classes take upon them the task of throwing the spanner in the works for the economic progress of the country, which cannot happen without the country's upper classes leading this development, then such an act can only be considered, in the author's opinion, as unpatriotic.

The arrangement which this book is advocating does not preclude the rise of any middle-class individual to the pinnacle of political power. Indeed, we see in all advanced democracies of the world that more often than not, it is individuals with humble or middle-class backgrounds who become the chief executives of those countries. But these individuals do not badmouth or sabotage the spinal economic structure of their countries, which ensures the prosperity of their upper classes and their businesses, which in turn ensures the prosperity of the people of that country at large.

Max Weber may have termed the middle class as the backbone of the capitalist system, but that is what they are: the backbone. They are not the limbs, which actually are the working class, nor can they be the heart or the brain, which can be attributed to being the commercial and the capitalist classes respectively. Any individual from any class can or may become the biggest influencer on the brain or heart or the limbs of a society, but when it comes to being studied as a class 'en bloc', the middle class cannot replace the upper class as being the prime driver and the leader class in the economy of a country.

This book does not deny the callousness, selfishness or snootiness that may very well exist among many if not most members of the upper classes, but merely highlights the empirically proven fact in history so far that, as a permanent successful economic model, it is only a free-market economy run by private capitalist ownership, management and advancement of the means of production which has withstood the test of history while constantly self-correcting and progressively humanizing itself more and more.

Indeed, through democracy and democratization in society, with the human development index of the larger part of growing populations rising ever more speedily, in modern times it becomes more and more easy to establish the oversight, regulation and corrections of democratic governments through legislation and its enforcement to check monopolies and human exploitation and ensure the protection of the rights of labor and consumers, and improvement in their quality of life.

It is this democratic struggle which the middle classes should indulge in impersonally, rather than in efforts to pull the rug from underneath their own upper classes

One caveat must be stated before the last subject specifically related to this chapter is discussed and the chapter concluded. This caveat deals with the direction the current upper classes of Pakistan will take in the future.

Because it is not inevitable that the upper classes of Pakistan will take the progressive direction as stated in this chapter. It is very much possible that the upper classes of Pakistan continue to behave in an archaic feudal manner and sell out the country entirely to foreign capital while enriching themselves through commissions and kickbacks or by merely buying themselves a share in the pie within these foreign capital investments without any structural changes in the economy to ensure maximization of local ownership, the transfer of technology, and the rise of indigenous mechanization and industrialization of the modes of production.

In such an event, these upper classes will only have become part of a 'mercenary economy' or 'casino economy' dominating the economic landscape of Pakistan, with the population of the whole country serving such an economy and the button to switch off the whole economy with a single click lying in the hands of foreign powers. With the undocumented economy being bigger than the documented one and continued tax evasion, money acquired through this undocumented economy, money of corruption, smuggling, and money laundering in the pockets of the public will be more than money in the pocket of the state. And while the market and the people on the ground will seem to be more affluent, the government will struggle to run the state effectively.

In that case, the upper classes of Pakistan will be guilty of having succumbed to neo-colonialism. Political entities representing such classes and this direction will be seen increasing the country's debt without investment in productive development, receiving foreign funding from dubious foreign quarters, shutting down projects of national interest like CPEC (China Pakistan Economic Corridor), giving away control of the country's state bank through legislation into the hands of international monetary bodies like the IMF (International Monetary Fund), writing letters to the IMF not to give money to Pakistan when not in power, and their cohort generals getting filthy rich by buying islands and building pizza franchises abroad[96].

Therefore, patriotic intellectual work calls for propagating and lobbying, in the media as well as in the legislature, for the avoidance or reversal of such an eventuality, and that would be the real revolutionary and progressive activism. Activism against corruption would fall in the same category, which will be touched upon in the next chapter.

The last subject which the author wants to deal with before concluding this chapter is about the significance of the business interests of Pakistan's military in the context of the discussion about the importance of a country's upper classes.

It is very well known that Pakistan's military actively runs many business enterprises, industries, and even a bank. Could we consider that the prosperity and advancement of business under Pakistan's military fall in the same category of the rise of the country's economic upper classes which this book advocates?

The answer to this question is that this could have been considered to be so, had this player in the country's economy not been in possession of 'the gun,' and due to the fact that the professionalism of any fighting machine is compromised once it has been seduced by the comforts, luxuries, and privileges enjoyed in the civilian way of life. The combination of these two facts can turn this very machine against its own people, whose protection is its duty, and result in lapses in its prime function of national defense.

The principle of a modern free-market economy is that of a level playing field, and legislation in democratic capitalist societies ensures that the element of coercion or the adverse effects of monopoly do not exist in the economy. If there is political dictatorship but there is 'economic

---

[96] Ardent followers of Pakistani politics will understand the context of these examples.

democracy,' an economy can thrive. But if there is democracy politically but no 'economic democracy,' the economy runs high risk of stagnating and running aground.

Without quoting specific examples, the author invites the reader to investigate and find that there are a few countries with prosperous economies which are not democracies per se politically, but the governments there ensure that the element of coercion or monopoly is minimized in their economies and every player in the economy gets the maximum level playing field to succeed and prosper.

In a country like Pakistan, where the military has directly taken over and ruled the country several times, and where the role of security agencies is all-pervasive, Pakistan being a security state to date, it is essential for the unhinged prosperity of all of Pakistan's economic classes that, while economic enterprises can exist which benefit and contribute to the welfare of retired military personnel and their families, the serving military and its influence should be divorced through legislation from any existing business interest, and any such influence or involvement be made unequivocally illegal.

The serving military has to be legally subservient to the defense ministry only and hence, by extension, to the country's executive and its chief, the prime minister. All control of funding the military should be in the hands of the elected government, and at any time, its doings should be able to be held accountable and punishable, if guilty of transgressing its constitutional mandate, by the parliament and its committees.

Rule of Law and Corruption

Laws are rules made for the citizens and people, residing or passing through, in any state to be abided by unconditionally. If a state is unable to ensure compliance with its laws, if it is unable to enforce these laws, and if it is unable to punish unconditionally those who violate its laws, then such a state starts losing its *raison d'être* (reason for existence). The continuance of such weakness ultimately results in its turning into a failed state.

The laws could have been made by a '*de jure*' government or a '*de facto*' government, but the first duty of any government and all state organs is to ensure that the rule of law prevails and is implemented and enforced ruthlessly. Any state asserts and seals its right to exist only by demonstrating its unconditional resolve through action, not just words, to enforce its laws, come what may.

If this penny has not dropped in the minds of those running a country or those residing in it or possessing its citizenship, then the game has already been lost before it even started. This is what happened to Pakistan in the early years of its existence, and this sloppiness continues to date and has seeped deep into the thought process of all state functionaries, including the judiciary.

In fact, it is the spinelessness and unprincipledness of the judiciary which lies at the root of the failure of effective law enforcement from the very first years of Pakistan's existence.

The moment that lawlessness took a judo hold of 'the rule of law' and threw it on the ground and then sat atop its chest in Pakistan can be traced back to the moment in 1954 when Chief Justice Muhammad Munir conjured the "doctrine of necessity" out of thin air and ruled in favor of the dismissal of Pakistan's first constituent assembly by the then governor general, Ghulam Muhammad.

From then on, as we see in the chequered history of the Pakistani state, it became open season for the country's judiciary. Every time a general staged a coup and took power, summarily violating the constitution in 'broad daylight', this judiciary stepped up with their services and each time attempted to give legal cover to the coups through disingenuous mental gymnastics.

It is like the losing of one's chastity outside of marriage. It is the first time which is the big hurdle. Once that is passed, it can become relatively easier to go down the path of open season for sex outside of marriage and become normal for the person practicing it.

If anybody thought that such an abandonment of principle and sloppiness on matters of law and constitution would not have sociopsychological repercussions up to the lowest rungs of society, then that person can be said to have been living in a fool's paradise.

It became subconsciously clear to all from the very outset that whoever had the 'gun to the temple of the state' was going to be the real wielder of state power and not those mandated by the written word of principle, as would be expected of a civilized people capable of ruling themselves.

In other words, the sword was going to be mightier than the pen in the new state. And so, it would be trickled down to the very roots of the new country that 'might is right' not 'law is right'. So whoever could wield more might behind the curtains could and would get their way, regardless of what the law may say.

Law was a formation of words which could be twisted to mean anything which a compromised judge wanted it to mean, and the underlying principle of jurisprudence at its base was thrown out of the window. This assertion of real might was expressed sometimes by way of threat of physical obliteration but increasingly started being expressed by way of material or monetary favors, i.e., bribery. This bribery could be monetary, but also could be the promise of granting material favors or of not upsetting the cart of a cushy job or respect in society for the judge or state functionary being compromised.

And so, it came to the situation that the state of Pakistan and its law enforcement increasingly became a sloppy affair. Eyebrows would be raised when a principled state functionary or judge would act or decide in strict adherence to the word of law, rather than being raised when violators of law were cajoled and let go scot-free.

Law enforcers increasingly became wary of going after and arresting criminals with such behind-the-curtains influence as they realized that the compromised judiciary would ultimately let them go, and they themselves became corrupt by engaging and negotiating for the best bribe from these criminals of influence.

When the ruler of the state could sit on top of everyone in complete contravention of the law and constitution of the land on the sole basis of his might of brute force, why would anyone below in different strata of the state shirk from using one's own monetary, societal, or physical power to sit atop those weaker than oneself and gain benefits in society regardless of what the word of law said?

An everyday indicator of such a situation of truth standing on its head can be observed when eyebrows are raised and a person is considered a fool when he or she stops one's car at a red light even when the roads are clear, rather than eyebrows being raised when the red light is jumped in that circumstance. This belies the extent to which the sloppiness and criminal compromise on matters of principles and the rule of law have seeped into the mindset of the country's populace in general.

But the ultimate irony, the ultimate twist, in this story of criminal compromise on the rule of law is the success of the country's military usurpers in building into the public's imagination and subconscious the narrative that the culprits of this compromise are the politicians of this country.

True, that the politicians of this country did not remain unaffected by the culture of sloppiness and seeking behind-the-curtains influence, specially those politicians who had come up under the umbrella and with the backing of the military usurpers, but the prime movers of this culture of compromise, the committers of this 'original sin' of making the sword mightier than the pen, the main culprits of preventing the country from becoming a civilized society where the rule and the word of law prevails, are without doubt in plain daylight those military adventurers who started conspiring against and toppling legal constitutional civil governments and the abettors of these military adventurers in the judiciary.

Again, in collaboration with the envious, hatred-ridden, myopic, and middle-class supremacist so-called educated intelligentsia in the media and urban areas of the country, inflicted with the three 'Ms' mindset identified by this book, the unelected military usurpers and their equally unelected abettors in the judiciary succeeded in turning the barrel of the gun towards the politicians who can only come to power through electoral democracy, and the 'silver bullet' which was loaded in that gun was called 'corruption'.

It was easy to do that since politicians operating in this culture of sloppiness, appeasement, and compromise on principles to garner votes from their constituencies naturally exuded an unintended aura of sleaziness and unprincipledness. Whether there was real substance beneath this aura did not matter. What mattered was to have this image successfully fixated in the public imagination.

Then along came these men in uniform or judicial robes, 'self-made' and duty-bound men, though unelected but pure from the requirements of pleasing anyone to get elected, so they had to be the ones who had no need to make any compromise on principle and therefore what they said had to be the truth, the right thing for the country. It is in this way that truth was made to stand on its head and those who were mandated by law to get enough votes to be elected and rule the country and would be the real legal representatives of the people were made to look as 'corrupt' and compromised and those who were completely unelected, had overstepped the constitutional mandate related to their jobs and duties in plain daylight, and were committing blatant 'corruption' by violating the rule of law, were considered as the very protectors of the rule of law.

Here there is a need to understand what the basic principles are on which the concept of the 'rule of law' rests and which will determine whether there is real 'rule of law' in a country or just 'rule by arbitrary force' (in other words, 'rule by virtue of subjective inclination' or 'rule by partisanship').

In the author's view, there are three maxims which can be considered to be the foundational philosophical bases of 'rule of law' in a society. The first maxim is: **'presumption of innocence until proven guilty'**. The second is: **'the monopoly of violence lies only with the state'**. And the third is that: **'at no moment should the state give the impression that it is afraid of enforcing its laws'**.

The first speaks more to the responsibility of the executive with respect to the modus operandi in going after a suspect or an accused and of the public in building their perceptions. The second speaks more to the responsibility of the public, that is, a citizen's responsibility towards the state, and to a lesser degree to that of the executive and the judiciary showing zero tolerance for unpeaceful means of protest by the public and the taking up of arms by non-state actors and vigilantes. The third speaks more to the responsibility and resoluteness of the executive and the judiciary in ensuring that the delivery of justice is not delayed (the cliché "justice delayed is justice denied") and that they will not be intimidated or influenced by threats or propaganda in any way to not enforce the law.

We will interrogate these maxims one by one in the context of our subject country.

We see in all civilized societies, specially successful democratic societies, that no person can be convicted by law till evidence has not been provided and this evidence accepted by the court as valid evidence. Mere allegations and slander are not enough to label a person as really guilty or a criminal. In fact, in many countries run under 'the rule of law', there are laws which would convict those who are found guilty of libel.

And this principle of proving guilt does not stop just there. In fact, we see in modern democratic states that even when it is known for a fact by hearsay, firsthand experience, and as an open secret that a person is a criminal, the law enforcement agencies do not and cannot crack down or arrest that person without obtaining sufficient evidence. Otherwise, the court immediately releases that person if such a false arrest is made for want of evidence, and turns around and can penalize those who made that false arrest, which meant that it was they who were not following the law.

This protocol is followed as a default system not for the protection of known criminals against whom enough evidence is absent but as a fail-safe guarantee that an innocent person will never be punished by society (more on the significance of this will be discussed in a while.)

There is no room for any vigilante action against perceived criminals in a society where the rule of law prevails. In fact, such a society punishes those who would indulge in vigilante action and calls it "taking the law in their own hands." This presumption of innocence as a starting point for any person and the requirement for the provision of evidence lies at the philosophical basis of humanity's journey over the course of centuries in assuring that justice is delivered to any member of a society and injustice to anyone is prevented.

Only with the assurance that the state will not come after anyone without solid evidence can a society function freely and efficiently, which results in collective good for all.

Whether it be monarchies of yore with just monarchs being the real wielders of power at the top or whether it be modern democracies, a just government would want that the citizens of its state feel secure, work confidently and loyally, and have respect for the way law is enforced in the country.

Even economically speaking, if a government was to crack down on businesses just on mere perception of corruption without bringing forth evidence to that effect, such a course of action would result in hesitation to invest in the economy by local or foreign investors, and the economic engine of the country would run the risk of first slowing down and then coming to a halt.

The notion of protecting an innocent person or a person who is not guilty lies at the very foundation of the philosophy of human jurisprudence universally, regardless of time and place. All great men, religions, and jurists converge on the concept of never punishing a person who is not guilty as the first basis of justice.

The most famous quote in this regard is by Maimonides, the 12th-century AD Jewish philosopher and an authority on the Torah and Jewish law and ethics, who is known to have stated that:

"It is better and more satisfactory to acquit a thousand guilty persons than to put a single innocent one to death."

The same philosophy is adopted in English law within what is known as Blackstone's Ratio, which states:

"It is better that ten guilty persons escape than that one innocent suffer" [97].

In the final scene of the 1961 movie 'Judgement at Nuremberg' when the German jurist Dr. Ernst Janning says to Chief Judge of the tribunal, Dan Haywood, referring to the people sent to death by Nazi courts during Hitler's rule in which verdicts he was a participant, that "*..those people, those millions of people, ..I never knew it would come to that, ...you must believe it, you must believe it*", Haywood replies, "*Herr Janning, it came to that the first time you sentenced a man to death you knew to be innocent*".

Even in Islamic jurisprudence, the burden of proof on the accusers is fundamental before proceeding to mete out any punishment to an accused,

---

[97] 'Commentaries on the Laws of England' by Sir William Blackstone (1765).

and there is strict reprimand for those indulging in libel and slander and then failing to provide evidence to substantiate their allegations.

Verses 11 to 21 of Surah Al-Nur of the Quran read as follows:

24:11. Verily, those who brought forth the slander are a group among you. Consider it not a bad thing for you. Nay, it is good for you. Unto every man among them will be paid that which he had earned of the sin, and as for him among them who had the greater share therein, his will be a great torment.

24:12. Why then, did not the believers, men and women, when you heard it, think good of their own people and say: "This is an obvious lie'.

24:13. Why did they not produce four witnesses against him Since they have not produced witnesses! Then with Allah, they are the liars.

24:14. Had it not been for the grace of Allah and His mercy unto you in this world and in the Hereafter, a great torment would have touched you for that whereof you had spoken.

24:15. When you were propagating it with your tongues and uttering with your mouths that whereof you had no knowledge, you counted it a little thing, while with Allah it was very great.

24:16. And why did you not, when you heard it, say: "It is not right for us to speak of this. Glory be to You (O Allah)! This is a great lie.'

24:17. Allah forbids you from it and warns you not to repeat the like of it forever, if you are believers.

24:18. And Allah makes the Ayat (verses) plain to you, and Allah is All-Knowing, All-Wise.

24:19. Verily, those who like that indecency should be circulated among those who believe, they will have a painful torment in this world and in the Hereafter. And Allah knows, and you know not.

24:20. And had it not been for the grace of Allah and His mercy on you, and that Allah is full of kindness, Most Merciful.

24:21. O you who believe! Follow not the footsteps of Shaytan (Satan). And whosoever follows the footsteps of Shaytan, then, verily, he commands indecency and the evil deeds. And had it not been for the grace of Allah and His mercy on you, not one of you would ever have been pure from sins. But Allah purifies whom He wills, and Allah is All-Hearer, All-Knower.

Surah Nisa, verse 112, reads:

"And whoever commits an evil or sinful deed then blames it on an innocent person, they will definitely bear the guilt of slander and blatant sin."

And Surah Al-Nur, verses 4 and 5, read:

24:4. Those who accuse chaste women 'of adultery' and fail to produce four witnesses, give them eighty lashes 'each'. And do not ever accept any testimony from them—for they are indeed the rebellious.

24:5. Except those who repent afterwards and mend their ways, then surely Allah is All-Forgiving, Most Merciful.

In the book of Hadith (sayings of Prophet Muhammad pbuh) by Tirmizi, the Prophet (pbuh) is quoted as having said to the effect that the use of laws to punish must be avoided if there are doubts in a case, and in such case, it is better for the judge to use the laws to show leniency towards the accused rather than to use them to mete out punishment.

Therefore, in any society where the rule of law has to prevail and justice is seen to be delivered, no person should be handed down a conviction without evidence, and the burden to produce that evidence lies on the shoulders of the accusers and the agencies of law enforcement, not on the shoulders of the accused.

In fact, in societies where the rule of law prevails, the police do not even proceed with an arrest until sufficient evidence has been gathered which would justify indictment in a court of law. A suspect or an accused may be called for interrogation, but then has to be let go free in the absence of evidence. This is the fundamental right of a citizen guaranteed by the state.

In Pakistan, governments have been toppled through illegal and unconstitutional coups and verdicts of the court influenced by mere force of slander, propaganda and public perception, on charges of corruption without producing the necessary evidence. The irony in this phenomenon in Pakistan is that, while production of evidence in court was found lacking to prove the allegations of corruption, the courts not only ignored the blatant 'corruption' committed in broad daylight for all to see, for which no further evidence was required but the eye witness of the entire nation, that is, the 'corruption' of carrying out illegal military coups and abrogating the country's constitution but in fact gave this 'corruption' their blessing through extra-legal and extra constitutional mental gymnastics thus becoming accomplices in this 'corruption'. The supreme judiciary became partners in this corruption by taking oaths of allegiance to the military usurper and by giving the usurper, to whom they should have been handing out the death sentence, ultra vires powers to alter the constitution singlehandedly[98]. And then arbitrary arrests were carried out of members of the ousted elected regime without sufficient evidence, creating a society where lawlessness and 'might is right' became the de facto law. The most infamous decisions against elected ousted prime ministers by the top courts of Pakistan without possessing the required sufficient evidence to reach those decisions, and violating the principle of 'presumption of innocence till found guilty' were two verdicts. One given against Zulfiqar Ali Bhutto in 1978 upheld in 1979[99], and the other against Nawaz Sharif in 2017[100]. In both cases, the principle of burden of proof lying with the accuser was thrown out of the window, and the adverse consequence of this unprincipledness was suffered not only by the two ex-prime ministers

---

[98] On 12 May 2000 Pakistan's supreme court rejected the petitions challenging General Musharraf's coup of 12 October 1999 and the military government was granted extensive powers to make new laws and even amend the constitution (Verdict of the Supreme Court of Pakistan regarding Constitution Petitions Nos. 62/99, 63/99, 53/99, 57/99, 3/2000, 66/99, and 64/99, May 12, 2000).

[99] There were gaping holes in the way the verdict was delivered against Bhutto for the murder of a political opponent, relying solely on witnesses implying direction having been given by Bhutto to carry out that murder while not being the direct murderer himself which would not definitely necessitate a death sentence. Much has been written about the deficiencies and bias that existed in the courts' verdict against Bhutto, and this was finally recognized and officialized by Pakistan's Supreme Court itself in 2024 (https://www.supremecourt.gov.pk/downloads_judgements/reference_1_2011_06mar2024.pdf).

[100] Court proceedings were initiated against the sitting Prime Minister Nawaz Sharif in 2016, although Nawaz Sharif himself had called for the formation of a judicial commission stating that he had nothing to hide, on allegations of corruption with reference to information publicly released internationally by the famous 'Panama Papers' of that time however, eventually when no evidence was found of Nawaz Sharif's corruption in that context, a verdict was delivered and Nawaz Sharif was convicted over the fact that he had been an employee of his son's company and had not declared the salary which he actually never received from that company.

individually, but socially, psychologically, and economically by the entire country.

The irony was that, at the time of Bhutto's verdict, the most obvious candidate for receiving the death sentence was sitting in broad daylight on the country's throne of political power, that is, General Zia ul Haq. While at the time of Nawaz Sharif's verdict, the most obvious candidates for receiving the death sentence under the rules of the constitution, as was evidenced conclusively later by their own vocal admissions of guilt of having involved themselves in politics, were the then and ex-chiefs of the country's army and military intelligence respectively.

A further irony, on top of a pile of ironies, is that historical record invariably shows that all regimes which replaced the ones accused of corruption by the 'anti-politicians' lobby proved to be more corrupt, and declared so by Transparency International ratings.

This book does not seek to defend or absolve politicians from the charges of high-handedness or corruption levelled against them. What this book is seeking to emphasize is that governments or regimes cannot be toppled or changed, least of all unconstitutionally, on mere allegations or perceptions of corruption.

Pursuance of corruption or criminal cases in court is one matter, but the move to change a government, specially an elected one, is entirely a different matter, and the two should not be connected in the interest of stability and the forward march of the economy and the healthy political process of a country.

True, a revolution can and should be instigated from the grassroots by the people of the country, using their constitutional and democratic rights, if corruption and physical suppression of critics and political opponents have pervaded and are visibly obvious up to the very lowest rungs of society.

However, if that corruption at the lowest level is minimal or is merely spontaneous as a societal phenomenon but not directly linkable to the ruler, or not seen to be condoned by the sitting government, and if law and order is being maintained by the sitting government and there is the least or no threat of political oppression from the government, then attempts to create political instability on the streets can safely be deemed to be not just unjustifiable but positively mischievous.

In a democratic society, where economic and social stability is being maintained by the government with no suppression of freedom of expression, the proper forums to raise issues and work for the implementation of one's agenda, cause, or manifesto are the elected assemblies, the courts, and organs of mass media.

In Western democratic societies, we have seen the examples of leaders like Ronald Reagan, Donald Trump, Nikolas Sarkozy, Ehud Olmert, Benjamin Netanyahu, etc. being brought into court over charges of irregularities and corruption, but such proceedings had no effect on the continuity of the political process of their countries, which derived its power and stability from the mandate of the people acquired through elections. And none were arrested; in fact, the question did not even arise of arresting them in the absence of substantial evidence gathered against them.

Even then, if the political opposition in any country considers it necessary to have the sitting government removed only because it perceives the government to be corrupt at the top, although the economy below is functioning stably and smoothly, still the patriotic way to go about it would be to gather enough votes to oust the government through a motion of no-confidence in the parliament or through impeachment of a president. Otherwise, all legal matters can be pursued in courts of law without creating political or economic instability in society, and the courts should deliver verdicts based on the availability or absence of evidence, as the case may be.

A culture of slander, defamation, libel, fake news, and character assassination, specially without evidence, or with fabricated 'evidence' which would not withstand scrutiny in a court of law, only creates a culture of unnecessary public dissatisfaction, cynicism, social divisiveness, hatred, and toxicity in society and should be discouraged and rejected by the people in general and the country's educated middle class in particular.

Sadly, this objective cannot be achieved by enforcement from the top, but has to be a voluntary decision and a voluntary act to be taken by the people and a responsible educated middle class.

However, if this voluntary course of action is not taken by the public, laws should be made by the legislature and strictly implemented by the executive as well as the judiciary against slander and false accusations.

Social consciousness and the cultural level of a society is elevated not just by preaching but also by making an example of those who break the law or indulge in slander.

The second maxim, which is considered by the author to be one of the foundational philosophical bases of 'rule of law' in a society, is that 'the monopoly of violence lies only with the state'.

A state is the political organization of a society within a territory over which that political organization asserts itself as the sole authority to determine how that society will be governed. The 'how it will be governed' can be termed to be the laws of that state, and the government of that state is the instrument which ensures that those laws are abided by and enforces the laws when it sees that there is risk of or actual deviation from those laws.

The word 'enforce' carries in it the word 'force'. It means that the government of a state is completely authorized and justified in using force, the most manifest form of which is physical force, to ensure that the laws of the land are complied with.

That the state will be the only legitimate wielder of physical force is a concept well considered and well established in the study of Political Science[101], not just for the modern state but also found applicable in history from the very first time a state came into being in human society.

Once a state and its government have allowed the existence and operations of armed militias or groups within their territory, and specially for them to operate without seeking prior authorization from the government of that state, then such a state is politically and internationally deemed to be on the path of progressively losing its credibility as a legitimate state and fast turning into a semi-failed or failed state.

When we say "allowed," we mean it in both ways: whether allowing through legislation or executive orders (that is, giving such existence and

---

[101] 'Les Six livres de la République' by Jean Bodin (1576), 'Leviathan' by Thomas Hobbes (1651), 'Politics as a Vocation' by Max Weber (1919)

operations legal mandate), or whether allowing by just turning a blind eye to this phenomenon. For a state to allow, through legal consent, the operation of armed non-state entities in its name is a sure sign of weakness of that state, but turning a blind eye to this phenomenon continuing with not even legal consent is suicidal.

Here we have to be clear that we are not talking about the possession of guns by the public. There is a difference between owning guns for hunting, practicing as a hobby, or self-defense purposes with authorization from the government in the form of a license, and using guns to take the law in one's own hands and asserting authority over pieces of territory within a state using those guns.

Even when the gun has been used in self-defense, in a state where the rule of law prevails, the user of that gun is immediately scrutinized by law enforcement agencies and interrogated in a court of law before that user is exonerated for having used the gun on another human. This is seen applicable in the foremost modern state of the present world, the United States, where laws regarding gun ownership are most lenient, but when it comes to using them on other humans or using them as a mode of political assertion, the laws of that land generally show no tolerance for homicide or the usage of that gun ownership for the purpose of creating "a state within the state."

In the context of Pakistan, however, the same cannot be said with respect to the existence of vast swathes of land where not only gun ownership, often unlicensed, exists, but also this arming of society translates into unlegislated and unauthorized "laws" made and enforced by the owners of arms in these areas. Similarly, in Pakistan there has been a history, specially since the 1980s under General Zia ul Haq's regime, of tolerating the possession of arms by religious seminaries and religiopolitical groups, even unlicensed, which subsequently time and again boiled to the surface and threatened and defamed the state, most notably as examples in the case of the 2007 Red Mosque insurrection in Islamabad or frequently unearthed links of these religious groups to terrorist operations abroad.

Therefore, tolerance of such non-state wielders of physical force is an existential question for any state, and the administrators and rulers of the

Pakistani state are no exception who can run away and hide themselves from this question, whether asked to them by the international community or whether asked by voices from within the boundaries of the state.

For Pakistan to exist and demonstrate itself as a successful state governed by the rule of law, it has to prove in no uncertain terms that the sole wielders and representatives of physical force for and within Pakistan are only and only its armed forces and its law enforcement agencies.

Even in modern democratic countries where the rule of law prevails, a physical assault and even worse, a murder of a member of the law enforcement, is considered an extreme violation of the law and the culprit immediately finds himself on the wrong side of the law, losing the sympathy of the courts and instantaneously qualified to be brought in or put down by all means available to law enforcement agencies.

But the buck for passing the test imposed by this maxim does not just stop at the door of Pakistan's state authorities only. It also rests with the responsibility which belongs to the social consciousness and understanding of the people of Pakistan, without which this maxim will not hold ground and the Pakistani state cannot become a successful state.

For a state which is one of the top most populous states of the world, which is in fact a federation with many diverse ethnic, linguistic, and sectarian groups, and where the stage of socioeconomic development varies from one territory to the other, it would be difficult to make this maxim hold true just by an executive effort on part of the government and the armed and law enforcement forces of the country.

Just as we determined earlier in the book that in Pakistan, for this very reason, even a military dictator has to indulge in realpolitik and engagement with political parties to succeed in his rule, similarly it is essential for this maxim to work in Pakistan that the public eventually understands and owns the trueness of this maxim.

It is true in its history, and some would argue that even now it happens, that the Pakistani state was taken over by its military forces, its constitution was violated, the rights of the people and sub-nationalities living within its boundaries were usurped and violated, dissenters and political opposition were incarcerated, and atrocities committed by state forces against the people.

But for the citizens of this country, and specially those who struggled for democracy, human rights, and the right to self-determination of the sub-nationalities, there was and always has been a choice to be made about the mode of struggle to be adopted in face of the state's repression.

There has been that political thought which chose to bear the hardships of this repression nonviolently but continued to speak out and mobilize the people against repression and never be silenced, and then there has been that trend which chose to resist that repression through violence against the state forces.

This book does not pass judgement on any of the above two stated political trends. It does not say that one was right, and the other was not. The Pakistani state has been resisted through violent means at various times by Baloch nationalists, by the Bengali Mukti Bahini, by Murtaza Bhutto's Al-Zulfiqar organization, by the Taliban, and by the perpetrators of physical attacks on its military symbols and installations on 9th May 2023[102]. In all such instances, those who indulged in these violent means had reasons good enough for themselves to view those in power in the Pakistani state, in fact the very state itself, in poor light and guilty of heinous injustices against them and the people whom they claimed to represent.

On the other hand, the Pakistani state has also been questioned and resisted when its military had usurped its power, since the first years of its existence and then subsequently and repeatedly decade after decade, imprisoning, hanging, assassinating and unseating from power, through illegal subversion of the political leadership of the other political trend, which bore this repression but questioned and resisted through nonviolent means politically only. That is, political forces like the National Awami Party (NAP), the Quaid's sister Fatima Jinnah, the Pakistan People's Party, the Pakistan Muslim League, and the parties which formed democratic alliances like the Combined Opposition Parties (COP), the Movement for the Restoration of Democracy (MRD), the People's Democratic Alliance

---

[102] This is in reference to the attacks that took place on Pakistan's military installations and symbols on 9th May 2023 as a reaction to the arrest of the former prime minister Imran Khan.

(PDA), the Alliance for the Restoration of Democracy (ARD), and the Pakistan Democratic Movement (PDM)[103].

In all elections held in Pakistan, the losing side always had reservations about the fairness of the process and the outcome. But it was those who chose the latter path who participated in the parliament to help the democratic institutions and process move forward with their imperfections rather than throw a spanner in the works through violence on the streets and implicitly weaken the state.

This book only proposes that if the path of violent means is taken by a political entity against the 'de jure' or 'de facto' state government and its forces, military or law enforcement, then it should be clear to those deciding to go this route that the possibility of the state itself unraveling is also part of the options on their table. Whether they want that to happen too or not is the choice that they then have to make.

Because by choosing to adopt violence also as one of the methods of providing resistance to perceived state repression and furthering one's cause, the choosing entity is deciding that the state is no longer going to be the sole wielder of physical force within the boundaries of the state and that there is 'a new kid on the block', that is, now there are more than one contestant claiming to be the state. Once that route has been chosen, then depending on the strength of this alternative political entity choosing that route, the existing state will now be combating not just a political movement it does not approve of, but the fight will be taken to the next level where it will be fighting for its very legitimacy to survive as a state.

The choice of such a route, whether one likes it or not, whether one says afterwards that the intention was not the unraveling or the breaking up of the state, most definitely opens a Pandora box and has the full potential to unleash forces of history which may no longer be controllable by even those who made that choice. This has been seen in the case of countries like Syria, Libya and Sudan as the dictatorships there lingering

---

[103] The book does not include the famous political alliances, Pakistan National Alliance (PNA), the Islami Jamhoori Ittehad (IJI) and the Grand Democratic Alliance (GDA) in this listing as it considers them suspect of serving the forces of martial law and military intervention and subversion in politics.

from the 20th century were challenged and brought down in the first quarter of the 21st century AD.

That is why it is safe to say that those political entities who struggle for democracy but always nonviolently and never take up the gun for this cause are the ones who are never anti-state, whereas those who think that arms can also be taken up in support of their cause may eventually land up in a situation where their actions could willingly or unwillingly become anti-state and deemed to be so also by any independent and objective observer.

This book considers the armed struggle of the East Pakistanis leading to the eventual breakup of the original state of Pakistan in 1971 and the armed struggle of the Baloch nationalists all through the history of Pakistan not just one-sided crimes against the Pakistani state but also views this armed tussle as an equal failure of those running the state and their criminal policies against the Baloch and the Bengalis, and views the armed attacks on the Pakistani state by the Taliban or the perpetration of the 9th May 2023 attacks as monstrosities in whose occurrence Pakistani state functionaries have also been complicit to begin with.

But since the book seeks the preservation and continuity of the Pakistani state in a successful democratic manner and does not principally believe in the concept of secession for any modern nation state per se, therefore it is the view of the author that those political leaders who chose not to resort to violence or even 'civil disobedience' (in a post-colonial state) can be termed as more 'pro-state' than the ones who included violence (or 'civil disobedience') in their modus operandi.

And it is particularly tragic when the lines between violent and nonviolent methods of political action are blurred, by an intellectually dishonest intelligentsia criminally confusing and misleading the people's consciousness, to place those adopting the former method in the same category with those who always chose to adopt the latter method.

The third maxim to be considered as one of the essential foundational bases for the rule of law relates to the very concept 'the rule of law' per se, that is, law enforcement. "At no moment should the state give the impression that it is afraid of enforcing its laws."

The moment the citizens of a state or anyone passing through that state are given the impression that the state is ready to turn a blind eye to, overlook, or compromise on a transgression committed by them in context of the laws of the land, that moment is the pivotal point at which the state starts losing grip of its writ, and the process of the unraveling of the state has commenced at that point, though it may not become immediately evident.

In other words, by choosing not to enforce its laws uncompromisingly, a state chooses to commit suicide by slow self-poisoning. Sloppiness, corruption, appeasement, and cajolement set in as second nature not just for state functionaries, including the police and judiciary, but for society in general as the predominant culture.

Sloppiness and corruption are not limited in meaning to the failure and compromise of forces of law enforcement only, but also mean criminal negligence of one's duty, and this extends into all branches of society including education, health, government services, business interactions, and personal relationships.

As has already been explained in the book, in the author's view the originating point of the downfall of law enforcement in Pakistan was when the 'doctrine of necessity' was resorted to by the judiciary to justify the dissolution of the constituent assembly in 1954 and then subsequently carried on by justifying martial laws and military coups and never punishing their perpetrators.

Ironically, the saving grace for the country, as also has been mentioned earlier in the book, was the intolerance of Pakistan's military towards any transgression of discipline within its ranks and towards violation of its writ which it imposed externally. In this way, de facto, Pakistan's military became the state, whereas this should not have been the case for any state which is to be governed by the rule of law wherein the military is only one of the state organs.

Because what the advocates of military rule did not, and do not, understand is that by imposing its writ while violating the constitution of the country, the military is basically proclaiming the "law of the jungle" in which "might is right." Thus, any militia or 'non-state' actor is made to understand that if it can exert enough might, then it will have the right to rule in the area where their might overpowers all others by brute force.

So ensued a race for maximum might, and the country has seen major swathes of territories out of bounds of the rule of Pakistan's constitutional law and where the brute force of the military and law enforcement agencies exhausts its limits. Even in territories where constitutional law is deemed to be implemented, armed groups and individuals of influence manage to create their own respective fiefdoms where only the law which they invent reigns supreme.

Chaudhry Aslam, a Pakistani police officer who became famous in the second decade of the 21st century for his successful prolonged campaign against terrorists and the Taliban and eventually paid the price of his work with his life, is known to have said about the Taliban that at no moment he wanted to let them feel that he was afraid of them.

A similar example of fearless law enforcement is found in the case of Pakistani Punjab's Home Minister Shuja Khanzada, who successfully cracked down on sectarian terrorist groups and was martyred in retaliation in 2015. The Pakistani state also came through when Mumtaz Qadri, the murderer of Punjab's governor Salman Taseer, was executed in 2016 and no compromise was made on the fact that Qadri had taken the law in his own hands.

Each time when the state makes no compromise on punishing those who break its laws, it recovers a little from the path of slow self-poisoning it was thrown on in 1954 by its superior judiciary. In 2019, for the first time, an ex-military dictator Pervez Musharraf was sentenced to death for having violated the constitution, which he himself was the architect of, on 3rd November 2007, but this sentence was overturned by the Lahore High Court the following year.

The fact is that historically, the prime culprit for the sloppiness in Pakistani law enforcement has been the superior judiciary. As already said, not only has the Pakistani superior judiciary been guilty of illegally justifying the 'law of necessity' and military coups but even did not stand firm on the principle of defending the constitution adulterated by the very military dictators they had supported.

The violation of his own adulterated constitution on 3rd November 2007 by General Pervez Musharraf was not the only such instance. In 1969, when the then military dictator 'Field Marshal' Ayub Khan resigned in face of mass protests against his rule, he did not hand over power to the speaker of the National Assembly as stipulated in his own adulterated constitution of 1962 and instead invited his deputy General Yahya Khan to impose another martial law. Neither General Ayub Khan nor General Yahya Khan were ever brought to justice and punished for their capital crimes.

The examples of approving the illegal power to amend the constitution by military dictators like General Zia ul Haq and General Musharraf and the legal lapses in the verdict of hanging Bhutto, have already been quoted in the book. And then this criminal lapse of duty of the judiciary was aggravated by the politicization of judges, where individual political leanings contributed to ridiculous and self-contradicting verdicts.

The example of convicting the prime minister Nawaz Sharif for not declaring the salary not taken from his son is already quoted, in which the personal political prejudices of judges like Justice Ijaz ul Ahsan and Chief Justice Saqib Nisar are well known.

Subsequent examples of this politicization are seen with the rise of the political party, the Pakistan Tehreek e Insaf (PTI), which many judges of the superior judiciary and their families were sympathetic to and supportive of.

This led to infamous court rulings like overlooking PTI's transgression of violating the court order not to enter forbidden zones of the capital during their protests, in which the then Chief Justice is known to have stated that "maybe Imran Khan did not know about our order." Or when the attacks of 9th May 2023 occurred and Imran Khan was brought in front of the then Chief Justice, the latter famously said, "good to see you," and later on the court ruled that the PTI chief could not be arrested even for any offence committed by him in the future.

The self-contradicting rulings in 2022 with respect to the implementation of Article 63A, related to the disqualification of parliamentarians due to defections in the Punjab Assembly, are another example of the judiciary's politicization. First, the Supreme Court ruled that those parliamentarians who had defected from PTI by voting in favor of electing the PML-N candidate as Chief Minister not only stood disqualified, but their votes would also not count since they had gone against their party.

Then, later on, in the second contest for the post of Chief Minister, when the Deputy Speaker of the Punjab Assembly rejected 10 PML-Q (Pakistan Muslim League – Quaid e Azam) votes in favor of the PTI-backed candidate against the specific direction of the PML-Q chief, the Supreme Court upheld those votes to make it possible for the PTI-backed candidate to win.

Another ridiculous verdict due to this politicization was seen in the 12th July 2024 decision of the Supreme Court, whereby reserved seats in the National Assembly were given to PTI, which did not even exist as a political party in the assembly and was neither a claimant in the case of the reserved seats being heard in the Supreme Court. Independent parliamentarians were given the opportunity to again choose party allegiance even though the procedural time limit had lapsed long ago and choices already made.

The book has already identified the seeds of such maladies and mental gymnastics of the judiciary to be sought in the three 'Ms' prejudiced mindset, as the originating subconscious behind such conduct. This politicization of the judiciary and the monopoly of such a politicized judiciary was sought to be cured by the passing of the 26th amendment to the Constitution of Pakistan on 21st October 2024.

Returning to the topic of law enforcement, that is, the rule of law, we ask the final question. What is the law enforcement agency to do if the judiciary is compromised or criminally negligent in following through with the punishment of the guilty party arrested by law enforcement, or if the prosecution fails to build a proper case against the guilty, backed by all available and sufficient evidence provided by law enforcement?

The answer is, no letup in efforts by law enforcement. Because there is no other way. There is no shortcut to the destination of a society governed by the rule of law. We have seen this throughout the history of nation-states who are now perceived as democratic civilized states where the rule of law prevails. These societies are where they are because of untiring, persistent efforts and sacrifices of law enforcement agencies who never gave up hounding lawbreakers, whether criminal or financial, gathering evidence against them and arresting them.

The executive arm of the state, which includes law enforcement agencies, utilized the maximum room for action provided to them by the constitution of their country to impose the writ of the state, to put down criminals, hound and trap them and, if not eliminated while escaping from the long arm of the law, bring them in front of a court of law to be tried for their crimes.

Of course, eventually the judiciary, the media, the intelligentsia and the legislature all have to step up and catch up to play their due part in ensuring that a real criminal never gets away. The elevation of a society to greater heights of law and order is, in the final analysis, a collective effort which is only voluntary. It cannot be achieved by merely a command or an action from the top.

A government in power, which is firm on the issue of the enforcement of law and order and is ready to provide full backing to law enforcement officers and prosecutors to relentlessly and repeatedly pursue suspects and bring them to a court of law after gathering sufficient evidence, does help in a big way towards the reduction of crime and corruption in the country.

But there is no other way.

We see the United States in debt as a state to the tune of trillions of dollars. We see allegations of corruption linked to even the presidents of the country during the course of its history up to the present. But never did any general violate the constitution of the United States and capture political power in the country using those allegations of corruption as a pretext. There were many instances, specially during the Cold War, when senior generals had reservations about policies of détente with the communist bloc and actions of US presidents may have been perceived by them to be soft to the degree of bordering on treason[104]. But never did any US general, or the military as an entity, overstep the constitution and

---

[104] As prime examples, reference is made to differences that are known to have existed between General Douglas MacArthur and President Harry Truman and between General Edwin Walker and President John F. Kennedy. An artistic rendition of this phenomenon in the form of the 1964 movie 'Seven Days in May' is also recommended for the reader.

depose the president of the country. We see similar stability in the Indian political system, where despite social upheavals and allegations as well as actual practice of corruption up to the lowest levels of society, the Indian military never overstepped the constitution of the country.

There is just no short cut. And there should also be no mercy for those who are ready to break the law or bypass it to take a short cut and jeopardize the whole legal system. This is the rule of law.

Pakistani Effervescence and Vagaries of the Outside World

Before we conclude this book, we have to go through this chapter of wrapping up whatever new aspects we discovered or rediscovered, since the author or the reader may have thought about them sometimes in their lives but may have forgotten about them, only to be rekindled in this book, in the preceding chapters in relation to the place where Pakistanis find themselves today. These aspects surfaced like effervescence after undergoing unique experiences in the brief period of the Pakistanis' existence as a separate nation-state, and this effervescence continues to stay afloat on the surface.

The outside world around them has changed substantially, and international trends of a few decades ago no longer exist and have been replaced by new trends. But the effervescence of perceptions floating on the surface as accepted narratives in Pakistan seems to remain the same as that of a few decades ago.

For instance, those external powers who used Pakistan during the Cold War, and were its perceived allies or backers, appear to be wary of and hostile to the very concept of the continued existence of Pakistan as a nation-state. The eastern neighbor, which previously used to have secular governments that made peace and reconciliatory overtures toward Pakistan emphasizing the commonalities of the two states, is now more overwhelmed by a religious-leaning populism and governments which look at Pakistan as "the other." It is now less inclined as a state to peaceful resolutions with Pakistan of any differences or disputes and is happy to see internal unrest in Pakistan. It tends to create barriers to possibilities of positive progress for Pakistan on the international arena.

Similarly, on its west, Pakistan has countries ruled and dominated by religious dogmatic fundamentalists, and the extent to which it can go to engage and befriend them is a question mark for Pakistan, not only in the context of its heavy reliance on receiving cooperation from the Arab countries and the US but also for itself as an existential question if it allows too much inroads of religious dogmatic fundamentalism inside its own territories.

For all practical purposes, the society inside Pakistan is less stifling and more democratic than its western neighbors, but the prevalent narrative remains the same, identifying increased political Islamism with some kind of perfection to be achieved and to be like that as being somehow more anti-imperialist or freer than a democratic society providing pluralism and complete freedom of expression to its citizens, men and women alike.

The existence of the communist ideological superpower bloc, which enabled generals in Pakistan to use it as a pretext in front of western democratic eyes to successfully stage coups and sustain them with Western help, and which on the other hand provided hope to wannabe revolutionaries to bypass capitalism and the indigenous upper classes through state ownership of the means of production, is a thing of a long-gone past. China is, for all practical purposes, a capitalistic economic power with no support, time, or sympathy forthcoming from its side for new communist revolutions in third world countries and views the whole world through capitalistic eyes and is a fellow member with India in the 'BRICS'[105] economic bloc. Pragmatically, it would prefer to engage more with individuals in a country who have the least of vested interests in the West, which brings us to the magnitude of the problematization caused by the vast numbers of Pakistan's ruling classes, including the military, and the country's middle classes having relations or themselves settled or seeking settlement in the West. And none of these classes have the stomach to live austerely, let go of the best of material comforts and thrills

---

[105] B.R.I.C.S. (acronym 'Brazil.Russia.India.China.South Africa').

provided by products and technological goods imported from the West, or let go of the entitlements of privilege and power they enjoy within their country over their less privileged compatriots.

In fact, if even a sincere leader inside Pakistan was to forego his or her ability to influence society by letting go of one's wealth, that leader would likely be abandoned by most comrades and allies and could become a lame duck, easy target for adversaries seeking elimination of that leader.

Ironically, to be able to do successful politics, even pro-people politics, a Pakistani leader or party in present times has to first entrench oneself in a fort of money or be from the landed or capitalist classes. To be able to do otherwise, which has not been impossible in human history, success should come immediately, or it would fizzle out and would not be institutionalized, and eventually would become legend and folklore only.

So, how far the friendship which is 'higher than the Himalayas, deeper than the Arabian Sea, and sweeter than honey'[106] can go has its own question marks and limitations which can only be overcome when a political leadership is completely clear about standing its own to all external powers including China, the US, Britain, Europe, India, the Arab states, Iran or Afghanistan without succumbing to compromise due to personal factors. The balancing act between China and the West was easier a few decades ago when India was almost completely in the Soviet bloc. Without the willingness to sacrifice on a personal level by the political leadership of the country, a policy of non-alignment coming out of Pakistan cannot be made to be accepted by external powers as Pakistan's rightful stand and replace the tendency of having either a pro-US policy, or an entirely pro-China policy, or a pro-Saudi or a pro-Iran policy for that matter.

It is time that the rulers of Pakistan take up only a pro-Pakistan policy and are able to convince the world that their country will neither serve as a client state for any external power nor be an engine for any ideological movement around the world. It will be a country, not a cause. It will be run just as another sovereign nation-state in the world.

---

[106] This is how the nature of friendship between Pakistan and China is commonly quoted inside Pakistan.

The West has ended its romance with immigration and multiculturalism and is predominantly being taken over by parties and narratives of reasserting the superiority of Western cultures which had previously conquered and colonized the lands of the 'colored' people. In the return of this narrative and its success, they have been historically helped by the failures, corruption, and dictatorships of third world leaders of most countries that emerged free after the end of colonialism in the world and the succumbing of the people of these countries to reactionary fanaticism and bloody fratricide.

In that sense, they have a point. Western democratic civilization, which emerged after the period of Western renaissance, specially after the end of the 19th century AD, has been progressively less and less dictatorial and repressive for 'its own people'. While it remained a colonizer of other nations, Western civilization was more and more democratic towards its own people, and stories of the kind of repression and torture that many third world leaders heaped on their own people after the end of colonialism are unknown or unheard of in modern Western nations.

The only digression happened with the rise of fascism and Nazism in Spain, Germany, and Italy, but it was eventually defeated convincingly not only physically but intellectually by Western democracies. So too was communism in Eastern Europe. Whether it be the 'white' modern Western democratic nations or even apartheid South Africa or Zionist Israel, these societies have consistently been democratic and pluralistic for 'their own people' and did not subject their citizens to violation of their human and democratic rights. And to top it all, in the end they even treated and still treat non-Whites as well as new legal immigrants belonging to non-White races and non-White countries of origin as equals before the law once they too became full citizens of their countries or their systems.

In the context of this resurgence of revisionist thinking regarding colonialism and the superiority of the values system of the ex-colonialists, the predominant political forces in the West now provide renewed support to Israel and voice rejection of even the two-state solution, which was the very basic condition for the creation of Israel by the United Nations (UN), as already mentioned earlier in the book, and rejection of the United Nations itself, which was the birthing body of Israel.

This support of Israel has also been strengthened as a reaction to the religious color that the anti-Israel movement has taken among Palestinians, whose struggle has predominantly changed from being a national liberation movement into a Jew-hating per se international fundamentalist movement. The secular premise has been thrown out of the window by both sides, and what was a land dispute between Israelis and Palestinians has become a matter of crusade for Zionist Jews and the Christian nations led by 'born again' Christian leaders on one side and Muslims of the world on the other.

As also mentioned earlier in the book, those types of political forces in the West who in the 1930s would have been at the forefront in the persecution of Jews in Europe are now acting as the champions of Israel. In this way, a colonialist mindset is returning in the West which rids itself of the guilt of hating and persecuting Jews and at the same time supports the last remaining colonial project of the world as a means to reassert and return a project of recolonizing, redistributing, and rearranging the lands of the world and continued supply of natural resources towards its own countries. Already, there is accepted talk of there never to be a Palestinian state, the extension of Israel much beyond its already illegal settlements which are not deemed illegal anymore, and the revival of US exceptionalism and redistribution to its advantage of lands and resources of the world.

At its end Russia asserts its control over lands that it considers Russian, as a vestige of the demographic management which occurred when the Soviet Union existed, and the world of international security and sanity which was propped up after the Second World War through the United Nations (UN) and NATO (North Atlantic Treaty Organization) is at the verge of unraveling.

This acceptance and resurgence of neo colonialist thinking in the West will only diminish if and when the ex-colonized countries get their acts right, build democracies and decrease repression within, focus more on their own technological development, build multiple new political, economic and military alliances externally in the multipolar world, and stand firm non belligerently on principles of sovereignty and a just international order against the neo colonialist political surge in the West, which will find them allies of reason and sense regaining political strength in the West.

These developments are specially problematic for Pakistan, because on the one hand these changes in international trends will give rise to increased influence of religiopolitical narratives inside the country and the demand to keep the official narrative effervescing to deem the Israel Palestine issue as a battle between Islam and World Jewry, but on the other hand, with pro-Israel forces gaining ascent in the West, Pakistan could be adversely affected in terms of international trade and finance if such a nihilistic and religion oriented narrative is maintained from its side.

This prime international issue is not to be avoided, dodged, or hidden from by Pakistan's leaders and intelligentsia but has to be taken head on bravely and to say in no uncertain terms what is really the right thing to be said without being intimidated by religious bigotry from within. Not in religious terms, but as a matter of principle which is more than enough to refute the stand of Israel regarding the right of the Palestinians to have a state. That no people existing on a land at a certain stage of history can be driven out of their homes or be deprived from having a say about the future of the land in which they and their children live.

And if, as per international law, Pakistan does accept the creation of Israel by the United Nations, then it can only be so if the fully sovereign Palestinian state is also created with no further delay. And if Israel and its Knesset now reject the two-state solution, then they immediately lose the right of Israel to exist as a state, because the creation of two states on that land was the basic starting premise of the United Nations resolution of 1947 which created Israel.

In that case, the only way forward would be the dismantling of the Israeli Zionist state just like the dismantling of the apartheid South African state and the establishment of one democratic state with all citizens equal and protected in the eyes of its law and constitution. This is a principled stand which Pakistan can easily take and defend without being accused of being an opposer of Israel per se and a vehicle for religious hatred against the Jews. In that sense, the narrative of Pakistan and inside Pakistan needs readjustment.

As has already been alluded to in the preceding chapter, "Statecraft, Upper Classes," the fascination and romance associated with revolutions and socialism, which still prevails as the ruling political correctness in the imagination of Pakistani intelligentsia, needs a relook and revisiting with the benefit of hindsight at hand now.

As European colonialism was ending and colonies gaining independence as sovereign states, there was an absence of upper classes in these ex-colonies possessing the necessary capital to initiate and manage large scale production. The necessary technological wherewithal was absent with them to spearhead the development and advancement of heavy industry to process the mineral and agricultural raw material produced in their country.

In that historical context, socialism, i.e. state ownership of the means of production, was an inherently essential component of the narrative of the anti-colonial struggle. It was also encouraged by the existence of the world socialist bloc at that time headed by the Soviet Union, which made it possible for newly independent states to make themselves technologically self-reliant if they played their cards right and borrowed and developed technology under state ownership. But what was needed to be understood, and was understood correctly by those newly liberated countries whose leadership was wise, was that such an arrangement would have to be a stop gap arrangement till their own economic classes did not grow and mature enough to invest in such technological ventures and take over from the state. In that case, it was necessary to keep their bourgeoning classes alive and give them special consideration to let them flourish and grow.

The success of such wisdom is best exemplified in the experience of India, where in the early Nehru years, although large scale economic ventures were launched by the state, the Nehru regime let the local capitalist classes grow in parallel and did not touch them. To a certain extent, that also holds true in a parabolic way even for countries like Kemalist Turkey, Iran, Malaysia, Botswana, South Korea, and similar countries which refuted and defeated the ideas of socialism and communism on a public level but used state ownership as a method of development for a certain time. All wise leaders knew, which as historical hindsight shows was proven true, that eventually it is market economy and private enterprise which is closer to human nature and its yearning for freedom than continuous state ownership of the means of production and economy.

Wise Chinese leaders like Chou En Lai and Deng Xiaopeng also succeeded in bringing China to this line of thinking after the death of Mao Tse Tung without the unraveling of their country, despite initially losing millions of lives at the altar of the foolishness of the 'Cultural Revolution' and 'The Great Leap Forward'. The Soviet Union did not succeed in this readjustment when it decided to go this way in the late 1980s, since its process of collectivization and the elimination of all potential for nascent economic classes to grow had been much longer and complete compared to China, and its composition much more multiethnic and less homogenous in that respect to be able to live up to the call of this readjustment.

As also mentioned earlier, with the collapse of the socialist economic bloc, the feasibility of implementing a fully socialist economy and sustaining it as a permanent way of running the economy is next to nil in the present international context. Moreover, any attempt to do so would also involve political repression and stifling dissenting voices. 'Public Private Partnership' and providing public services like health, education, and communication under state ownership is still doable and is done so even in several Western countries. But the main thrust of economic growth in a country can now only be provided by developing and backing the concentration of capital in the private sector, enhancing the ability of one's country's economic classes to thrive on their own and, if and when needed, build partnerships with the public sector or foreign direct investments with the laws of the country providing oversight and protection of national and public interest.

In this international situation, to talk about revolution and rail against the upper economic classes of one's own country and specially call for a violent revolution targeting state manifestations and protections of such an economic order, as if this revolution and uprising were being brought about against a foreign colonial power, is not just infantile idiocy but suicidal for one's state. Only channels of democracy, freedom of expression, and lobbying for correct legislation and its strict uncompromising implementation have to be used with revolutionary fervor, without the element of hatred, to protect the interests of the people and prevent their social, political, or economic exploitation. Pakistani intelligentsia has to explore the cultural, literary, and sociopsychological aspects and complexities of the human experience manifested in societies which did not go the socialist route and not only succeeded but in the final analysis are at the forefront of advanced human society.

So far, Pakistani intelligentsia has been oblivious to an understanding of the dynamics of such societies and still views in its zeitgeist, the capitalist as always the bad entity and the socialist always the good one, the (US) Republican always bad and the Democrat always good, the (UK or Commonwealth) Conservative always bad and Labour always good, Latin American socialists always good and those who oppose them as always bad and wrong. Pakistanis have to outgrow the romance associated with socialism and revolution. These phenomena, although having catalytic significance in history, are not that romantic in the long run.

Pakistani effervescence needs to be revisited so that the Pakistani zeitgeist does not become like stagnant water, gathering fungus and bacteria, throwing out stench and disease. It has to be like flowing water with its effervescence clear and sparkling.

Epilogue

The Promise of Pakistan and the Agents of This Promise's Undoing

There are various seminal reasons why, when Pakistan spurted forth on the international map as a new country, this endeavor was looked upon more as a promise than a mere embellishment on the tapestry of post-British India. This promise was not just for the capitalist West, who at the time needed a strong ally in the region against international communism, but also by the Muslims of the Indian subcontinent themselves as the 'promised land' where they could be in charge of their own lives and live their lives unfettered according to their own religious and cultural values. The reasons of this promise were not superficial but enrooted in genuine sociopolitical developments in the subcontinent, as have been touched upon in this book. The author believes that despite the ugliness of this new state's breakup in 1971 and the various martial laws it suffered from in its history, this promise is still not dead. Certain inherent premises exist in the very nature of this state which provide promise of a land that can become a place where people of different ethnicities and religious beliefs can coexist in a civilized manner under democratically legislated law and economic growth achieved, thus serving as an example to follow for ex-colonized countries of the Third World, specially the Muslim world.

The first inherent premise of this promise is that the country is a federation. It is no great achievement for a country to form and exist where the populace is culturally, linguistically, and religiously homogeneous. That is easy; anybody can do that. The true test of civilizational greatness which a country can pass and ascend to the greatest heights of nation building is when people different from one another can coexist in one federal state as civilized people with their rights to self-expression, self-assertion, and self-determination assured in a federal democratic system.

The second promising premise is that the state of Pakistan emerged out of a movement of Muslims who had broken away from religious orthodoxy and were forward-looking in terms of science, the role of women, and the usage of modern structures of state building. This second premise is intrinsically linked to the third promising premise, which is that the country came into existence not through an armed struggle but by the force of the ballot. The utilization of the 'Westminster' mode of democracy is ingrained in the historical political experience and the federating nature of the state. Abandoning this mode of existence would strike at the very modus operandi of its existence, as it did when the presidential form of rule resulted in its breakup in 1971, and that is why this democratic mode of existence is also the very promise and the saving grace of this state.

The fourth and the most important premise which provides promise to the world and itself is its people, one of the most populous peoples of the world, spread across the globe, a resilient, hard-working, cerebrally advanced, and pragmatic people who can deliver much if the country at home is run like a country and not an ideological cause.

But if ideology supersedes the prerequisites of running a modern nation state, if the compartmentalization in society and personal solipsism as has been discussed in this book continues, if compatriots are ethnically, linguistically, and religiously looked at as 'the other' and dehumanized in subjective political discourse, if reasons of being different from one another are sought more eagerly than seeking reasons of being similar, if politics is considered to be the elimination, even physical, of the political opponent, and hatred and dehumanized ridicule of 'the other' and of the political opponent is espoused as the norm among the educated and the intelligentsia of the country, then these promising premises will evaporate into thin air just like the oceans of the earth would evaporate if the planet were to lose its atmosphere.

All sophisticated political or economic analyses aside, including the hue and cry about 'corruption' which has sufficiently proven to be a bogey as those crying hoarse about it the most from rooftops are themselves found drowned in it, the real malady of Pakistan is the poison that exists in the mindset of its so-called educated middle class and its intelligentsia.

On 12 June 2019, a Pakistani government minister sat on a television channel and advocated the extrajudicial killing of 5000 persons to rid the country of its problems[107], showing all that is wrong and flawed in the mindset of the reactionary and fascistic element of Pakistan's educated middle classes. That it is ok to kill people without due process or evidence, that it is ok for a person to publicly call out for the murder of other people, and that this finds resonance among a large number of so-called educated middle classes, belies the fascist makeup of their mentality which has brought harm and self-destructiveness to state and society from the very inception of this state.

It is this mindset which called for killings and torture of dissenting or critical voices, which called for the persecution and military actions against Bengalis, Baloch, and Pashtuns (and Sindhis during the MRD movement in the 1980s) during various military rules, dehumanizing them in the prevalent narratives of those times. It is this mindset which was cheering the butchering of Bengalis in 1971 who were Pakistani citizens at the time, while the military government was doing something which was anti-people as well as anti-constitution and anti-law. It is this mindset which turns stone cold in compassion when ordinary Punjabi common folk are murdered in the name of the so-called 'national liberation' struggle of smaller provinces, a struggle which would almost always lose on the altar of popular mandate if it opted for going into elections rather than choosing violence as the mode of its operation. It is this narrow mindset which prevents the acceptance and assimilation of descendants of the non-Punjabi migrants from India by the indigenous population of the country, although the former were born and bred in this land and the latter view the former still as 'the other'. It is this mindset which, when it bypasses the legal and constitutional process just because of its personal like or dislike of this or that leader, and which considers itself justified in trampling the legal and constitutional rights of its opposition just because it considers itself high and mighty and holier than everyone else, that such a mindset results in the breakdown of all: state, society, and respect of law.

It is Pakistan's tragedy that the predominant mindset in its so-called educated middle classes, in all provinces, is fascistic, whereas in other democratically successful countries it is the educated middle classes who

---

[107] https://images.dawn.com/news/1183012, 'The scary 'kill' fetish' by Abbas Nasir (https://www.dawn.com/news/1488355)

are very clear about the rule of their country's law and constitution and never compromise on the due process of law, evidence, and constitution when solving any problem, including problems of corruption, dissent, and bad governance. In those democratic countries, the educated middle classes are the backbone and bedrock of democracy and the rule of constitution. In Pakistan, sadly, the same classes are the bedrock and backbone of fascism and cheerleaders of violence or martial law.

So, in Pakistan the salvation lies with the democratic-minded upper classes (who are organically also the engine of economic growth), the vast population of the lower working classes, the traders and the rural classes, and the remaining of the educated middle classes who are right-minded about due process, the rule of law, and constitution as being the essence of a successful civilized state. Otherwise, Pakistan has already been half undone in 1971 due to this sickly mindset, and there is every possibility of its being fully undone if this mindset is not checked and defeated. The founder of Pakistan is famously known to have said that *"there is no power on earth which can undo Pakistan."* Maybe then he did not even think about this internal Achilles' heel, otherwise he would have said: *"there is no power on earth which can undo Pakistan... except Pakistanis themselves."*

Index

1

18th Amendment, 135, 150, 177
1973 Constitution, 80, 140, 150,
    168, 177, 218, 219

2

26th Amendment, 247
2nd Amendment, 140

A

A. K. Fazlul Haq, 121, 123
A. Masroor, 173
Abbas Nasir, 260
Abbasid, 9, 12, 65, 66
Abdul Ali Malik, 48
Abdul Aziz bin Muhammad bin
    Saud, 10
Abdul Ghaffar Khan, 54, 132, 201
Abdul Maalik, 89
Abdul Samad Achakzai, 132
Abdul Wajid Rana, 141
Abdus Salam, 48
Abu Bakr, 64, 98, 102
Abu Salama, 99
Abu Sufyan, 64, 101, 102
Abul Fazl, 32
Abul Kalam Azad, 5
Adhikari, 46
Afghanistan, 3, 12, 13, 29, 30, 44,
    58, 83, 84, 144, 147, 173, 185,
    200, 204, 221, 251
African, 18, 26, 76, 114
Ahmadi, 6, 48, 61, 75, 83, 84, 85,
    140
Ahmed Rashid, 173
Aisha, 95, 98, 103

Akbar, 32
Akbar Bugti, 200
Akhtar Hussain Malik, 48
Al Beruni, 12
Al Ghazali, 60, 69
Al Qaeda, 163, 221
Alexandria, 103
Ali, 64, 65, 70, 71, 108
Aligarh, 36
Aligarh Muslim University, 36,
    120, 125
All India Muslim League, 39, 54,
    112, 113, 121, 123, 198
Al-Zulfiqar, 241
Ameer Muawiya, 64, 65
Anatolia, 12, 13
Anglo Afghan War, 27
Anna Fleck, 216
ANP, 173
Anwar ul Haq, 155
Arab, 8, 9, 10, 11, 12, 15, 17, 21,
    22, 23, 27, 29, 43, 52, 59, 61, 63,
    64, 65, 73, 76, 88, 89, 90, 96,
    100, 104, 114, 130, 250, 251
Arabia, 11, 43, 62, 63, 68, 79, 82,
    90, 96, 203
Arabian Sea, 181, 251
ARD, 135, 242
Armenia, 44
Arya Samaj, 37
Asharites, 60, 67, 82, 167, 168
Asifa, 174
Asma, 102
As-Sakran ibn Amr, 97
Aurangzeb, 27, 29, 30
Australia, 205
Austro Hungarian Empire, 18

Averroes, 60, 66, 89, 169
Avicenna, 12
Awami League, 125, 133
Awami National Party, 173
Ayesha, 64
Ayesha Jalal, 111
Ayesha Siddiqa Agha, 111
Ayodhya, 45
Ayub Khan, 80, 126, 128, 129, 130, 131, 132, 135, 136, 137, 138, 139, 155, 246
Azerbaijan, 11, 44

B

Baathist, 58
Babar, 29
Babri Mosque, 45
Baghdad, 10, 60, 126
Bahawalpur, 200
Balfour Declaration, 22, 23
Ballot Act, 162
Baloch, 30, 54, 132, 147, 241, 243, 260
Balochistan, 27, 127, 131, 132, 138, 140, 141, 142, 147, 200
Bangladesh, 70, 107, 129, 133, 134, 149, 153
Banu Aws, 104
Banu Mustaliq, 101
Banu Nadir, 102, 104
Banu Qurayza, 95, 103, 104
Banu Umayya, 64, 68
Barrah, 102
Basic Democracies, 132
Basra, 64
Battle of Badr, 99
Battle of Camel, 64
Battle of Khaybar, 102
Battle of the Trench, 102, 104
Battle of Uhud, 99

Benazir, 81, 135, 137, 150, 174, 178, 221
Bengal, 25, 113, 121, 123, 124, 130, 147
Bengali, 52, 116, 117, 120, 121, 122, 123, 124, 126, 127, 128, 129, 130, 131, 133, 134, 135, 137, 138, 144, 147, 148, 149, 150, 153, 154, 155, 202, 207, 241, 243, 260
Benjamin Netanyahu, 237
Bezmenov, 86
Bhutto, 55, 136, 137, 138, 139, 140, 141, 142, 143, 144, 150, 152, 154, 155, 174, 179, 187, 188, 219, 220, 221, 235, 236, 246
Bible, 91
Bihar, 116, 117
Bilawal, 174
Bill of Rights, 78
Black Plague, 213
Blackstone's Ratio, 232
Bombay, 46, 113, 121
Bosnian, 44
Botswana, 255
BRICS, 250
Britain, 181, 212, 213, 214, 221, 251
British, 6, 21, 22, 23, 25, 29, 30, 31, 32, 36, 37, 38, 39, 44, 45, 46, 47, 54, 69, 108, 109, 112, 113, 114, 115, 125, 126, 131, 134, 182, 183, 184, 185, 198, 199, 205, 211, 212
British India, 5, 7, 25, 27, 30, 35, 36, 53, 54, 109, 115, 116, 117, 120, 123, 127, 130, 134, 138, 149, 171, 187, 195, 258
Brunei, 14

Buddhists, 30
Burki, 187

C

C. Raja Mohan, 173
Cambodia, 58
Canada, 45, 158, 205
Catholicism, 76
CENTO, 126
Central Asia, 29, 43, 64
Charter of Democracy, 135, 150, 177
Chaudhry Aslam, 245
Chaudhry Mohammad Ali, 125
Chaudhry Rehmat Ali, 147, 148
Chechen, 18
China, 3, 16, 58, 77, 86, 197, 214, 250, 251, 256
China Pakistan Economic Corridor, 185, 225
Chou En Lai, 256
Christian, 19, 21, 47, 48, 56, 57, 68, 91, 103, 166, 167, 253
Christianity, 47, 66, 67, 68, 74, 79, 101, 167
Chundrigar, 125
CoD, 135, 150, 177
Cold War, 21, 47, 70, 115, 125, 126, 127, 132, 143, 164, 168, 177, 208, 248, 249
Combined Opposition Parties, 133, 135, 241
Commonwealth, 257
Communist Party, 46
Communist Party of Pakistan, 133
Congress, 113, 214, 215
Constantine, 68
Convention Muslim League, 126
Council of Islamic Ideology, 168
CPEC, 185, 225

Cyprus, 44

D

Dalits, 6
Darwin, 36
David Loyn, 106
Dayananda Saraswati, 37
Declaration of Independence, 91
Deepika M, 216
Delhi Sultanates, 27
Deng Xiaopeng, 77, 256
Dennis Kux, 45
Dhaka, 123, 128, 130
Dilawar Hussain, 139
Dome of the Rock, 44
Donald Trump, 237
Douglas MacArthur, 248
Durand Line, 30

E

East Pakistan, 107, 121, 124, 126, 127, 128, 130, 133, 136, 137, 139, 140, 148, 153, 155, 180, 208
East Punjab, 116, 121, 122, 124, 154, 155
Eastern Europe, 18, 252
Edhi, 163
Edwin Walker, 248
Egypt, 10, 11, 13, 62, 64, 65, 73, 103
Ehud Olmert, 237
Eric Fromm, 74, 75, 176, 194
Ethiopia, 101
Europe, 21, 24, 51, 66, 75, 76, 88, 89, 92, 118, 165, 182, 196, 251, 253
European Union, 107, 108

F

Faisalabad, 116
Fatima Jinnah, 80, 131, 132, 133, 135, 138, 241
Federal Shariat Court, 168
Feroze Khan Noon, 125
Fiqh, 12, 93, 98, 105, 167
France, 158
Franco, 76
French Revolution, 196, 212
FSF, 143

G

G.M. Syed, 54
Gandhi, 39, 45, 113, 183, 198, 201, 215
GDA, 242
George the Sixth, 204
George Washington, 91
Germany, 58, 145, 252
Ghaus Bux Bizenjo, 132
Ghulam Ahmed Parvez, 62
Ghulam Muhammad, 125, 128, 227
Ghulam Murtaza Malik, 62
Godot, 93, 94
Gorbachev, 88, 272
Gramsci, 41, 162
Great War, 21
Gujrat, 116, 117
Gupta Empire, 27

H

Hadhramaut, 63
Hafez al-Assad, 143
Hafsa, 98, 99, 103
Hafsa Khawaja, 130
Han Chinese, 18
Hanafi, 59
Harry Truman, 248

Haryana, 121
Hasan, 65
Hassan Al Banna, 69
Hejaz, 64
Henry Byroade, 143
Hilali Tribe, 102
Himalayas, 251
Hindko, 139
Hindu, 5, 6, 15, 26, 30, 37, 38, 39, 40, 45, 46, 47, 48, 52, 53, 54, 55, 108, 109, 110, 111, 115, 116, 120, 121, 122, 123, 127, 130, 132, 134, 144, 146, 147, 149, 150
Hindu Mahasabha, 39
Hindu Rashtra, 108
Hindustan, 147, 148
Hindutva, 40, 76, 106, 108, 145
Hitler, 76, 176, 232
Holy Roman Empire, 56
Hudaibiyya, 102
Huma Yusuf, 180
Husain Suhrawardy, 121, 125
Hussain Haqqani, 111, 131
Hussein, 65, 143
Hyderabad, 25, 45, 115, 116, 117
Hyderabad Conspiracy, 141

I

Ibn e Khuldun, 66, 89, 169
Ibn e Rushd, 60, 66, 169
Ibn e Sina, 12
Ibn e Taymiyyah, 11, 69
Ibn Saud, 22
Ibrahim, 103, 125
Iftikhar Khan Janjua, 48
Ijaz ul Ahsan, 246
IJI, 150, 242
Ijtihad, 105, 167
Ikhwan, 22

Ikram Sehgal, 139
Ikramullah Khan Niazi, 187
Imam Abu Hanifa, 59
Imam Ghazali, 61, 66, 67
Imam Hanbal, 10, 60
Imam Shaafi, 106
IMF, 185, 225
Imperial Legislative Council, 112
Imran Khan, 135, 178, 179, 180,
    181, 183, 184, 185, 186, 187,
    189, 192, 241, 246
India, 5, 6, 8, 15, 25, 26, 27, 28, 29,
    30, 31, 32, 34, 36, 37, 38, 39, 40,
    42, 43, 44, 45, 46, 47, 48, 49, 52,
    53, 54, 55, 56, 59, 76, 106, 108,
    109, 110, 111, 112, 113, 116,
    120, 121, 122, 130, 132, 133,
    134, 137, 138, 139, 140, 144,
    145, 146, 147, 148, 149, 150,
    154, 158, 170, 172, 183, 198,
    199, 200, 201, 211, 212, 214,
    215, 216, 250, 251, 255, 260
Indian National Congress, 6, 39,
    42, 53, 70, 108, 112, 122, 198
Indian Nationalism, 109
Indira, 55, 144
Indonesia, 14
Indus Valley, 55
International Monetary Fund, 185,
    225
Iqbal, 6, 48, 113, 148, 163
Iran, 3, 13, 58, 62, 64, 77, 84, 88,
    200, 251, 255
Iraq, 13, 22, 58, 62, 64, 65, 78
Ireland, 162
Irving Kristol, 82
ISIS, 78
Iskander Mirza, 122, 125, 126, 127
Islam, 7, 8, 9, 10, 11, 12, 13, 14,
    15, 17, 19, 20, 21, 22, 24, 26, 27,

28, 29, 31, 39, 47, 49, 50, 59, 61,
    62, 64, 65, 67, 68, 69, 73, 78, 79,
    80, 81, 82, 84, 86, 89, 90, 91, 92,
    93, 94, 95, 96, 97, 98, 99, 100,
    101, 103, 104, 106, 126, 130,
    133, 141, 147, 149, 166, 167,
    170, 188, 254
Islamabad, 239
Islami Jamhoori Ittehad, 150, 242
Islamic Socialism, 144
Ismaili, 6, 61
Israel, 20, 21, 23, 24, 25, 26, 107,
    252, 253, 254
Italy, 58, 252

J

Jahangir Khan, 181
Jains, 30
Jamaat e Islami, 70, 83
Jamaat-e-Islami, 5, 80, 133
Jamiat Ulema-e-Hind, 5
Jang e Jamal, 64
Jansher Khan, 181
Japanese, 18
Javed Ghamdi, 62
Jean Bodin, 238
Jerusalem, 44
Jew, 19, 22, 23, 44, 75, 95, 104,
    253, 254
Jinnah, 37, 39, 43, 46, 48, 69, 70,
    108, 112, 113, 121, 131, 164
Jogendra Nath Mandal, 6
John K. Cooley, 106
Judaism, 67
Judgement at Nuremberg, 75, 232
Jullundur, 155
Junagadh, 45
Junejo, 178
Justice Munir, 128, 155
Juwayriyyah, 101, 102, 103

K

K. K. Aziz, 111, 135
Kaaba, 95
Kalat, 200
Karachi, 45, 115, 121
Karbala, 65
Karnal, 121
Kashmir, 45, 46, 47, 48, 84, 137, 147
Kaswar Gardezi, 132
Kemalist, 255
Kenana bin Rabi, 102
Kennedy, 76, 248
Khadija, 95, 97, 103
Khairpur, 200
Khaled Ahmed, 111
Khalid Bin Sayeed, 111
Khalistan, 48
Kharijites, 64
Khawaja Nazimuddin, 121, 125, 128
Khilafat Movement, 6, 113
Khorasan, 11, 12
Khyber Pakhtunkhwa, 27, 173, 185
Knesset, 26, 254
Krishak Praja Party, 123
Kunwar Khuldune Shahid, 48
Kurdish, 13

L

Lahore, 116, 140, 143, 245
Latin America, 113, 118
Lawrence Ziring, 125
Levant, 11, 64, 73, 90
Liaqat Ali Khan, 121, 125, 126, 127
Libya, 242
Lyallpur, 116

M

Maamoun, 60
Madhya Pradesh, 116, 117
Magna Carta, 212
Mahmud Ghaznavi, 29
Mahzarnama, 85
Maimonides, 232
Majlis e Shura, 81
Majlis-e-Ahrar, 5
Malabar Hill, 46
Malaysia, 14, 206, 255
Malik Ghulam Mohammad, 125
Manavadar, 45
Manmohan Singh, 215
Mao, 58
Mao Tse Tung, 88, 256
Maratha, 31
Maratha Empire, 27, 30, 31
Maren Clay, 213
Mariyya, 103
Mariyya Qubtiyya, 102
Martin Luther, 74
Marxism, 82, 196
Maudoodi, 69, 80
Maulana Bhashani, 133
Maulvi Tamizuddin, 128
Maurya Empire, 27
Max Weber, 74, 223, 238
Maymunah, 102, 103
Mazhar Ali Khan, 132
Mecca, 9, 17, 22, 64, 95, 99, 100, 101, 102, 103
Medina, 17, 63, 99, 100, 101, 102, 104
Mesopotamia, 11
Mian Iftikharuddin, 132
Mian Tufail, 70
Middle East, 24, 113, 117, 118, 200
Mirza Ghalib, 31, 32, 34
Mirza Nasir Ahmad, 85

Modern Prince, 41, 162
Moghul, 29, 32
Moghul Empire, 27, 29
Mohammad Ali Bogra, 121, 125, 127, 128
Mohammad Bin Qasim, 29
Mohammedan Anglo Oriental College, 36
Mongol, 10, 60, 90
Montgomery Watt, 100, 104
Moplah Rebellion, 16
Morocco, 12
Mount Hira, 95
MQM, 172
MRD, 135, 241, 260
Muhajir, 115, 117, 138, 141, 146, 171, 172
Muhajir Qaumi Movement, 172
Muhammad ibn Abdul Wahab, 10
Muhammad Munir, 128, 227
Mujahideen, 173
Mujib ur Rehman, 70, 133
Mukti Bahini, 241
Mumtaz Qadri, 245
Murtaza, 241
Murtaza Haider, 130
Murtaza Kamran, 132
Musharraf, 135, 150, 159, 173, 177, 178, 180, 187, 188, 189, 220, 221, 235, 245, 246
Muslim, 3, 5, 6, 7, 8, 10, 11, 12, 13, 14, 15, 16, 17, 18, 19, 20, 21, 22, 24, 25, 26, 27, 28, 29, 30, 31, 32, 35, 36, 37, 38, 39, 40, 42, 43, 44, 45, 47, 48, 49, 50, 51, 52, 53, 54, 55, 57, 59, 60, 63, 65, 66, 67, 71, 72, 73, 78, 81, 82, 84, 85, 89, 90, 92, 93, 94, 95, 96, 97, 98, 99, 100, 101, 102, 103, 104, 105, 108, 109, 110, 116, 119, 120,
121, 122, 123, 125, 127, 130, 131, 137, 144, 147, 148, 149, 152, 163, 166, 167, 169, 182, 204, 211, 219, 253, 258
Muslim Conference, 48
Muslim League, 5, 6, 39, 45, 48, 54, 113, 121, 123, 125, 130, 133, 159, 173, 174, 205, 241, 247
Mussolini, 76, 176
Mutazilites, 9, 60, 61, 82
Mysore, 30

N

Nadeem Farooq Paracha, 85, 111
Nakba, 24, 107
Nanda Empire, 27
NAP, 133, 137, 138, 139, 140, 141, 142, 150, 241
Napoleon, 197
Narsimha Rao, 215
National Awami Party, 133, 141, 241
NATO, 253
Nawab Nauroz, 132
Nawab of Bahawalpur, 137
Nawab of Kalabagh, 137
Nawaz Sharif, 135, 143, 150, 174, 175, 178, 179, 185, 186, 187, 188, 189, 235, 236, 246
Nazi, 58, 75, 76, 145, 232
Nazism, 3, 23, 252
Nehru, 39, 45, 113, 198, 200, 212, 214, 215, 216, 255
New Zealand, 205
Nigeria, 14
Nikolas Sarkozy, 237
Norman Stillman, 104
North Africa, 10, 62
North Atlantic Treaty Organization, 253

North India, 29, 30, 121, 124
North Korea, 58, 77
Northern Africa, 12
Northern Ireland, 56
Nubian, 12
Nuremberg Laws, 75
NWFP, 127, 131, 132, 139, 140,
    141, 201

O

Objectives Resolution, 43, 70, 83,
    126, 164, 168
OIC, 140
Old Testament, 91
Oman, 63
One Nation Theory, 110
One Unit, 127, 128, 131, 132, 137,
    171
Operation Gibraltar, 47
Operation Searchlight, 3
Organization of Islamic Countries,
    140
Osama bin Laden, 185
Osama Bin Laden, 83
Ottoman, 10, 21, 22, 66
Oudh, 30

P

Pakhtun, 138, 173
Pakistan, 1, 3, 5, 6, 7, 13, 16, 20,
    24, 25, 26, 27, 28, 29, 30, 36, 37,
    39, 40, 41, 42, 43, 44, 45, 46, 47,
    48, 49, 50, 51, 52, 53, 54, 55, 57,
    59, 61, 62, 67, 69, 70, 71, 75, 80,
    83, 84, 85, 86, 106, 108, 109,
    110, 111, 112, 113, 114, 115,
    116, 117, 120, 121, 122, 123,
    124, 125, 126, 127, 128, 129,
    131, 132, 133, 134, 135, 136,
    137, 138, 139, 140, 141, 143,
    144, 145, 146, 147, 148, 149,
    150, 152, 153, 154, 155, 156,
    158, 159, 163, 164, 168, 169,
    170, 171, 173, 174, 175, 176,
    177, 179, 180, 181, 182, 183,
    184, 185, 186, 187, 188, 189,
    190, 191, 192, 193, 194, 195,
    198, 199, 200, 201, 202, 203,
    204, 205, 206, 208, 209, 210,
    211, 217, 218, 219, 220, 221,
    222, 224, 225, 226, 227, 228,
    234, 235, 239, 240, 241, 242,
    243, 244, 245, 246, 247, 249,
    250, 251, 254, 258, 259, 260,
    261, 272
Pakistan Army, 47, 114, 115, 130,
    171, 185, 186
Pakistan Democratic Movement,
    242
Pakistan People's Party, 137, 159,
    172, 174, 187, 241
Palestine, 22, 23, 25, 62, 117, 254
Palestinian, 20, 24, 26, 44, 52, 253,
    254
Pathan, 120, 129, 139, 147, 148,
    187
Paul Alling, 45
PDA, 242
PDM, 242
Persia, 11, 13, 73
Pervez Hoodbhoy, 111, 173
Peshawar, 25, 116
PML-N, 174, 175, 177, 247
PNA, 242
Pol Pot, 58
PPP, 137, 139, 174, 175, 177, 187,
    188
Prophet Muhammad, 17, 63, 64,
    73, 77, 92, 95, 97, 234

Protestantism, 165, 166, 167
Protestants, 168
PTI, 150, 173, 175, 176, 179, 187, 188, 189, 246, 247
Punjab, 5, 6, 25, 27, 30, 46, 113, 121, 122, 123, 127, 131, 132, 137, 138, 139, 143, 147, 150, 172, 174, 175, 186, 187, 200, 245, 246, 247
Punjabi, 5, 6, 42, 43, 48, 117, 120, 122, 123, 124, 125, 128, 129, 138, 139, 141, 148, 150, 154, 155, 160, 171, 173, 175, 186, 187, 260

Q

Qaddafi, 143
Quaid e Azam, 43, 45, 61, 69, 80, 108, 121, 122, 126, 131, 134, 199, 200, 204, 205, 206, 247
Quetta, 116
Quran, 36, 49, 60, 67, 69, 72, 79, 80, 81, 82, 89, 90, 96, 104, 105, 166, 167, 168, 219, 233
Quraysh, 68, 98, 99, 100

R

Ram Mandir, 45
Ramla, 101, 103
Ranjit Singh, 30
Rashidi Emirate, 22
Rashidun, 9, 11, 12, 64, 67, 72
Rawalpindi, 46, 115
Rayhana, 102, 103
Red Mosque, 239
Republican Party, 125, 127
Reza Pirbhai, 132
Romans, 62, 63, 89, 167
Ronald Reagan, 237

Rothschild, 22
Roy Beck, 119
Russia, 18, 58, 197, 250, 253
Russian Revolution, 196

S

Saad bin Muaadh, 104
SAARC, 108
Saddam, 143
Sadiq Khan, 185
Safa, 95
Safiyya, 102, 103
Safwan Ibn Muattal, 104
Salafi, 84
Sally Hemmings, 91
Salman Taseer, 245
Samuel Beckett, 93
Saqib Nisar, 246
Sardar Daud, 144
Sarfraz Husain Ansari, 131
Sassanid, 62, 63, 65
Saudi, 83, 251
Sawdah, 97, 103
Sayyid Qutb, 69
Scotland, 56
SEATO, 126
Seraiki, 187
Serb, 44
Seven Days in May, 248
Seyed Vali Reza Nasr, 71
Shafi, 6
Shahid Javed Burki, 125
Shamsur Rahman Faruqi, 32
Sharif al Mujahid, 69
Sharif family, 175
Shaukat Aziz, 178
Shaukat Khanum, 187
Sher Baz Khan Mazari, 132
Sher Mohammad Marri, 132
Shia, 6, 61, 65, 84, 171, 188

Shuddhi Movement, 37
Shuja Khanzada, 245
Sialkot, 116
Sikh, 30, 31, 46, 47, 48, 116, 120, 121, 122, 123
Sikhs, 47
Sind, 6, 27, 29, 30, 113, 127, 131, 138, 139, 140, 147, 172, 174, 200
Sirajudaulah, 30
Slavic, 18
South Africa, 26, 117, 250, 252
South Indian, 16, 18, 52
South Korea, 255
South Pacific, 14
Southeast Asia, 14, 117, 126
Soviet, 18, 21, 44, 70, 71, 77, 78, 83, 84, 86, 88, 106, 125, 133, 197, 201, 214, 217, 251, 253, 255, 256, 272
Spain, 8, 10, 76, 252
Sri Prakasa, 45, 46
Stanley Wolpert, 143
Statute of Labourers, 213
Sudan, 13, 242
Sufi, 30, 165
Sufism, 12
Sukkur, 116
Summer Sultana, 132
Sunni, 59, 61, 65, 84, 171, 188
Surah Al-Nur, 233, 234
Surah Nisa, 80, 96, 234
Surah Nuh, 36
Swami Vivekananda, 37
Swat, 200
Syed Ahmed Khan, 32, 35, 40, 121, 163, 199
Sykes-Picot Agreement, 21, 22
Syria, 58, 62, 64, 65, 78, 242

T

Tajikistan, 147
Talha, 64
Taliban, 44, 58, 169, 173, 184, 185, 221, 241, 243, 245
Tatar, 18
Tehreek e Insaaf, 175
Tehreek e Nizam e Mustafa, 83
Tehreek-e-Taliban Pakistan, 173
Tenancy Act of 1950, 124, 202
Tenures Abolition Act, 213
Thabit bin Qays, 101
Thomas Hobbes, 238
Thomas Jefferson, 91
Timur, 29
Tom Holland, 89
Torah, 232
Transjordan, 22
Transoxiana, 12
Transparency International, 189, 236
TTP, 173
Turkey, 13, 66, 255
Two Nation Theory, 109

U

Ubayda bin Haaris, 99
Ubaydullah bin Jahsh, 101
UK, 56, 146, 158, 162, 204, 212, 257
Umar, 64, 98, 99
Umayyad, 9, 12, 64, 65, 68, 89
Umm Habiba, 101
Umm Salama, 99, 103
United Arab Emirates, 206
United Kingdom, 56, 204, 212
United Nations, 20, 26, 87, 252, 253, 254

United States, 45, 56, 69, 78, 82, 83, 86, 91, 106, 118, 125, 127, 168, 173, 184, 239, 248

Urdu, 31, 42, 43, 46, 117, 121, 135, 141, 147, 160, 166, 187, 189

USA, 16, 158, 185, 188

Usman, 64, 98, 99

USSR, 3, 4, 6, 47

Uttar Pradesh, 116, 117, 121

Uzbekistan, 29, 147

V

V. S. Naipaul, 15

Venus, 91

W

Wahabi, 22, 84, 143, 171, 188

Wali Khan, 132, 133

War of Independence of 1857, 31

War on Terror, 84, 115, 173, 221

West Pakistan, 115, 120, 123, 124, 125, 127, 128, 129, 130, 131, 132, 133, 134, 136, 137, 138, 139, 153, 154, 171, 195, 199, 200, 202, 203, 207, 208

West Punjab, 116, 122, 154

Westphalian, 51, 52, 54, 58, 108, 111

William Blackstone, 232

World War 1, 21

World War 2, 21, 24, 106

Y

Yahya Khan, 71, 139, 246

Yasser Latif Hamdani, 48

Yemen, 63

Yugoslavia, 3, 18, 52, 107

Z

Zac Goldsmith, 185

Zafar Chaudhry, 48

Zafarullah Khan, 48

Zafarullah Khan Jamali, 178

Zahid Hussain Gardezi, 133

Zahir Shah, 204

Zardari, 174

Zayd, 100, 102

Zaynab, 99, 100, 101, 102, 103

Zia ul Haq, 49, 81, 83, 84, 135, 143, 150, 153, 154, 155, 156, 164, 168, 171, 172, 177, 178, 186, 187, 188, 220, 236, 239, 246, 272

Zimbabwe, 197

Zionist, 22, 26, 252, 253, 254

Zubair, 64

Zulfiqar Ali Bhutto, 55, 70, 136, 179, 235

About the Author

The author is a civil engineer by profession. He was politically active during the era of General Zia ul Haq's military regime in Pakistan and was a member of the now defunct Pakistan Socialist Party of C. R. Aslam up to the early 1990s. He views favourably the policies of Gorbachev in the last years of the Soviet Union without ascribing to the view that the dissolution of the Soviet Union was historically a foregone conclusion. However, he conclusively considers communism and socialism as systems to be obsolete for the modern world. Email: *mhikhalid@yahoo.com*.

www.ingramcontent.com/pod-product-compliance
Lightning Source LLC
Chambersburg PA
CBHW051137120626
46547CB00012B/834